Eckhart's Way

Dedicated
to the memory of
James A. Weisheipl, OP,
Ursula Fleming,
Peter Talbot Willcox,
Maurice O'Clare Walshe
and
John O'Donohue
'Friends of God'

Eckhart's Way

Richard J. Woods, OP

VERITAS

First published 1986 by Glazier (United States); 1987 by Darton, Longman
and Todd (United Kingdom)

This edition published 2009 by
Veritas Publications
7/8 Lower Abbey Street
Dublin 1, Ireland
Email publications@veritas.ie
Website www.veritas.ie

ISBN 978 1 84730 157 4

10 9 8 7 6 5 4 3 2 1

A catalogue record for this book is available from the British Library.

Designed by Paula Crehan
Printed in the Republic of Ireland by ColourBooks Ltd, Dublin

Veritas books are printed on paper made from the wood pulp of managed
forests. For every tree felled, at least one tree is planted, thereby renewing
natural resources.

CONTENTS

FOREWORD

In 1984, Michael Glazier asked me to provide a one-volume introduction to the life and teaching of Meister Eckhart, the great fourteenth-century German Dominican mystic and preacher, as one of the first volumes under the general editorship of Noel Dermot O'Donoghue in the series on 'The Way of the Christian Mystics'. After two years of research and writing, *Eckhart's Way* was published in 1986 in the United States by Glazier (reprinted in 1990 by the Liturgical Press) and in England by Darton, Longman and Todd in 1987.

Critical Eckhart scholarship has advanced considerably since 1986, owing largely to the work of scholars in Europe and the United States, notably Alois Haas, Niklaus Largier, Bernard McGinn, Georg Steer, Loris Sturlese and Frank Tobin. McGinn's masterful work, *The Mystical Thought of Meister Eckhart: The Man from Whom God Hid Nothing*,[1] adjunct to his multi-volume history of western Christian mysticism, *The Presence of God*,[2] remains an outstanding contribution to Eckhart studies. Michael Demkovich's recent *Introduction to Meister Eckhart*[3] is a highly readable overview of Eckhart's life and teaching with a selection of excerpts from his sermons and treatises.

Why, then, should a new edition of *Eckhart's Way* be of interest? Although both editions of the book were out of print by 1998, there has been a fairly constant request by members of the Eckhart Society and others for a reprint. Further, many of the studies that appeared after the publication of *Eckhart's Way*, notably Oliver Davies' excellent introduction *Meister Eckhart: Mystical Theologian*[4] and Frank Tobin's magisterial *Meister Eckhart, Language and Thought*,[5] are no longer in print. Other works have appeared, pre-eminently the two studies by Professor Bernard McGinn, both of which are epoch-making scholarly works but aimed at a professional readership. Reissuing *Eckhart's Way* therefore presented an opportunity to provide more than a basic introduction to Eckhart's life and teaching, but less than a massive treatise that a comprehensive grasp of the Meister's teaching merits.

On the other hand, a good deal of research over the last two decades has altered some of the details we know of Eckhart's career, and there were corrections to be made and some points that I needed to clarify as well as updating the references considerably. A thorough revision of *Eckhart's Way* was thus a real temptation. But in the long run that would amount to virtually writing a new book, which was beyond my purpose and more than my correspondents asked for. A companion volume is a real possibility, but that is a matter for another day. I have made changes where errors of fact or expression required it, and I have tried to update the references where helpful. But *Eckhart's Way* remains essentially the same work.

Richard Woods, OP
May 2009

NOTES

1. New York: Crossroad, 2001. It would be a daunting and unnecessary task to attempt to reference all the pertinent sections of McGinn's watershed account in this edition of *Eckhart's Way*, especially since serious scholars will have ready access to the book itself. Occasional passages will be noted, however.
2. New York: Crossroad, 1996–2005. McGinn's fourth volume in the series, *The Harvest of Mysticism in Medieval Germany* (New York: Crossroad, 2005), contains much of the same material but expands and elaborates on many important aspects. As it situates Eckhart's life and teaching in the context of the mystical currents of medieval Germany from the thirteenth to the fifteenth centuries, it is an indispensable resource.
3. Ottawa/Notre Dame: Novalis/Fides, 2005.
4. London: SPCK, 1991.
5. Philadelphia: University of Pennsylvania Press, 1986.

INTRODUCTION

At the General Chapter of Walberberg in 1980, the Order of Preachers initiated official procedures to reopen the case of an aged Dominican friar, fifteen articles from whose writings were condemned for heresy by a papal bull in 1329, a year after his death.[1] Today, with the world in uncommon turmoil and the Church facing grave crises of faith and trust both within and outside the official institution, the question naturally arises, why bother to rehabilitate Meister Eckhart?

To begin with, scholars have reexamined Eckhart's works and the proceedings against him in Cologne and Avignon for over a century now. The growing conviction that he was in fact the victim of deliberate or indeliberate ecclesiastical injustice clearly warrants a rehearing. To be sure, agreement that Eckhart was innocent of the charges against him has never been univocal. William of Ockham, himself under house arrest in Avignon for suspected heresy at the same time, complained in fact that Eckhart was treated far too leniently. However unworthy Ockham's motives, his opinion has been echoed many times, at least with regard to Eckhart's teachings.[2]

A broad range of opinion has always existed with regard to Eckhart's life and doctrine. This should not be surprising. He had patrolled the nether borders of the unnameable Mystery we call God and strained human language to its limits in describing that experience. It is my own conviction, and only fair to state in advance, that even so Eckhart remained an orthodox and creative proponent of the classical tradition of Christian spirituality, a heritage whose extensive roots can be traced back to the desert mystics of Christian Egypt and Syria, the Bible, and the philosophical theologies of Plotinus, Aristotle and Plato.

Perhaps the most pressing reason for another look at the 'Eckhart case' concerns just those crises in the Church today which at first glance make the whole notion of a rehearing seem preposterously backward-looking. For many of these challenges and dilemmas are surprisingly like those of Eckhart's own times – a massive loss of confidence in the Church as an institution, a sense that God is remote or, indeed, 'dead', a sometimes overwhelming awareness of social violence and corruption against which the message of the Nazarene stands pale and ineffective, a proliferation of alluring cults and mean-tempered sectarianism, a pervasive fear of the future and, hardly least, a vast and consuming hunger for meaning, value and love on the part of people everywhere. In the fourteenth century Eckhart's preaching and teaching revitalized the faith of much of Europe. That same mystical spirit, freed from the lurking suspicion of unorthodoxy, may well help to dispel the spiritual confusion of our time, springing up into the parched lands of trust and friendship like a fountain in the wilderness.

The Master

Eckhart never claimed to be an original thinker, nor has he commonly been considered one by the academy. Even there, however, opinion is beginning to change. When his long-forgotten Latin works were rediscovered at the end of the nineteenth century, Eckhart's daring flights of theological speculation were found to be as intellectually stimulating as in the more familiar vernacular works his heroic call to self-renunciation and wholehearted dedication to God and neighbour were still able to arouse the spirit.

Regrettably, it is impossible in a work of this size and character to attend adequately to both theology and spirituality. I must therefore pass only cursorily over Eckhart's dogmatic and exegetical works. But it is well to remember, as Bernard McGinn has rightly emphasised, that the integral Eckhart is the Master of both the German and the Latin works.[3] Ultimately, he must be studied whole.

Eckhart and German Mysticism

Was Eckhart himself a mystic? If the world commonly regards him as such, scholarly opinion has also been mixed on this issue. Much of the dispute concerning whether Eckhart was in fact a philosopher merely preempting the mystical language of the time, as C.F. Kelley and others have claimed, or in truth a mystic himself revolves around the meaning of mysticism and its related areas.[4]

Following the example of William James in his immortal *Varieties of Religious Experience*, and interpreters such as Rudolf Otto and Frits Staal, some Eckhart scholars do not attempt to define mysticism at all, but simply point to the lives and teachings of the men and women to whom the world has extended the accolade of 'mystic'. Such an approach tends to beg the question, and we are still left wondering why were such people called 'mystics' to begin with?

Sufficiently for present purposes, the great scholar of German mysticism Jeanne Ancelet-Hustache described mysticism as '... the mysterious desire of the soul – felt to be sacred, preceding any rational justification and sometimes unconscious yet profound and irresistible – which urges it to enter into contact with what it holds to be the absolute. This will normally be its God, but sometimes also a vaguer concept such as Being in itself, the great All – nature or the world soul.'[5] A Christian mystic, then, is a person who experiences a profound sense of union with Ultimate Reality or at least, as Evelyn Underhill wisely added, wants to.[6]

Speculation and Praxis

Generally, Eckhart has been categorised as a speculative mystic. His teaching is in fact thick with philosophical and theological query and implication. His complex train of thought is often difficult to follow. The very language he used to express his profound insights into the mystery of the human encounter with God is challenging and yet elusive. Much of it, at least in his German writings, Eckhart had to invent.[7]

Ideally it is possible, if risky, to extrapolate from theory to practice in the lives of great spiritual figures. With Eckhart, this is particularly hazardous because we know so little about his life and personality. The record of his doctrine itself is incomplete. Still, I have become convinced from studying his sermons and treatises and the records of his trials that Eckhart knew from direct, first-hand experience the concrete truth of what he preached, particularly when he expressed himself with the candid and utter conviction that typifies his work at his best.

Eckhart's doctrine is in fact rich in practical advice, most of it far more sound than the spiritual writings of the next three centuries. We can learn much from the old Lebemeister. To disengage the practical aspects from his speculative concerns would nevertheless distort and misrepresent his teaching as well as impoverish it. No matter how demanding on the temperament of late twentieth century spiritual seekers, if Eckhart is to be truly grasped, here too he must be taken whole.

The Rhineland Mystics

Whether or not one considers Eckhart a mystic in practice, his doctrine and name became virtually synonymous with the magnificent flowering of mysticism of the fourteenth century Rhineland. This rich and turbulent area extends from the great Rheinwaldhorn Glacier to the North Sea, encompassing even in the fourteenth century some of the most densely populated portions of the western world. For over eight hundred miles, the great river runs like the spine of Europe through large sections of Switzerland, Liechtenstein, Austria, Germany, France and the Netherlands. It is navigable to Cologne by ocean-going vessels, and by barge as far as Basel.

The Rhine brought life to the extensive farmlands and bustling commercial centres of the Middle Ages; Eckhart invigorated the spirit of a God-seeking people through a lifetime of preaching and teaching. But he was not the first.

Mysticism appeared in Germany comparatively late in Christian history, for Germany itself was not fully evangelised until the end of the first millenium.[8] When it appeared, however, mysticism swept across the Rhineland like a flash-flood. The first mystical work written in the German language was probably St Trudperter Hohelied, composed anonymously around 1140.[9] But Eckhart's more immediate predecessors were the remarkable women mystics of the twelfth and thirteenth centuries, Hildegard of Bingen, Mechthild of Magdeburg and Gertrude the Great.[10] Significantly, his immediate followers, the German Dominican friars and nuns, also drew from those elder sources. But Eckhart himself had become the primary channel through which the stream of Rhineland mysticism now passed from generation to generation.

Heretic

On trial at Cologne and Avignon for his mystical teaching toward the end of his life, Eckhart argued that heresy is primarily a matter of the will, which pertinaciously clings to proved doctrinal error. As he insisted, his own will remained loyal to God and the Church unto death. However, the posthumous condemnation of some of the Meister's teachings, although only a minuscule portion of his writings, has cast a centuries-long shadow over his doctrine as a whole.[11]

Was Eckhart in fact a heretic? Or was he simply misunderstood or even a scapegoat for ecclesiastical and imperial politicians, as some have maintained? We may never really know. For now, whatever the outcome of the Dominican petition to have the papal condemnation re-examined and withdrawn, whether Eckhart's life and teachings will again provide nourishment for women and men whose spirits have been parched by the demand of times manifestly as turbulent as those of the fourteenth century, a new generation of readers must decide for itself.

Translations

To many American and English readers, Eckhart represents a discovery of the last few years. For half a century, the most comprehensive translation available was Miss C. de B. Evans' two-volume translation (1923 and 1931) of Pfeiffer's 1857 edition of Eckhart's German sermons.[12] The most popular abridgement was a compendium of sermons and treatises sometimes inaccurately translated by Raymond Blakney.[13] The best general treatment at hand was perhaps a brief sample of sermons and treatises translated by Hilda Graef in Jeanne Ancelet-Hustache's superb little book, *Master Eckhart and the Rhineland Mystics* (1957). In the same year, James M. Clark published a selection of twenty-five well-translated German sermons and related documents with an excellent introduction.[14] The following year, Clark and John V. Skinner published an additional volume containing translations of equal merit of the German treatises, eight Latin and two German sermons and short excerpts from Eckhart's Latin biblical commentaries.[15] But of the above, only Blakney's edition is still in print.

During the next twenty years, to the best of my knowledge the only other work of Eckhart's translated into English was Fr Armand Maurer's edition of the Latin *Parisian Questions and Prologues* – five theological disputations and several introductory sections intended for incorporation into Eckhart's unfinished summa, the *Opus Tripartitum*.[16] In 1978, however, eight German sermons were brilliantly translated by Reiner Schürmann as the basis of an extensive philosophical analysis and commentary.[17] Then, between 1979 and 1985 the late Maurice Walshe published a new translation of Pfeiffer's 1857 collection in a monumental three-volume edition of sermons and treatises.[18] In 1980, a translation of thirty-four German sermons and treatises and three Latin sermons was edited with short commentaries by Matthew Fox.[19] The following year, another and very valuable collection appeared, a representative selection of sermons and treatises from both the Latin and German writings with extensive critical notes and commentary by Edmund Colledge, OSA and Bernard McGinn,[20] followed in 1987 by a second collection edited by McGinn, Frank Tobin and Elvira Borgstädt.[21] A number of shorter anthologies appeared in the following years.[22] Eckhart had found a new and growing readership in both scholarly and popular circles.

Perhaps the majority of scholarly Eckhart studies are still in German, although a considerable number exist in French, Dutch and Italian. A growing number are appearing in English. Comprehensive bibliographies can be found in the editions by Colledge-McGinn, Schürmann, and in particular the special *Thomist* issue of April, 1978 (Vol. 42, No. 2), which supplements and updates Ernst Soudek's extensive bibliography in *Meister Eckhart*.[23] Niklaus Largier's on-going bibliography in the annual *Eckhart Review* is now an indispensable reference.[24] (In the bibliographical section at the end of this volume, I have included a select list of books and articles in English and some foreign language studies published since 1987.)

Texts and References

Despite occasional scholarly idiosyncrasies, over the past two decades references to Eckhart's German and Latin works have become almost standardised. In keeping with contemporary practice, in this book Josef Quint's critical edition of the German works will be abbreviated DW (for *Deutsche Werke*), followed by Roman numerals for volume number and Arabic numerals for sermon and page numbers. Similarly, the Latin works will be abbreviated LW (for *Lateinische Werke*), followed by Roman numerals for volume and sermon number and Arabic numerals for page numbers. [25] Quint's 1955 modernisation of a selection of Eckhart's Middle High German Sermons will be referred to as DP (for *Deutsche Predigten*), with Arabic numerals indicating sermon and page numbers. [26]

Over the centuries, hundreds of sermons were spuriously attributed to Meister Eckhart. Pfeiffer's 1857 attempt at a critical edition reduced that number to 110 sermons. Of these, Josef Quint included seventy-one in the eighty-six unquestionably authentic sermons in the Kohlhammer edition (DW) – 5-14, 19-25, 27, 29-36, 38, 40-43, 45-49, 52, 55, 58-60, 62-66, 69, 72-74, 79-91, 94-100 and 102. [27] Sermons are listed in DW according to the strength of evidence for their authenticity, from highest (1) to lowest (86). [28] Fifteen others were added from a variety of sources, primarily single manuscripts edited by Jostes, Jundt and Strauch. In his 1955 modern German translation (DP), Quint added five more (1, 2, 4, 15 and 56) from the Pfeiffer collection to forty-four from DW and ten (3, 5, 14, 15, 18, 19, 20, 21, 40 and 51) from other sources. Walshe lists ninety-seven sermons in his edition. Because of double numbering in four cases, however (13a and 13b, 14a and 14b, 24a and 24b, and 32a and 32b), there are in fact 101 sermons. Of these, ninety-one are taken from DW, five from DP and five more from Pfeiffer as amended by Quint. Modern scholarship currently recognises 114 sermons as most probably authentic.

For the sake of convenience to the general reader, whose access to the critical German editions of Eckhart's works is understandably limited, unless otherwise noted all numerical references to the German sermons in this book will be to Walshe's translation, abbreviated W and followed by Arabic numerals. [29]

Since for the most part I have relied for citations principally on Walshe's version and occasionally on other modern translations of Eckhart's difficult Middle High German, I have not attempted to substitute more inclusive references to God (which are usually masculine), the human soul (usually feminine), and other customary medieval usages so unpalatable to contemporary tastes. As has become evident with the Bible and Shakespeare, efforts to 'degenderise' sublime poetry serve mainly to dilute it. Neither Eckhart nor Jesus, nor for that matter, Shakespeare, were misogynists. With that in mind, I think it possible to tolerate the inadequacies of their language in the interest of accuracy and respect without succumbing to undesirable cultural presuppositions reflected in the speech patterns of their times. It is, in any event, a goal worth striving for.

Like the householder in the gospel (Mt 13:52), Eckhart himself drew out of the considerable treasury of his learning and prayer goods both new and old. But he was always selective and creative, rarely leaving his plunder unembellished, if not sometimes thoroughly recast. Even when he reinterpreted the meaning of his predecessors almost past recognition – a tendency for which he was judiciously upbraided by the theological commission at Avignon – Eckhart's intention remained what it had always been (as he patiently reminded his examiners): to preach the gospel, to bear blessing to his hearers, and to glorify God. *Laudare, benedicere, praedicare*: he was, after all, a Dominican. Truth was the star he followed and found, the divine Truth that would set the world alight with freedom. Over the centuries, Eckhart's long-silent voice still directs us to that star through the startling, ingenuous poetry of his undying word.

Special thanks is due to Watkins Publishing Co., Ltd. for their generous permission to cite from *Meister Eckhart: Sermons and Treatises*, M. O'C. Walshe, ed. and trans., 3 vols., London, 1979, 1981 and 1985. Similarly, I wish to thank Paulist Press, Mahwah, NJ, for permission to cite passages from *Meister Eckhart: The Essential Sermons, Commentaries, Treatises and Defense*, translation and introduction by Edmund Colledge, OSA and Bernard McGinn, New York, 1981. For their unstinting assistance in locating reference materials, I remain indebted to Rev. Phillip McShane, OP, Mark and Anne Primavesi, Rev. Timothy Sparks, OP, and Mr Randy Wilhelm. I also wish to express special fraternal gratitude to Dr Suzanne Noffke, OP, and to Professors Joachim Stieber and Jochanan Wijnhoven of the departments of history and medieval studies at Smith College, Northampton, Massachusetts, for their timely encouragement and support. Most particularly, I wish to thank my confrere and former teacher, Rev. Benedict Ashley, OP, whose kind and painstaking reading of the original manuscript prevented a host of major and minor errors. Those which survived remain my sole responsibility. For them, as would the Meister, I ask pardon in advance.

NOTES

1. *Acta Capituli Generalis Provincialium Ordinis Praedicatorum apud Walberberg*, Rome: S Sabina, 1980, p. 74, n. 122 ('De Studio').

2. On Ockham's lack of candour, see Edmund Colledge, OSA, 'Meister Eckhart: His Times and His Writings', *The Thomist*, 42 (No. 2, April, 1978), p. 246. Among contemporary, even sympathetic critics who have either concluded to or assumed the unorthodox content of Eckhart's doctrine are Edmund Colledge, John Loeschen, Daisetz Suzuki and Shizuteru Ueda.

3. Bernard McGinn, 'The God beyond God: Theology and Mysticism in the Thought of Meister Eckhart', *Journal of Religion* 61 (1981), pp. 5–6.

4. For Kelley's appraisal of Eckhart, see below, pp. 179f. Mysticism is a relatively late addition to the English language, first appearing in 1736. The term has been defined in a number of ways, all of them unsatisfactory in one respect or another. To his classic *Christian Mysticism* (1899), Dean William Inge was able to append a fourteen-page list of twenty-six lengthy definitions or descriptions of mysticism from that century alone. Similar attempts will be found in W.K. Fleming (ed.), *Mysticism in Christianity*, London: Robert Scott, 1913, pp. 3, 10–11. Other classic definitions can be found in Rufus Jones, *Studies in Mystical Religion* (1909), New York: Russell and Russell, 1970 ed., p. xv; Evelyn Underhill, *Mysticism* (1910), New York: World Pub. Co., 1955 ed., p. xiv; Dom Cuthbert Butler, *Western Mysticism* (1922), New York: Barnes and Noble, 1968 ed., p. 5; and W.T. Stace, *The Teachings of the Mystics*, New York: New American Library, 1960, pp. 14f. For a more recent but still reticent effort, see Nelson Pike, *Mystic Union: An Essay in the Phenomenology of Mysticism*, Ithaca and London: Cornell University Press, 1992, esp. pp. 166ff.

5. Jeanne Ancelet-Hustache, *Master Eckhart and the Rhineland Mystics*, New York and London: Harper and Row: Longmans, 1957, p. 5. Hereafter referred to as Ancelet-Hustache.

6. 'Mysticism is the art of union with Reality. The mystic is a person who has attained that union in greater or less degree; or who aims at and believes in such attainment.' *Practical Mysticism*, New York: E.P. Dutton and Co., 1915, p. 3.

7. Cf. Bernard McGinn, 'Meister Eckhart's Condemnation Reconsidered', *The Thomist*, 44 (1980), p. 414. Maurice de Gandillac similarly hailed Eckhart as 'le vrai fondateur de la prose allemande'. ('La "dialectique" de Maitre Eckhart', *La Mystique Rhénane*, Paris: Presses Universitaires de France, 1963, p. 60.) More recently, however, McGinn has observed that 'Older claims that Eckhart single-handedly created German mystical and/or philosophical-theological language must be abandoned. The Dominican was part of a broad effort in the thirteenth and fourteenth centuries to make MHG [Middle High German] an apt instrument for speculation and mysticism. But there is no doubt about Eckhart's genius in forging a distinctive mystical style of preaching, one that was famous and controversial in his day as in ours.' *The Mystical Thought of Meister Eckhart*, op. cit., p. 31.

8. In regard to the origins of Christian mysticism, the first volume of the monumental multi-volume history by Bernard McGinn, *The Presence of God*, is

an indispensable resource for serious study: *The Foundations of Mysticism*, New York: Crossroad, 1991. For early Christian mysticism, see Louis Bouyer, 'Mysterion', in *Mystery and Mysticism*, London: Aquin Press, 1955, pp. 18–32; Andrew Louth, *The Origins of the Christian Mystical Tradition*, Oxford: Clarendon Press, 1981; and Richard Woods, *Mysterion: An Approach to Mystical Spirituality*, Chicago: Thomas More Press, 1981.

9.   Cf. M.O'C. Walshe, *Meister Eckhart: Sermons and Treatises*, 3 vols., London / Shaftesbury: Watkins / Element Books, 1979, 1981 and 1985, I, p. xiv. Hereafter referred to as Walshe (W in reference to particular sermons). Walshe's groundbreaking work is undergoing revision and will be published soon by Crossroad in a single volume. Because the original edition of this work was keyed to the three-volume set, I have retained that usage. The numbering of individual sermons will remain the same.

10.   For a discussion of these women and their influence on Dominican spirituality and Eckhart in particular, see Ancelet-Hustache, pp. 15–18; William W. Hinnebusch, OP, *The History of the Dominican Order*, 2 vols., Staten Island, NY: Alba House, 1966 and 1973, I, p. 389 (hereafter Hinnebusch); Jean Leclercq, OSB, 'From St Gregory to St Bernard', *The Spirituality of the Middle Ages*, ed. by J. Lerclercq et al, London: Burns and Oates, 1968, pp. 177–80; Francois Vandenbroucke, OSB, 'New Milieux, New Problems', ibid., pp. 358–64, 373–79; and Walshe, I, p. xiv.

11.   In Sr Mary Jean Dorcy's *St Dominic's Family*, a compendious volume containing thumbnail biographies of more than 300 famous Dominicans including Henry Suso, Johann Tauler and even Heinrich Denifle, Eckhart is not only excluded, but when mentioned in passing, not even identified as a Dominican. (Washington, DC: Dominicana Publications, 1983.)

12.   For these and other standard references, see the bibliography, pp. 196–207.

13.   Raymond Blakney, *Meister Eckhart*, New York: Harper and Row, 1941.

14.   James Clark, *Meister Eckhart: An Introduction to the Study of His Works with an Anthology of His Sermons*, Edinburgh and London: Nelson, 1957. Hereafter referred to as CL.

15.   James M. Clark and John V. Skinner, eds and trans., *Treatises and Sermons of Meister Eckhart*, New York: Harper and Row. Reprinted by Octagon Books, New York, 1983. Hereafter referred to as CL-SK.

16.   Armand Maurer (ed.), *Master Eckhart: Parisian Questions and Prologues*, Toronto: The Pontifical Institute of Medieval Studies, 1974. Hereafter referred to as Maurer.

17.   Reiner Schürmann, *Meister Eckhart, Mystic and Philosopher*, Bloomington, Indiana: Indiana University Press, 1978. A translation and new edition of *Maître Eckhart ou la joie errante*, Paris: Editions Planète-Denoël, 1972. Hereafter referred to as Schürmann.

18.   Walshe, op. cit.

19.   Matthew Fox, *Breakthrough: Meister Eckhart's Creation Spirituality in New Translation*, Garden City, NY: Doubleday, 1980.

20.   Edmund Colledge, OSA and Bernard McGinn, eds and trans., *Meister Eckhart: The Essential Sermons, Commentaries, Treatises and Defense*, New York: Paulist Press, 1981. Hereafter referred to as C-McG.

21. Bernard McGinn with Frank Tobin and Elvira Borgstädt, eds and trans., preface by Kenneth Northcott, *Meister Eckhart: Teacher and Preacher*, New York: Paulist Press / London: SPCK, 1987.

22. Outstanding among the latter is Oliver Davies' selection, *Meister Eckhart: Selected Writings*, London and New York: Penguin, 1994.

23. Ernst H. Soudek, *Meister Eckhart*, Stuttgart: Metzler, 1973, pp. 24–33.

24. *The Eckhart Review* is available from the Eckhart Society, in care of the Secretary at Summa, 22 Tippings Lane, Woodley, Reading, Berkshire RG5 4RX, UK, and online at www.eckhartsociety.org.

25. *Meister Eckhart: Die deutschen und lateinischen Werke. Herausgegeben im Auftrage der deutschen Forschungsgemeinschaft*, Stuttgart and Berlin: Verlag W. Kohlhammer, vols I–V, 1936. For these and other critical works and commentaries, see the bibliography at the end of this volume. A list of abbreviations used will be found on p. 194.

26. *Meister Eckehart: Deutsche Predigten und Traktate*, ed. and trans. by Josef Quint, Munich: Carl Hanser, 1955. N.B.: Walshe refers to this volume as QT, Fox as Q.

27. See Walshe, II, p. vii.

28. For a brief description of Quint's criteria of authenticity, numbering and consequent divisions of the sermons into groups, see C-McG, p. 67.

29. Unlike other recent versions, such as those of C-McG, Fox and Davies, Walshe largely retains Pfeiffer's 1857 numbering system, which as he notes enjoys greater manuscript authority and allows for the inclusion of sermons omitted from DW but nevertheless very probably authentic. Fortunately, he always supplies the corresponding Quint numbers and other references as well. For comparisons of the numbering systems of the critical editions, Quint's modernisation, Walshe, McGinn, Davies and other major English translations, see Appendix A, p. 208.

PART ONE
ECKHART'S WAY

THE FRIAR'S WAY

His name was Eckhart.[1] Known later as Eckhart von Hochheim, he was born about 1260 in a Thuringian village in northeastern Germany, possibly Tambach, of a family of the lesser nobility. Hochheim might then be a family name.[2] There are, however, two villages in the district called Hochheim, one northwest of Gotha and the other near Erfurt. Little else is known of Eckhart's origins, the formative influences of his family, childhood experiences or early youth.[3] As a member of the Dominican Order, he would have initially been called Friar or 'Bruder' Eckhart. But when he completed his magisterial studies in theology at the University of Paris in 1302, the honorific title 'Master' (*Meister* in German) was added to his name as was customary. Since then, he became known and venerated throughout the world simply and forever as Meister Eckhart.

At a very young age by modern standards, probably between fifteen and seventeen, Eckhart was accepted into the novitiate of the Order of Friars Preachers (Dominicans) at Erfurt. After professing his vows, or possibly before, he was probably sent to the University of Paris for initial studies. There, he seems to have studied under Siger of Brabant, whose radical Averroist-Aristotelianism was condemned on 7 March 1277 along with certain propositions of Thomas Aquinas.[4]

From Paris Eckhart went in 1280 to the *studium generale* established in Cologne in 1248 by the great Dominican teacher and bishop, Albert the Great, master of Thomas Aquinas. On his arrival it is not certain but likely that Eckhart actually met 'Bishop Albrecht', who spent his last years at Cologne and died there on 15 November 1280, shortly after Eckhart would have begun his formal theological studies.[5] However, it is altogether unlikely that he could have met Thomas, who died in 1274, probably well before Eckhart entered the order. But he lived to see the Angelic Doctor exonerated and canonised in 1323 by the very pope, ironically, who would posthumously condemn fifteen of Eckhart's own propositions six years afterwards.

Eckhart's Times: The Beginning of the End

As the thirteenth century drew to a close, the great edifice of medieval Christendom was beginning to crumble. Forty years earlier, there had been only distant rumblings in the remoter vaults. But despite growing discontent and occasionally ominous crises, the years of Eckhart's youth were not a period of unusual conflict, confusion and catastrophe. The debacle still lay ahead. But even during the tempestuous century that followed, as in all periods of cultural transition and political upheaval, there were moments of sparkling achievement in religion, the arts, humanities, science and the experiences of ordinary life.[6]

During the decades immediately before and after Eckhart's birth, scholastic theology and philosophy attained their greatest heights at the universities of Paris and Oxford. Bonaventure had interrupted his brilliant teaching career to become Minister General of the Franciscan Order in 1257. In 1263, the year Balliol College was founded at Oxford, Thomas Aquinas finished the *Summa Contra Gentes*. The following year he began his masterpiece, the *Summa Theologiae*, left unfinished by a premature death a decade later. The Franciscan Roger Bacon was then teaching at Oxford at the newly founded Merton College while Albert the Great presided over the Dominican *studium generale* (house of study) at Cologne.

Spiritual ferment was also in the air: it was an era of saints – friars such as Albert, Bonaventure and Thomas Aquinas, queens and kings such as Elizabeth of Hungary, Brigit of Sweden and Louis IX of France, lay people such as the Franciscan Angela of Foligno and Ramon Lull, even popes, such as Gregory X and the bewildered holy man Peter of Murrone, who became Pope Celestine V. In 1296, the gentle Dominican friar Henry Suso was born and in 1300, his junior contemporary, Johann Tauler. The year the Black Death first appeared in Europe, 1347, also witnessed the birth of one of the greatest mystics and the first woman Doctor of the Church, the Dominican laywoman, Catherine of Siena.

It was also an era of emerging lay spirituality. Fundamentally orthodox but misunderstood associations such as the Beguines were first reported in the densely populated areas of the Netherlands in the late twelfth century. Within a few decades, the movement had spread throughout the Rhineland. Fertilised by the prophecies of the Calabrian apocalypticist, Abbot Joachim of Fiore, a wilder variety of mystical cults also flourished throughout Europe. Strange sects and religious scoundrels proliferated. The anarchic, erotically-prone 'Brethren of the Free Spirit' roamed from country to country attacking organised religion and conventional morality. The first flagellant movements sprang up in southern Germany and northern Italy.

By the end of the thirteenth century, moreover, the Church that had presided spiritually and even politically over a shakily unified Christendom for several centuries found itself torn between opposed forces intent on controlling Europe – the French dynasty of Anjou, rulers of the largest and most powerful nation in Europe, and the Germano-Austrian Kings, especially the Holy Roman emperors, whose dreams of conquest were hardly less grandiose. The papacy frequently found itself under attack from both directions, sometimes simultaneously, even while its power was slowly eroded from within by the restive Italian republics and a growing secularist movement.

Only a century later, however, as the Black Death cut its terrible swath over the continent, internecine political and dynastic struggles would have seriously weakened the power of the German Imperium to threaten national or ecclesiastical interests for several generations to follow. The papacy, too, having moved to a safer position at Avignon under the 'protection' of the French monarchy, would never regain even under the Borgias the power and prestige it enjoyed during the High Middle Ages. France, finally, would find itself reduced by a seemingly incessant war with England to a state of economic and political desperation. Eckhart, however, would know none of this, no matter how gifted his prophetic powers, even though murmurs of destruction must have been audible by the time he began his scholastic career in Paris.

Eckhart the Student

In its earliest years, the Dominican Order provided no courses in the arts and humanities for its student members, who were instructed only in scripture and theology. Once professed, Dominican students were actually forbidden to take courses in the liberal arts, medicine, law and philosophy, especially that of 'pagans and unbelievers' such as Aristotle (although they were allowed to 'consult' them privately). Postulants were expected, as today, to have completed their initial studies prior to entrance. As ever-greater numbers of young candidates flocked to the Order, however, it became necessary to modify this custom.

At the time Eckhart entered, sometime in the latter part of the 1270s, matters were in transition. He could have already finished his preliminary studies at the University of Paris as Hinnebusch suggests, or he may have been sent there to do so. In either event, the course of studies he would have first been exposed to consisted of grammar, logic and dialectics, natural science, psychology, astronomy, metaphysics and moral philosophy – the sequence imposed by decree at the University of Paris in 1255 and followed by the Dominican *studium generale* at St Jacques as part of the University.[7]

Dominican students in prioral schools who showed particular aptitude for studies were selected to go on for more advanced work in general houses of study such as that founded at Cologne in 1248 by St Albert, which would one day be incorporated into the new university. (Both the university, founded in 1388, and the Cologne studium were destroyed by revolutionary French troops in 1797.) 'It was the intellectual elite, finally, who matriculated in the universities,' Hinnebusch relates, 'and not all of them advanced to the mastership.'[8] Eckhart, however, did so, advancing from Cologne to the University of Paris in 1293 at the age of thirty-three as a lecturer on the Sentences.

Merely to qualify to become a Master of Sacred Theology, the ultimate medieval academic achievement, a candidate would thus have already completed at least seven years of preliminary study in theology, having lectured as a bachelor on scripture and the Sentences and remained in active residence for five or six years.[9] Fortunately, because of their previous work in the order's houses of study, Dominican aspirants such as Eckhart would not have had to repeat the preliminary requirements. But overall, 'The bachelorship and residence requirement extended over a period of at least fourteen to fifteen years before licensing and graduation as a master'.[10]

The Priesthood and Paris

After finishing his higher studies at Cologne and before returning to Paris to undertake studies for the prestigious title of Master in Theology, Eckhart was ordained to the priesthood. The date and place are not known and this biographical detail is usually passed over in accounts of Eckhart's life. As a Dominican friar, however, his ordination would have figured greatly in Eckhart's own spiritual life and his eventual career as pastor and preacher. I suggest that at the centre of the multiplicity of offices, duties, commissions and disputes that would preoccupy him until his death, the 'unwobbly centre' of Eckhart's life as a Dominican remained the pastoral call that first led him to the door of Erfurt priory and eventually to the ministry of pulpit and altar.

Josef Koch dates the first part of Eckhart's second stay in Paris between 1293 and 1294, during which time he composed the *Collatio in libros Sententiarum*, his inaugural lecture as Master of the Sentences of Peter Lombard.[11] From the end of that period came his Easter sermon, 'Pascha nostrum immolatus' of 18 April 1294, which contains an early reference to 'Bishop Albrecht'.

Eckhart must have enjoyed the confidence of his brethren from the beginning, for the next we hear of him, he has been elected prior of his home convent at Erfurt in 1294. About the same time, and well before 1298, when holding multiple offices was forbidden, he was appointed vicar of Thuringia. It is perhaps at this point in his life that he dictated the *Reden der Unterscheidung* (*Talks of Instruction*), discourses or 'collations' given to the younger members of the community on a variety of topics concerning the spiritual life. One of the treasures of German vernacular literature, these talks reflect the young Eckhart as priest and pastor, but a man himself already possessed of keen spiritual discernment and balance. In them, almost all the major themes of his mature spiritual doctrine are present at least in germinal form.[12]

After his term of office expired in 1298, Eckhart resumed his studies in Paris, where, in 1302, he was granted the coveted title of *Magister in Theologia*. During the next year, he was Regent Master for Externs. From this period come three 'Parisian Questions', the third debated with the Franciscan Master Gonzalvo of Spain, and the great sermon for the feast of St Augustine delivered on 28 August 'Quasi vas auri solidum'.[13] But while Eckhart prepared himself for what everyone no doubt expected to be the career of a distinguished teacher and theologian, events in the wider world of church and state had, however, already begun to determine a vastly different future for him.

Evangelical Poverty, Radical Reform and Spiritual Dissent

Throughout the twelfth and thirteenth centuries, religious, even apostolic fervour percolated among both clergy and laity. Not even the papacy was immune from the zealous efforts of reformers. Outstanding among the more formidable proponents of twelfth and thirteenth century religious revolutions were the major heretical groups, the so-called Cathars, Albigensians and Waldensians, all of whom preached and practiced forms of voluntary poverty, radical obedience to their leadership and an anti-institutional spirituality. The two former groups were all but extinguished by papal crusades. Near the turn of the century, however, the Waldensians, also known as the Poor Men of Lyons, merged with a similar group called the *Humiliati*, and became known as the Poor Lombards. Pockets of Waldensians continue to exist to this day.

At least two groups were known as *Apostolici*, one centred on Cologne and Périgueux in France, the other founded in Parma by Gerard Segarelli in the year of Eckhart's birth. Influenced by the doctrine of the Spiritual Franciscans, the latter group was twice condemned by Rome, in 1286 and in 1291. Segarelli was burned to death at Parma in 1300, but his followers regrouped under the apocalyptic preacher and anarchist, Fra Dolcino, who met a similar fate seven years later.

There were also the Bogomils, the Luciferians, the Almaricans, the *Fraticelli*, the Beghards and, of course, the Beguines. The most pervasive and elusive of the movements for religious freedom and spiritual anarchy were, however, the Brethren of the Free Spirit. With such a plethora of similar, even competing movements, the dividing line between heterodoxy and orthodoxy must surely have wavered at times in the minds of bishops and theologians. For those such as Archbishop Henry of Virneburg, such a confusion of tongues was all the more reason for stern methods of discernment and repression.

The Pope, the Emperor and the King

Eckhart's fate was closely tied to that of his native land as well as his Church. Throughout the thirteenth century, German political interests had centred on preserving the tentative unity created by the hereditary investiture of the imperium in a German prince – six of whom between

1138 and 1268 were of the Royal House of Hohenstaufen. Assuring German ascendency in Europe required keeping two other powerful forces at bay – the papacy and the French. To this end, the last great Emperor of the Middle Ages, Frederick II, 'the Cunning Fox' who was elected King of Germany in 1212 and Emperor in 1220, shifted his considerable military attention to southern Italy. At first, he succeeded. In 1237, invading imperial forces soundly defeated the Lombard League at Cortenuova.

The Church fought back with spiritual power as well as the military and political weapons at papal disposal. In 1239, Pope Gregory IX excommunicated Frederick for the second time and convened a General Council against him. The Emperor forestalled him by an assault on Rome itself in 1241, during which the old pope died. Under his successor, Innocent IV, Frederick was declared deposed in 1245 by the First Council of Lyon. Undaunted, the Emperor seized the vacant Duchy of Austria and Styria. By 1248, however, the tide of war had turned. Frederick was seriously defeated by Lombard forces at the Battle of Parma and died two years later. In 1254, the year in which Robert Sorbon founded the great theological school at the University of Paris named in his honor, Frederick was succeeded by Conrad IV, who himself died only four years later, inaugurating the violent and fatally debilitating Interregnum that would last until 1273.

In 1258, Frederick's bastard son Manfred claimed the succession and was proclaimed King of Sicily. Sensing disaster, Pope Alexander IV appealed to Charles of Anjou, brother of the saintly Louis IX and would-be King of Naples, inviting him to occupy the disputed southern lands. But in 1260, the year of Eckhart's birth, the Florentine Ghibellines, allies of the Hohenstaufens, defeated the pro-papal Guelphs at Montaperti. The pope was driven from Rome, and, 'unable to heal the ills of the Church, succumbed to his grief in 1261. Even his successor Urban IV could not return to the City'.[14] Two years later, however, Manfred was defeated and killed by Charles of Anjou at Benevento.

Aided by the substantial influence of Pope Clement IV, Charles succeeded to the throne of the Kingdom of Naples and Sicily in 1266. Infuriated, in 1268 the Ghibellines called on Conradin, the fifteen-year-old grandson of Frederick II and a cousin of Thomas Aquinas, to reclaim the southern kingdom of the Hohenstaufens. But he, too, was defeated and captured by Charles. Then to the horror of Europe, the youth was beheaded in the public square of Naples, thus at least temporarily forestalling the German threat to papal and French interests in Italy. A crime winked at by the beholden papacy, the merciless execution of Conradin, last of the Hohenstaufens, also destroyed the Duchy of Swabia as an integral political unit. At the height of its power, this vast area had extended from Strassburg to Ulm and from Baden to the Italian frontier. As Charles had no doubt intended, Germany was thereby plunged into internal turmoil regarding both the imperial succession and the redistribution of territory, further reducing its threat to France and the Pope.

Ironically, perhaps fittingly, Clement IV died within the year, inaugurating a three-year vacancy in the papacy. He was succeeded by the saintly Gregory X, who lived only five more years. In the meantime, Rudolf of Hapsburg was elected King of Germany in 1273 and recognised as Emperor by Gregory X, thus ending the Interregnum. In 1282, however, with the famous 'Sicilian Vespers', the nobles and people of Palermo revolted and massacred their French overlords. Once again the balance of power was threatened with upset.

The Overlord of France

In 1285, Philip IV ascended the throne sanctified by his grandfather, Louis IX, inaugurating a reign of political brutality which would bend two popes to his will, see to the death of another and, before his own death in 1314, succeed in removing the papacy from Rome to Avignon. In that same fateful year, with the reluctant connivance of the pope, Philip would engineer the final destruction of the Templars, the largest and most powerful of the Church's military orders, thus ensuring the virtual captivity of the papacy at Avignon for sixty-four more years.

In 1305, after the brief pontificate of the Dominican Pope Benedict XI (1303–1304), Bertrand de Got was elected Pope as Clement V. In fact the candidate of Philip IV, Clement was crowned at Lyons in the king's presence. And, in 1309, Clement fixed the papal residence at beautiful Avignon, thus inaugurating the 'Babylonian Captivity of the Church'. (Although not part of the Kingdom of France, Avignon at that time was a fiefdom of the Kingdom of Naples and Sicily, and thus under the 'protection' of Philip's cousins, Charles II and his successor, the brilliant Robert of Anjou.)

Not without skill and strength, Clement nevertheless remained subservient in most respects to Philip, who actually sat beside him during the Council of Vienne to assure the condemnation of the Templars. Not surprisingly, the six popes following Clement would also be French and also effectively vassals of the kings of France.

In the meantime, Adolf of Naussau had been elected German King in 1292. Deposed and killed in battle six years later, he was succeeded by Albert I, son of Rudolf of Hapsburg. But Albert was himself assassinated in 1308, possibly eliciting one of Eckhart's finest spiritual works, the *Book of Divine Consolation*, which he may have composed for Albert's grieving widow, Agnes of Hungary.[15] In the same year, Henry VII, Count of Luxembourg, was elected king. In 1312, he was proclaimed emperor but lived only a year longer. Almost immediately, Ludwig of Bavaria was elected emperor by five of the German prince-electors in Frankfurt. On the same day, the Count Palatine of the Rhine and the Archbishop of Cologne, Henry of Virneburg, elected Frederick of Hapsburg to the same office. Civil warfare broke out at once, raged intermittently and ended only with Frederick's defeat at Mühldorf in 1322. In 1325, however, Ludwig was constrained to accept Frederick as co-ruler.

Though he could not have known it, Eckhart, who by 1325 had returned to the *studium generale* in Cologne, was being drawn inexorably into the whirlpool of these conflicting interests — imperial, papal and national. In the eyes of the world they would eventually precipitate him as well as the Franciscans William of Ockham, Michael of Cesena, and their confederates to lasting disgrace and ruin.

The Pastor

In 1303, however, the year in which the aged Pope Boniface VIII was in effect brutally murdered by French troops and Eckhart concluded his first tenure as regent master in Paris, the Dominican General Chapter meeting at Besançon divided the province of Germany into two new provinces, those of Saxony and Teutonia. On 9 September, Eckhart, the new 'Meister', but already a middle-aged man, was elected the first provincial of the Saxon Province, in which Erfurt now lay. His election was confirmed the following year by the Chapter of Toulouse. He was also placed in charge of the Dominican nuns of the region.

Administrative successes mounted. In 1307, he was appointed Vicar of Bohemia by the Provincial Chapter of Strassburg and commissioned to reform the houses which had apparently fallen into dissolution there. Between 1309 and 1310, he founded three new houses of the order at Braunschweig, Dortmund and Groningen. And in 1310, Eckhart was elected Provincial of Teutonia. However, this election was canceled by the General Chapter meeting at Naples the following year. It was not a censure: the Meister was needed elsewhere.

The Second Paris Residence

For the third time, Eckhart journeyed to Paris, where once again he occupied the Chair for Externs. It has been suggested that his mission was to combat the influence of the great Scottish Franciscan, John Duns Scotus there – although Scotus himself had died in Cologne in 1308. From this period, there are extant two more disputations, the scriptural commentaries and other fragments of the monumental *Opus Tripartitum* ('The Three-Part Work') which Eckhart planned to be the crowning work of his scholastic career.[16] He apparently sought to complete the efforts of the Cologne School with his projected work, which was to contain an *Opus Propositionum* ('Work of Propositions') of more than one thousand propositions divided into fourteen treatises, an *Opus Questionum* ('Work of Questions') dealing with theological issues, and an *Opus Expositionum* ('Expository Work'), a vast biblical theology consisting of a Book of Commentaries and a Book of Sermons. Fragments of the first and third parts have been found, but nothing has come down to us of the *Opus Questionum*.[17]

Eckhart was not destined to finish his projected masterwork. Having completed his second magisterial residence at Paris, the Meister was recalled to Germany. Rather than returning to Erfurt, however, he appears in Strassburg in 1313 as professor of theology, prior, spiritual director and preacher – an all-consuming ministry that was to change his life forever.

The Pastor and Preacher

Eckhart was already well-known for his preaching before he came to Strassburg. In addition to the Latin sermons from his magistral periods in Paris, an important German sermon, 'On the Noble Man' *(Vom edeln*

Menschen), was committed to writing around 1313 but was probably delivered before Queen Agnes of Hungary in 1308 after the assassination of her husband, King Albert I, by his nephew at Königsfelden.[18] But it was in Strassburg that Eckhart's preaching career blossomed in unexpected ways and so fruitfully that his plans to complete the *Opus Tripartitum* would never be realised.

Perhaps Eckhart grasped this from the outset of his residence in this bustling, mystical city. The fact that there is no hint of regret in his later writings suggests that he accepted this change of itinerary gracefully. He was, after all, a member of an order illustrious for its ministry of preaching. One can also only wonder whether Eckhart would have felt some anxiety had he known that with this fateful transition to the active life of a preacher, forces that would lead to his eventual downfall had also been set in motion. From what we know of his spirituality from that preaching, it seems unlikely.

In 1314, Eckhart was elected Prior of the Dominican convent at Strassburg. He was also named vicar by the Master of the Order, Berengar of Landora, and with Matthew of Finstingen placed in charge of the nuns of the region. (A letter of Eckhart to the nuns of Unterlinden near Colmar dates from 1322, under Hervé of Nedellec, Master from 1318–1323, who renewed the charge.) Thus it was that shortly after his arrival, Eckhart began his preaching ministry among that most remarkable group of mystics of the fourteenth century Rhineland, the contemplative sisters of the Dominican monasteries that surrounded Strassburg like the rim of a great wheel.

St Dominic's Daughters

Throughout the fourteenth century, mystical spirituality of a high order flourished among the cloistered Dominican nuns of southern Germany and northern Switzerland. Their many convents were havens for large numbers of religiously gifted, well-educated women otherwise deprived of position, authority and creative outlets in an age of growing social confusion and psychological anxiety. The teachings and example of Meister Eckhart, and, in later years, that of his disciples, Tauler and Suso, greatly influenced the language, tone and content of the sisters' mysticism, although they also drew heavily on other sources, such as the writings of Mechthild of Magdeburg, the lives of the Dominican

Brethren and the chronicles and legends of other Dominican convents. It was the sisters who would also preserve the memory and teaching of their beloved Meister.

Cologne

Sometime after 1322, Eckhart returned to the great city of Cologne, now as regent master of the *studium generale* where he had laboured as a youth more than forty years before. He was at the pinnacle of his career. Here he would have as a student and his most loyal disciple the remarkable and lovable mystic Henry Suso. Here, too, after 1325 he may have briefly known Suso's younger contemporary, Johann Tauler, also to become a follower of Eckhart's 'way', and later the greatest preacher of his generation.

Cologne (Köln in German) was the Roman city of Colonia Agrippina, founded in the first century of the Common Era. During the twelfth and thirteenth centuries, it particularly flourished under the great prince-archbishops such as Henry II of Virneburg who held office as one of the seven imperial Electors. By the fourteenth century it boasted over one hundred churches. The cornerstone of its great cathedral, one of the finest in all of Europe, and which contains the relics of the Magi, was laid by Archbishop Conrad of Hochstaden on 15 August 1248. It was not finished until the nineteenth century. The magnificent choir was consecrated by Henry of Virneburg in 1322, just as Eckhart returned to the city. The splendid Dominican church built by St Albert, where his tomb lay and Eckhart would have preached and prayed, was destroyed by French troops in 1799.

To this great city, the finest Franciscan scholar of his age, Duns Scotus, came from Paris in 1307 to teach. But here, tragically, he died the following year at the age of forty-three. Here, too, at the peak of his success as a preacher and teacher, calamity finally engulfed the venerable and esteemed Master of the Dominican studium.

Heresy and Death in an Alien Land

To his own amazement and that of his colleagues and students, at the age of sixty-six Eckhart was summoned on charges of heresy before the stern and unyielding Archbishop of Cologne, Henry II of Virneburg. The aged friar defended himself vigorously but to no avail. Supported by his fellow friars, he appealed to the pope. And thus at the age of sixty-seven or sixty-eight, this great teacher and preacher began the last great journey of his life, walking the five hundred miles with several of his brethren in order to plead his case at the papal court, now at Avignon. Both Eckhart and his companions fully expected acquittal.[19] But the process dragged on for over a year without result. Sometime before the final, tragic resolution, the old man died, adamantly convinced of the orthodoxy of his doctrine, but willing as always to retract anything that could be proved erroneous.

The bull of condemnation issued in March, 1329, mentions Eckhart's death as well as his retraction. Eleven months earlier, however, a letter concerning the process of examination sent by Pope John XXII to Archbishop Henry of Virneburg had referred to him as already dead.[20] Thus, the date of Eckhart's death can be fixed as late in 1327 or early 1328. He probably died in Avignon at the Dominican priory.[21]

NOTES

1. Occasionally it is supposed that Eckhart's forename was Johannes (John). No contemporary source warrants the appellation, however, which may have arisen from confusion with either his Dominican disciple Johann Tauler or the 'Bruder Hans' or 'Johannes', several of whose treatises were erroneously ascribed to Eckhart by Franz Pfeiffer in 1857. See Walshe, ed. cit., Vol. I, pp. ix–x, xlv, CL pp. 11, n. 4, 114; John Caputo, *The Mystical Element in Heidegger's Thought*, Athens, Ohio: Ohio University Press, 1978, p. 100. Apparently Eckhart was not an uncommon name in Germany at this time. Thomas Kaeppeli lists three other Dominicans of that name during the period of Eckhart's life – Eckhart the Younger, a disciple of the Meister; Eckhart of Groningen (possibly the same person); and Eckhart Rube, also a disciple of the Meister. All were preachers, some of whose sermons are extant. Cf. *Scriptores Ordinis Praedicatorum Medii Aevi*, Vol. I, Rome: Santa Sabina, 1970, pp. 354–62.

2. See Bernard McGinn, *The Mystical Thought of Meister Eckhart*, p. 2, n. 8. A note in a capitulary relates the death of Eckhart's father, 'a knight of Hochheim' in 1305.

3. It has been proposed by Heinrich Denifle, Clark and others that he was descended from a knightly family of Thuringia named Eckhart. However, the late Fr Josef Koch, one of the greatest Eckhart scholars and editors, concluded that this is an error based on confusion with the different Eckhart family of Gotha. Joseph Koch, OP, *Kleine Schriften*, Rome: Edizioni di Storia e Letteratura, 1973, Vol. 2, p. 249, n. 12, which represents a change in the position he held previously, cf. Koch, KS I, pp. 203, 248ff [hereafter KS]. See also C-McG, p. 5, n. 3.

4. William Hinnebusch suggests without further comment that Eckhart studied at Paris before entering the Dominicans, which is possible and perhaps more likely given Siger's intransigent anti-Thomism. (See Hinnebusch, II, p. 304.) In either event, Eckhart seems to have studied under Siger and may have been in Paris when Bishop Stephen Tempier's condemnation was promulgated. Cf. Koch, KS II, p. 254 and C-McG, p. 6.
5. Eckhart refers in a familiar manner to Albert in several of his sermons and in his defence before the Inquisition. Cf. C-McG, pp. 5f. On Albert and Eckhart, see below, pp. 77–8.
6. For a historical overview of the events of the late thirteenth and fourteenth centuries, see Barbara Tuchman's still-compelling volume, *A Distant Mirror: The Calamitous Fourteenth Century*, New York: Alfred Knopf, 1978. For a general interpretation of social and economic conditions, see Lester Little, *Religious Poverty and the Profit Economy in Medieval Europe*, Ithaca, NY: Cornell University Press, 1978, M.M. Postan, *The Medieval Economy and Society*, New York: Penguin Books, 1975, Henri Pirenne, *Economic and Social History of Medieval Europe*, New York: Harcourt, Brace and World, 1937, and Sir Richard Southern, *Western Society and the Church in the Middle Ages*, New York: Penguin Books, 1970. The intellectual situation has been described by Johan Huizinga, *The Waning of the Middle Ages*, Garden City, NY: Doubleday, 1954, and David Knowles, *The Evolution of Medieval Thought*, New York: Random House, 1962, esp. pp. 291–340. With particular respect to events surrounding Eckhart's life, see Richard Weber, 'The Search for Identity and Community in the Fourteenth Century', *The Thomist*, 42 (April, 1978), pp. 182–96.
7. Established by St Dominic himself in 1220, the Dominican school was effectively incorporated into the university that year when Dominic secured the services of the English secular master, John of St Albans, as professor of theology, thereby establishing the first of its chairs. In 1270, when John of St Giles, another English secular master, suddenly became a Dominican, St-Jacques acquired its second chair. By custom thereafter, Dominican masters from the Province of France held the chair of St Albans and taught French students, while masters of other provinces usually occupied that of St Giles and normally taught non-French students or 'externs'. Albert the Great was the first German to hold the chair for externs, and Thomas Aquinas the first Italian, occupying it twice. Eckhart would in time succeed to the same chair and like Thomas, hold it twice.
8. Hinnebusch II, p. 30.
9. As a bachelor, the *biblicus* or *cursor biblius* was required to give brief, expository comments on the Bible and assist the principal lector for a year. A 'second bachelor', the *sentenarius* or *cursor sententiarum*, lectured in the same manner on the *Sentences* of Peter Lombard, the fundamental theological textbook of the Middle Ages. As regent master for yet another year, he gave detailed lectures on biblical texts, addressed special problems in theology and presided over student debates. The principal lector presided over the studium as a whole, holding his position indefinitely.
10. Hinnebusch, II, p. 59. Cf. also p. 31.

11. LW V, pp. 3–26.

12. DW V, pp. 185–309. Edited and translated by Edmund Colledge in C-McG, pp. 247–84. Cf. Koch, KS I, pp. 258ff. (Sometimes referred to as 'Counsels of Discernment', recent scholarship has preferred to translate *Reden der Unterscheidung* as 'Talks of Instruction'.) Several of the propositions objected to in the proceedings at Cologne some twenty-five years later were taken from these 'table-talks'.

13. LW V, pp. 27–54, 87–99. Cf. Koch, KS I, pp. 249, 260. In a register of Latin sermons delivered at the University of Paris in the late thirteenth century which Thomas Kaeppeli discovered in the Benedictine abbey at Kremsmünster are listed the titles of several other sermons attributed to Eckhart, none of which have yet been found. Cf. Thomas Kaeppeli, *'Praedicator Monoculus*: Sermons parisiens de la fin du XIIIe siècle', AFP XXVII (1957), pp. 124–5. The disputed questions of 1302–1303 and those of Eckhart's second magisterial residency in Paris in 1311–1312 were discovered simultaneously by Martin Grabmann and Ephrem Longprè as recently as 1927. See LW V, pp. 27–83. Together with the prologues to the *Opus Tripartitum* (LW I 35–49, 129–32, 148–84), they were translated and published by Fr Armand Maurer in 1974 under the title *Master Eckhart: Parisian Questions and Prologues*, op. cit.

14. Ancelet-Hustache, p. 23.

15. Recent scholarship has cast some doubt on whether Eckhart did in fact compose this work for Queen Agnes. See McGinn, *The Mystical Thought of Meister Eckhart*, op. cit., p. 12.

16. Neither the idea of such a work nor its title was original with Eckhart. Humbert of Romans, the fifth master of the Order, had already composed a work of that name but which had a vastly different character. (Cf. Hinnebusch, II, pp. 294f.) Ulrich of Strassburg, Albert's favourite disciple, had also advanced the idea of an *Opus Propositionum* that unfortunately came to nothing. (Cf. Alain de Libera, *Introduction á la Mystique Rhénane*, Paris: OEIL,1984, p. 236.)

17. Cf. Maurer, op. cit., pp. 80–2, and de Libera, op. cit., pp. 235–7. For discussion, see McGinn, *The Mystical Thought of Meister Eckhart*, op. cit., pp. 7–8.

18. Cf. Koch, KS 1, p. 281. With the *Book of Divine Consolation (Buch der göttlichen Tröstung)*, it comprises the *Liber Benedictus*, which Eckhart may have presented as a gift to the grieving queen. Her step-daughter, Elizabeth, eventually took up residence in the Dominican convent of Töss, in Switzerland, which Eckhart had occasion to visit several times. English translations in Ancelet-Hustache (partial) and C-McG, pp. 209–47.

19. Colledge, art. cit., p. 251.

20. Colledge, art. cit., p. 253, n. 41. The reference is to Koch, KS 1, p. 316.

21. Recent research suggests that Eckhart may have died on 28 January 1328, according to an annotation in a late seventeenth-century Dominican chronicle to the effect that Eckhart's memory was observed on that day in certain German convents. See McGinn, *The Mystical Thought of Meister Eckhart*, p. 18, n. 102.

THE MASTER'S WAY

'When I preach,' Eckhart said, 'it is my wont to speak about detachment, and of how man should rid himself of self and all things. Secondly, that man should be in-formed back into the simple good which is God. Thirdly, that we should remember the great nobility God has put into the soul, so that man may come miraculously to God. Fourthly, of the purity of the divine nature, for the splendour of God's nature is unspeakable.'[1]

Eckhart's self-characterisation is accurate so far as it goes. These four great themes – detachment (*Abgescheidenheit*),[2] transformation (*Wiedereingebildet*) into God, the nobility (*Adel*) of the soul and the unutterable simplicity (*Luterkeit*) of God – appear directly in a great number of treatises as well as sermons and inform the background of many more.[3] Each in its way figured in his trial and condemnation. But while emblematic, these four themes by no means encompass even the major features of his spiritual doctrine. Considered by themselves, further, they in fact tell us very little. Other prominent and even more characteristic elements in Eckhart's teaching include the spark of the soul (*Seelenfünklein*), the ground (*Grunt*) of the soul, *Gelassenheit* – 'letting go,' the nothingness (*nihtes Niht*) of God and the nothingness of creatures, and the birth of the Word in the soul (*Gottesgeburt*).

Eckhart provided no systematic overview or summary of his spiritual doctrine as a whole. But it should be clear from even a cursory reading of his sermons and treatises that for him not only these four major themes but many others as well were integrated into a coherent, organic vision of the spiritual life. In all, the vast storehouse of interconnected ideas and counsels found in the Meister's writings will probably never be exhausted, and not least because of their depth as well as their richness.

A beginner will probably approach the Meister through the eyes and ideas of one of his many interpreters. Another way to approach

Eckhart's doctrine in search of its salient features is through the propositions condemned in the Bull *In agro Dominico*. Even many scholars have done so. In fact, both the condemned and deplored propositions clearly cluster around many of Eckhart's major teachings – detachment (nos. 7–9), the nothingness of creatures (no. 26), the spark of the soul (no. 27), transformation into God (nos. 10, 13, 23–24), the birth of the Word in the soul (nos. 20–22), and identity with the Son of God (nos. 11–12).[4] But such an approach, as Edmund Colledge observes, inclines towards as one-sided an interpretation of Eckhart as that shown by his inquisitors.

Spiritual Theology: An Architectonic View

It can be shown, I believe, that the whole of Eckhart's spirituality rests on three tenets: the transcendent and ineffably unknowable unity of the Godhead, union with God as the origin and goal of human existence, and the dialectic of reconciliation – the reciprocal is-ness and no-thingness of both God and creatures that provides the way towards ultimate integrity.[5] As an admittedly inchoate system, Eckhart's spiritual doctrine rises from this three-fold basis in successively higher levels in a kind of spiral which opens at last onto the infinite expanse of the Godhead 'beyond God'.

The full scope of this organic, dynamic and yet architectonic system, at once both speculative and practical, is breathtaking. It is possible, however, to consider various stages or elements of his teaching in a gradual manner. We can explore Eckhart's spiritual theology structurally from the simple groundwork 'upwards', that is, in ascending gyres of complexity and consciousness, as Teilhard de Chardin might have put it. It is also possible to view his organic system dynamically, that is, in terms of the emanation of all reality from the simple unity of the Godhead and the return there as a function of the birth of the Eternal Word in the souls of the just: the expansion and contraction of the universe of Personal Being.[6]

The first turn of Eckhart's ascending gyres involves his elaboration of a Trinitarian theology on the foundation of the utter oneness of God. He accomplishes this by employing the ancient Christian Neoplatonic theme of *emanation* – the emergence or effulgence of the Divine Persons from the dynamic unity of the Godhead. This overflowing wealth of life and energy expresses itself in creative activity, calling forth every being out of the sheer nothingness of what is not-God. Having become fully manifest in both image and likeness in humankind through the *birth of the Word* in time and place, the indwelling Triune God retracts the universe into itself through the birth of the soul back into God – Eckhart's great theme of *breakthrough*.

Following Albert and Thomas Aquinas, Eckhart similarly sought the ultimate realisation of human beatitude, the vision of God, principally in terms of intellectual experience. His entire theology is in fact centred on Mind – the *Logos*, Word and Wisdom of God manifest in the rational form of human existence. Thus for Eckhart the order of salvation, the whole divine economy of creation, redemption and sanctification, was not only entailed, mutual and simultaneous, but focused on mentality – the creative mind of God, the intellectual generation of the Word, and the transformation of human consciousness by the grace of Christ.

Eckhart's theological anthropology is no less a continual discourse on personal knowledge in as much as human persons reflect the image of God. Nevertheless, human salvation, indeed *deification* in the language of the mystical theology of the ancient church which supplies so much of the background of Eckhart's teaching, depends on human cooperation with what in the final analysis is the gift and life of grace beyond both love and knowledge. It would thus be a serious error to conclude that Eckhart was only a speculative theologian, much less one trapped in a purely mentalistic frame of reference. The second turn of the ascending spiral therefore opens onto the practical, spiritual dimension of his Trinitarian theology.

In the practical as well as in the speculative order, attempting to correlate the classical (or any other) scheme of spiritual development with Eckhart's categories can be only approximative and even perilous. Schürmann in fact implies that Eckhart was unconcerned with linear patterns of spiritual growth.[7] Perhaps the closest he comes to articulating a model of progressive development is found in his description of the six-fold stages of human spiritual progress which he freely adapts from St Augustine in his German treatise *Vom edeln Menschen* (*On the Noble Man*).[8]

Evil, Sin and Suffering

Similarly, Eckhart was little concerned with temptation, sin, the Fall, suffering and evil unlike so many spiritual writers of later, more worrisome times. But he did not so much neglect these elements of orthodox dogma and speculation as presuppose them. Ebulliently positive despite his deeply Augustinian and Dionysian roots, references to hell, damnation and the devil will be found here and there in Eckhart's writings, but never as the focus of attention.

Istikeit: The Supreme Is-ness of God

Eckhart was all but exclusively fascinated by the identity of unity, being and intellect in God. Unlike many Christian Neoplatonic thinkers, however, he did not elevate unity above being and understanding. His most salient emphasis is in fact on God's supreme 'is-ness', which he expressed by coining the German word *Istikeit* (or *Isticheit*). For Eckhart, God alone supremely is: 'A master says that being is so pure and lofty that all God is, is being. God knows nothing but being, He is conscious of knowing but being: being is His circumference. God loves nothing but His being, He thinks of nothing but His being ... God's characteristic is being ... in being alone lies all that is all. Being is the first name.'[9] Compared to God, therefore, all else is simply nothing: '... God alone is, for all things are in God and from Him, since outside of Him and without Him nothing truly is: all creatures are worthless and a mere nothing compared with God.'[10] In developing this theme from the perspective of creation, Eckhart found himself confronted by the Inquisition. For he had realised that from such a viewpoint, God in turn must figure as nothing.

But from God's point of view, if to speak of such a perspective makes sense, not only is the divine existence necessary and absolute, it is equally and necessarily one. Like most Christian theologians who drew upon the ancient theology, Eckhart emphasised the unity of God, if not as higher than the Trinity, at least as logically prior to it. So far, he did not deviate from the traditional position. But the unity of God had for him a special philosophical pre-eminence; that alone guaranteed, as it were, the divinity of the Persons.

In German Eckhart customarily referred to this undifferentiated divine unity as *Gottheit*, which is usually translated as 'Godhead'. His teaching about this 'Godness' of God, the divine nature shared equally by the Persons, gave rise to some of his most original and daring propositions. Eckhart said, for instance, 'Everything that is in the Godhead is one, and of that there is nothing to be said. God works, the Godhead does no work: there is nothing for it to do, there is no activity in it. It never peeped at any work. God and Godhead are distinguished by working and not-working'.[11]

Theological uneasiness over the logical distinction between the Godhead and God as the Trinity of Persons had become acute a century before when Gilbert of Poitiers was summoned before the Council of Rheims in 1148 and his doctrine eventually condemned. Some of Eckhart's statements seem at first glance to veer perilously close to Gilbert's teaching: 'God and Godhead are as different as heaven and earth.'[12] But in this matter, strangely enough, Eckhart's doctrine escaped final censure.

The Absolute Nothingness of Creatures

The fundamental elements of Eckhart's theology are strikingly affirmative or, in the classical terminology of the ancient Church, 'kataphatic'. For such a vision, there is no darkness, no limitation of any kind in God. All is light and the fullness of existence: '... in God there is light and being, and in creatures there is darkness and nothingness, since what is in God is light and being, in creatures is darkness and nothingness.'[13]

Turning in this light more fully towards creatures, Eckhart simply denies that they are anything at all in their own right: 'All creatures are pure nothing. I do not say they are a trifle or they are anything: they are pure nothing.'[14] This bold statement became the substance of article 26 in the bull of condemnation. Clearly, however, Eckhart was affirming not the absolute non-existence of creatures, but their relative non-existence, their total and absolute dependence on God. For in the original sermon, Eckhart immediately added, totally in accordance with orthodox teaching, that 'What has no being, is not. All creatures have no being, for their being consists in the presence of God. If God turned away for an instant from all creatures, they would perish'. Elsewhere, the Meister similarly said, 'God alone is, for all things are in God and from Him, since outside of Him and without Him nothing truly is: all creatures are worthless and a mere nothing *compared with God'*.[15] The important and saving qualification at the end of the sentence was omitted, significantly, from the inquisitors' citation.

For Eckhart, as for the orthodox tradition, what being creatures do in fact have, they have by God's mercy and it shall not be taken from them. But such existence, *compared with God's sovereign being*, is equivalent to nothing, for as the ancient theology had held since Philo, it is out of nothing that all creatures are fashioned, towards nothing they always incline, and to nothing they would instantly return without the creative support of God's power maintaining them in existence.

At first glance, Eckhart here seems to have gone radically beyond Thomas Aquinas, for whom creatures and God truly share a common bond of being, although proportionate (which is to say infinitely disproportionate) to their respective status as Creator and creatures. God's being is primarily distinguished in that only in God are essence and existence identical. From Eckhart's primordial (or 'principial') perspective, however, there can be no mutual bond of being which unites creatures and Creator across the infinite abyss. As distinct in themselves (if never actually separate) from God, creatures are just nothing. For Eckhart, a creature's being is always 'borrowed' – never possessed. Christ is the only substantial Word; creatures are only 'adverbs', *bî-worts*.[16] Our dependence on God is radical, total, infinite, absolute and final. (Nonetheless, as we shall see, Eckhart maintained that by grace, at least human creatures could become one with God through identification with the Word, the God-human Christ. Although this notion, too, was a theme of ancient Christian theology, the commissioners found cause to condemn it in various articles.)[17]

But Eckhart could seemingly reverse himself by a sudden shift of viewpoint and commonly did. The following remark, already cited, earned him an accusation of heresy at Cologne not because it denied existence to creatures, but because it exalted that existence excessively: 'A master says that being is so pure and lofty that all God is, is being. God knows nothing but being, He is conscious of knowing but being: being is His circumference. God loves nothing but His being, He thinks of nothing but His being. *I say all creatures are one being.*'[18]

In sum, despite the intransigent narrowness of his prosecutors' interpretation of Eckhart's teaching regarding the nothingness of creatures, it is abundantly clear from many passages in his sermons as well as from Eckhart's own clarifications that, as always, he meant nothingness *in comparison with God*. Eckhart clearly stated as much: 'All creatures are too base to be able to reveal God, they are all nothing *compared to God*. Therefore no creature can utter a word about God in his works.'[19]

The Nothingness of God

A more radical shift in viewpoint to the obvious reality of creatures in the phenomenal world finds expression in Eckhart's reciprocal doctrine of the nothingness of God, an aspect of his theology also easily twisted into heretical form when in fact not only sound doctrine but the consistent teaching of the great mystics of the Church. No one can see God, as John's Gospel has it.[20] For God has no material embodiment to see. God never appears, as William Ernest Hocking phrased it, as an object among other objects, a being among other beings, not even the Supreme Being at the end of a chain of infinite extent. God's being is so far beyond human grasp as to seem like nothingness. God is, in this sense, nothing – *no thing*. Therefore even comparatives and superlatives lose all significance: 'God is not being or goodness. Goodness adheres to being and does not go beyond it: for if there were no being there would be no goodness, and being is even purer than goodness. God is not "good," or "better" or "best". Whoever should say God is good would do Him as much injustice as if he called the sun black.'[21]

Condemned as proposition no. 28 in the bull of John XXII, Eckhart's orthodox meaning is clearly evident in the parallel passages: 'But if God is neither goodness nor being nor truth nor one, what then is He? He is pure nothing: He is neither this nor that. If you think of anything He might be, He is not that.'[22] In accents of the ancient negative or *apophatic* theology of Alexandria and Dionysius, Eckhart remarks that God 'is beingless [*weselôs*] being'.[23]

The Darkness of God

Apophatic theology, the negative correlative of positive or 'kataphatic' theology, denies attributes to God only in the same sense in which we apply them to creatures. From this perspective, God is not light to the mind, but darkness – a theme found in Philo and developed by St

Gregory of Nyssa and the later theologians of the Alexandrian as well as the Augustinian tradition for over a thousand years before reappearing in Eckhart's writings: '... the hidden darkness of the eternal light of the eternal Godhead is unknown and shall never be known. And the light of the eternal Father has eternally shone in this darkness, and the darkness does not comprehend the light (John 1:5).'[24]

Thus for Eckhart God's being is simply not being in any way comprehensible to a finite intellect. God does not lack being but wholly transcends it. God 'is as high above being as the highest angel is above a midge. I would be as wrong to call God a being as if I were to call the sun pale or black. God is neither this nor that.'[25] Logically, it has the elegance of simplicity. Perhaps too much so. Compared to God, creatures are nothing; compared to creatures, God is nothing. Yet – and yet (as is usually the case with Eckhart) – *God is there*, in all things, beyond all things, supporting and preserving all things. Thus, all things mediate the presence and activity of God.

Pantheism and Panentheism

Such a vision of the intimate presence of God veered perilously close in the minds of Eckhart's investigators to the heretical position called *pantheism* – the view that everything is somehow God. Eckhart never taught pantheism. But he did develop the classical Christian teaching which for a century now has been known as 'panentheism' – the belief that God is present in all things, and conversely that all things mediate God's presence to those able and willing to grasp the reality of that presence.[26] Further, God is present in particular acuteness in the spiritual essence of the human soul – another classical tenet that Eckhart made a touchstone of his preaching and teaching. That belief, too, came under official scrutiny and condemnation. The Meister said: '... God is unseparated from all things, for God is in all things and is more inwardly in them than they are in themselves.'[27] Again, he said: 'God is in all things. The more He is in things, the more He is out of things; the more in, the more out, and the more out, the more in. ... God is in all things; but as God is divine and intelligible, so God is nowhere so truly as in the soul, and in the angels if you will, in the inmost soul, in the summit of the soul. And when I say the inmost, I mean the highest, and when I say the highest, I mean the inmost part of the soul. In the inmost and the highest part of the soul – there I mean them both together in one.'[28]

For Eckhart, God was everywhere, both in the streets and chapel,[29] but most of all present interiorly to the human spirit. Again citing Augustine, he sounded the mystical theme of conscious awareness of God's presence within: 'God is closer to me than I am to myself: my being depends on God's being near me and present to me. So He is also in a stone or a log of wood, only they do not know it.'[30]

The logic of such claims led Eckhart to conclude paradoxically that although separated by a fathomless abyss, God and the human soul were so intimately present one to another as to share a common ground, the divine Ground itself: 'As surely as the Father in his simple nature bears the Son naturally, just as surely He hears him in the inmost recesses of the spirit, and *this* is the inner world. Here God's ground is my ground and my ground is God's ground.'[31] The all-important transition from darkness to light was for Eckhart the passage from ignorance to awareness of God's constant presence in the depths of conscious experience – the birth of the Word in the soul.

God as Eternal Mind: Eckhart's Cartesian Revolution

Eckhart's appropriation of the ancient mystical doctrine of the eastern Church led him to claim ultimately and to the consternation of his Franciscan critics that God was above and beyond all else Pure Intelligence: 'The joy of the Lord is the Lord Himself and no other, and the Lord is living, essential, actual intellect which understands itself and is living itself in itself and is *the same*. [In saying this] I have attributed no mode to Him: I have taken from Him all mode, for He is Himself modeless mode, living and rejoicing in that which he is.'[32]

Commenting on a passage in the *Book of the Twenty-Four Philosophers* (mistakenly) ascribed to Hermes Trismegistus, 'God is an intellect that lives solely by understanding itself,' Eckhart said, 'God is something that necessarily transcends being. Whatever has being, time or place, cannot reach God: He is above it. God is in all creatures, in so far as they have being, and yet He is above them.'[33] Thus, as all-transcendent, God cannot be a being, but his being is his intelligence: 'Intellect is the temple of God. God dwells nowhere more truly than in His temple, in intellect ... God in His own knowing knows Himself in Himself.'[34]

God's supreme self-consciousness as Intellect sometimes takes precedence for Eckhart over being itself as the prime attribute of divinity. While a disputed point among theologians, the Meister's teaching here followed one path of Thomas Aquinas' logic, if it ultimately went beyond the Angelic Doctor's carefully nuanced positions.[35] Eckhart's departure lay in making intellect also the foundation and not only the perfection of being in God. In the first of the disputed *Parisian Questions* he asserts: 'it is not my present opinion that God understands because he exists, but rather that he exists because he understands. God is an intellect and understanding, and his understanding itself is the ground of his existence.'[36]

Again, the difference is perhaps more a matter of a shifting viewpoint than a radical divergence. What remains evident is that at least in the *Parisian Questions*, Eckhart, more than Aquinas, identified God with pure intelligence, a position which had important consequences with regard to the emphasis on the human mind in his spiritual doctrine. For if the human spirit would be truly one with God, union must necessarily occur in respect to humankind's most God-like property. For Eckhart, this could only be the mind, and at the highest point of the mind.

Eckhart's Mystical Anthropology

For Eckhart as for his confreres, the human person was an integrated whole composed of various dimensions or aspects which he refers to in the traditional manner as soul and body. These do not exist or operate independently of each other as in commonsense or later Cartesian views. The whole predominates. Body and soul are essentially coordinated and correlated. They are isolable only rationally and never interchangeable: 'One priest said, "I wish your soul were in my body." Then I said, "Truly she would be foolish in there, for she could do nothing with it, nor could your soul in my body." No soul can do anything except in the body to which she is allotted.'[37] Evidently Eckhart would not have regarded very patiently the contemporary fascination with reincarnation.

The Meister also subscribed at times to the time-honoured view of the person as a tri-unity of mind, body and spirit – a part of the legacy of Middle-Platonism that appears in the Pauline writings as well as in most classical works of mystical theology in the Alexandrian and

Dionysian traditions: 'Just as the sun illumines the air and the air the earth, so his [St Paul's] spirit received pure light from God, and the soul from the spirit and the body from the soul.'[38] From Paul, Jerome and especially Augustine he also took the distinction between the outer or 'fleshly' person and the spiritual, inner one, with its all-important emphasis on the unfathomable depths of consciousness, Eckhart's *Innerkeit*.[39]

The Image of God

Like his Augustinian predecessors, Eckhart sometimes interpreted the threefold higher powers of understanding, memory and will as the joint reflection or image in human persons of the Trinity. He was more wont to stress the intellect alone as the *imago Dei*.[40] Whatever aspect he might have stressed for various purposes, the biblical and theological foundation of Eckhart's characteristic doctrine of the interior birth of the Word was itself 'man's soul, which He has made exactly like Himself, just as we read that the Lord said: "let us make man in our image and likeness" (Gen 1:26). And this He did. So like Himself has God made man's soul that nothing else in heaven or on earth, of all the splendid creatures that God has so joyously created, resembles God so much as the human soul.'[41]

For Eckhart, as for St Thomas Aquinas, God had made the soul 'not merely like the image in Himself, or like anything proceeding from Himself that is predicated of Him, but He has made her like *Himself*, in fact like everything that He is — like His nature, His essence and His emanating-immanent activity, and like the ground wherein He subsists in Himself, where He ever bears His only-begotten Son and where the Holy Ghost blossoms forth: it is like this outflowing, indwelling work that God has formed the soul.'[42]

On the basis of his teaching, Eckhart would later be accused of claiming that the intellect was in fact divine, although even the papal bull itself distinguished this view from Eckhart's authentic doctrine (in article 27). In fact, the Meister carefully avoided such a conclusion in his preaching: 'This is a natural image of God which God has impressed by nature in every soul. More than this I cannot ascribe to the image; to ascribe more to it would make it God Himself, which is not the case, for then God would not be God.'[43]

Such caution was not always typical of Eckhart's pronouncements, a feature of his doctrine that ultimately led to misunderstanding and condemnation, although such apparently rash statements as the following in fact echo Christian doctrine from the days of Athanasius himself: since '... the eternal Word took on human nature imagelessly, therefore the Father's image, which is the eternal Son, became the image of human nature. So it is just as true to say that man became God as that God became man. Thus human nature was transformed by becoming the divine image, which is the image of the Father.'[44]

The Ground of the Soul

As creature, the human person retains the impress of God within it; God, too, intentionally and divinely possesses the eternal idea of the person, as of all creatures. But as a spiritual creature and particularly one created to the image and likeness of God, humankind enjoys a privileged region of communion with God that Eckhart often referred to as the ground or abyss of the soul. There God is primordially but unrecognisably present. As the soul rids itself of preoccupations with other creatures, self, even its concepts of God, that Presence becomes increasingly manifest, ultimately becoming overwhelmingly evident in the mystical birth of the Word: 'As surely as the Father in his simple nature bears the Son naturally, just as surely He bears him in the inmost recesses of the spirit, and *this* is the inner world. Here God's ground is my ground and my ground is God's ground.'[45]

At first, therefore, consciously only *capax Dei* ('receptive to God'), the soul possesses no experiential knowledge of its commonality with God. As awareness grows, however, the soul's true nature is progressively realised: 'The soul, which has no nature in her ground, in that ground of love which is not yet called love – this soul must emerge from her nature, and then God lies in wait for her to lead her home into Himself. Whatever is borne into this essence comes almost to share that essence.'[46]

The Spark of the Soul

God-consciousness for Eckhart is grounded and consummated in what he, following the ancient tradition, called the 'spark' of the soul (*Seelenfünklein, scintilla animae*), and elsewhere the peak or apex or even the abyss of the soul, depending on the particular nuance of doctrine he is stressing: '... the highest peak of the soul which stands above time and knows nothing of time or of the body.'[47] It is clear in many references that Eckhart has in mind the intellect or understanding itself, the highest power of the soul which in high scholasticism was called the *ratio superior*, the mind as turned toward God: 'The spark of intellect, which is the head of the soul, is called the husband of the soul, and is none other than a tiny spark of the divine nature, a divine light, a ray and an imprint of the divine nature.'[48]

The spark of intellect is more, however, than the higher aspect of the natural human mind. It contains, as has been noted, or rather is, the trace in the mind of its divine origin in the mind of God: 'I recently said in one place that when God created all creatures, if God had not previously begotten something that was uncreated that bore within itself the images of all creatures – that is the spark, as I said at St Maccabees if you were listening – this spark is so akin to God that it is a single impartible one, and it contains in itself the images of all creatures, imageless images and images above images ...'[49]

Eckhart's emphasis on the intellect, like that in Zen Buddhism, is not concerned with discursive thought (*ratio inferior*), but with the capacity of *mind*, of conscious awareness, and particularly with the enlightenment of the ordinary mind in the contemplative realisation of oneness with God. The mind is for the Meister as for the Dominican tradition as a whole the most distinctive and, as *ratio superior*, the highest characteristic of all. It is also the point of access to the presence of God within: 'I have a power in my soul which is ever receptive to God.'[50] Again Eckhart said: '... as I have said before, there is something in the soul that is so near akin to God that it is one and not united. It is one, it has nothing in common with anything, and nothing created has anything in common with it. All created things are nothing. But this is remote and alien from all creation. If man were wholly thus he would be wholly uncreated and uncreatable.'[51]

The charge of heresy attached to this and similar passages has been disputed, not least by Eckhart himself. His plain meaning was that if the human soul were pure intellect, as only God is, it would be God. But (as he insists) the soul is *not* wholly intellectual and therefore not divine. Nevertheless it is in its limited and partial way most Godlike because that aspect of the human person created as God's image and likeness. Further, and also like God, the higher intellect is no thing, but a subsisting activity, radically unlimited by the physical restrictions of time, space and matter: 'There is a power in the soul, which is the intellect. From the moment that it becomes aware of God and tastes Him, it has five properties. The first is that it becomes detached from here and now. The second is that it is like nothing. The third is that it is pure and uncompounded. The fourth is that it is active and seeking in itself. The fifth is that it is an image.'[52]

The Nothingness of the Intellect

From the perspective of his theological anthropology, the parallel or analogy Eckhart carefully drew between God and human creatures found its most striking expression in his doctrine of the 'nothingness of the intellect'.[53] Based on Aristotelian psychology and the doctrine of Thomas Aquinas, it is the capstone of Eckhart's teaching, supported by his more general doctrines of the nothingness of creatures and even more, the nothingness of God. Here, too, he does not mean that intellect does not exist; for Eckhart intellect is the supreme reality of God, not just the highest form of being, but the divine being itself. God is no being with a mind, but subsisting intelligence. In as much as human persons embody the image and likeness of God, what is also most real about human existence is likewise intellect. But here too intellect is no *thing*. It is a *power* in the particular sense in which Eckhart uses that term. It is not merely the activity of a faculty, but the radiance of an immaterial dynamism, an ideal openness to all reality. 'By virtue of being like nothing, this power is like God. Just as God is like nothing, so too this power is like nothing.'[54]

Because *like* no-thing, the intellect is potentially everything, open to an infinity of possibilities of knowing, and therefore also of knowing God.

The Knowledge of God

Recognising the divine Presence within requires effort – a turning inwards away from what Chinese mystics call 'the ten thousand things' that occlude our spiritual vision. More will be said of this later. Here, Eckhart's theological anthropology is concerned with inwardness itself

(*Innerkeit*) and the discipline necessary to exercise and develop it as a power or quality of experience.

Once more calling on Augustine, Eckhart said: 'God is closer to me than I am to myself: my being depends on God's being near me and present to me. So he is also in a stone or a log of wood, only they do not know it. If the wood knew God and realised how close He is to it as the highest angel does, it would be as blessed as the highest angel. And so man is more blessed than a stone or a piece of wood because he is aware of God and knows how close God is to him. And I am the more blessed, the more I realise this, and I am the less blessed, the less I know this. I am not blessed because God is in me and is near me and because I possess Him, but because I am aware of how close He is to me, and that I *know* God.'[55]

Knowing God is not simply a matter of finding a peaceful spot for prayer, much less thinking *about* God. It requires a shift of consciousness, a reversal of the natural mode of thinking, or, better yet, a conversion of attention: 'For whoever would enter God's ground, His inmost part, must first enter his own ground, his inmost part, for none can know God who does not first know himself. He must enter into his lowest and into God's inmost part, and must enter in to his first and his highest, for there everything comes together that God can perform.'[56]

Eckhart is clearly not advocating a merely theoretical consideration of God as a concept, but advertence to the Presence of a person, true experiential knowledge: '... as for the man who has no acquaintance with inward things, he does not know what God is, just as a man who has wine in his cellar: if he has not drunk it or tried it, he does not know that it is good. So it is with people who live in ignorance: they do not know what God is, and yet they think and imagine that they are living. That knowing is not from God ...'[57]

Such knowledge, as William James might say, is not knowledge *about* but knowledge *of* – direct apprehension, an intuitive gaze on present reality: 'I have said before, knowledge and intellect unite the soul with God. Intellect penetrates into the pure essence; knowledge runs ahead, preceding and blazing a trail so that God's only-begotten Son may be born.'[58] In consonance with the ancient theology, Eckhart is referring to truly *mystical* intuition, the insight of immediate consciousness, ultimately the perfection and goal of all human experience.

The Primacy of Knowing

It is hardly surprising that Eckhart gave understanding the highest priority among the activities of the soul, a characteristic of all Dominican spirituality and one which involved him in a collision with the Franciscans: 'The intellect is the head of the soul. Those who put the matter roughly say that love has precedence, but those who speak most precisely say expressly – and it is true – that the kernal of eternal life lies in understanding more than in love. You should know why. Our finest masters – and there are not many of them – say that understanding and intellect go straight up to God. But love turns to the loved object and takes there what is good, whereas intellect takes hold of what makes it good. Honey is sweeter in itself than anything made from it. Love takes God as He is good, but intellect presses upwards and takes God as He is being.'[59]

Eckhart surprises us, however, with several reversals in his teaching, turning from the theme of knowing to unknowing, and then to the relative superiority of love, and finally transcends both love and knowledge in seeking union with God. In accents, first, that herald a later English disciple, the author of *The Cloud of Unknowing* and other works of mystical spirituality, Eckhart said: 'For you to know God in God's way, your knowing must become a pure unknowing, and a forgetting of yourself and all creatures.'[60] Also like Thomas Aquinas and the *Cloud* author, Eckhart was well aware that the imperative movement of love provided the motive and energy for seeking God in the present life: 'Nothing brings you closer to God or makes God so much your own as the sweet bond of love. A man who has found this way need seek no other. He who hangs on this hook is caught so fast that foot and hand, mouth, eyes and heart, and all that is man's, belongs only to God.'[61]

Knowledge and love require each other for completeness; Eckhart was too holistic a psychologist to bifurcate his spirituality. 'The perfection of blessedness,' he said, 'lies in both, knowledge and love.'[62] Again he said, 'God and I are one. Through knowledge I take God into myself, through love I enter into God.'[63]

Nevertheless, in the Meister's final reckoning the true and lasting happiness of union with God transcended both knowledge and love. Apparently denying what he has already affirmed, Eckhart said: 'Some teachers hold that the spirit finds its beatitude in love. Some make him find it beholding God. But I say he does not find it in love, or in gnosis, or in vision.' 'But,' he then asks rhetorically, 'has the spirit in eternal life no vision of God?' Eckhart's answer is, as might be expected, enigmatic: 'Yes and no. Once born, he neither sees nor pays heed to God: but at the moment of birth, *then* he has a vision of God. The spirit is in bliss then because it has been born, and not at being born, for then it lives as the Father lives, that is in the simple and naked essence.'[64]

The Meister's meaning becomes clearer in light of supporting passages where he states that beyond love and vision lies that which is far greater and infinitely beyond any human achievement: 'The best masters declare that intellect strips everything off and grasps God bare, as He is in Himself, pure being. Knowledge breaks through truth and goodness and, striking on pure being, takes God bare, as He is, without name. I say that neither knowledge nor love unites. Love takes God Himself, insofar as He is good, and if God were to lose the name of goodness, love could go no further. Love takes God under a veil, a garment. Understanding does not do this: understanding takes God as He is known to it: it can never grasp Him in the ocean of His unfathomableness. I say that above these two, understanding and love, there is mercy: there God works mercy in the highest and purest acts that God is capable of.'[65]

For Eckhart, as for Paul, Augustine and Luther, no merely human act can unite us with God. The perfection of salvation is the accomplishment only of God's grace, which supplants and completes the feeble reach of our spiritual powers. He therefore concludes, 'To know what the soul is requires supernatural understanding. When the powers go out from the soul into works, we know nothing of that, or at least we know a tiny bit about it, but our knowledge is small. What the soul is in her ground, nobody knows. What we can know of it must be supernatural: it must be by grace. Therein God works His mercy. Amen.'[66]

Thus it is for Eckhart that 'blessedness lies neither in intellect nor in will: blessedness lies above them, where blessedness lies as blessedness not as intellect, and God is there as God and the soul as God's image. Blessedness is there, where the soul takes God as God. There soul is soul and grace is grace, blessedness is blessedness and God is God.'[67]

Conclusion

Taken out of context and debated by canonists and theologians far inferior to Eckhart himself and largely unfriendly to the trend of his thinking, such statements, while completely orthodox, could easily led to misunderstanding and condemnation. Eckhart would not be the last victim of ecclesiastical myopia. But his teaching would someday find acceptance and comprehension in both East and West. Centuries would pass first and Eckhart himself, as well as his persecutors, would long have been dust.

In any event, after the Meister completed his second regency at Paris, he was called again to undertake in the burgeoning, troubled city of Strassburg the pastoral and administrative work that not only permanently interrupted his scholarly enterprises but led to the tribunals of his downfall. How much of his great *Three-part Work* he lived to finish is still unknown, and perhaps will be forever.

NOTES

1. W 22, p. 177 (DW 53). For an investigation of these themes in comparison with Zen Buddhism, cf. Reiner Schürmann, 'The Loss of Origin in Soto Zen and in Meister Eckhart', *The Thomist* (April, 1978), pp. 281–312. Cf. also McGinn, 'God beyond God', p. 4.

2. The word may be spelled either *abgeschiedenheit*, which is later, or *abgescheidenheit*, which is closer to the Middle High German of Eckhart. In either case, the root means 'to part' or 'cut', and the word signifies separation, detachment, or 'abscission'.

3. Among the German sermons, cf. the following (Walshe nos.): *Abgescheidenheit*: 1, 22, 51, 57, 63, 66, 72, 74, 88, 96; Transformation into God: 22, 43, 47, 95; Nobility of the Soul: 6, 10, 13b, 22, 24b, 32, 46, 51, 52, 60; Purity of Divine Essence: 8, 13a, 13b, 16, 17, 20, 22, 24a, 26, 31, 35, 36, 37, 49, 53, 61, 63, 64, 83, 84, 94, 96, 97.

4. The remainder deal with a variety of related issues: the eternity of creation (nos. 1–3), unity with the will of God – *Gelassenheit* (nos. 4–6, 14–15), incomparability of God (no. 28), equanimity in human and divine love (no. 25) and the goodness of exterior acts (nos. 16–19).

5. In many respects, this characterisation is very similar to the subsumption of themes under the rubric of 'the mysticism of the Ground' by Bernard McGinn. See especially *The Mystical Thought of Meister Eckhart*, op. cit., pp. 35–52 and *The Harvest of Mysticism*, op. cit., pp. 83–93, 118–24.

6. Structurally, the theological framework which most closely fits Eckhart's spiritual doctrine is that common to almost all medieval theologians, beginning at least with Peter Lombard and including, perhaps especially, Albert the Great

and Thomas Aquinas. It is formulated on the model of the Apostles' Creed –
God as One and Three; Creation; the human person, particularly the powers
and operations of the soul; Christ and the Redemption of the World; the Holy
Spirit; the Church with its liturgical life and structure; and, finally, the Last
Things – death, judgement, heaven and hell. Dynamically, it is represented by
the exitus-redditus model – the origin from and return to God of all things
through Christ. Eckhart evidently and understandably followed this pattern in
setting out his teaching, as indicated by the proposed order of the *Opus
Propositionum*, which was to be divided according to the subject matter of 'the
Summa of the illustrious and venerable Friar Thomas of Aquino ...' (Maurer, ed.
cit., p. 81.) The latter elements – ecclesiology and eschatology – Eckhart almost
entirely neglected, however, at least in his extant works. Scattered seeds of a
rich theology of the Church as the mystical body of Christ are nevertheless
surely present. Cf. K. Kertz, SJ, 'Meister Eckhart's Teaching on the Birth of the
Divine Word in the Soul', *Traditio*, 15 (1959), esp. pp. 355–62.

7. In describing what he terms 'the Eckhartian itinerancy' of Dissimilarity,
    Similarity, Identity and Dehiscence, Schürmann avers that Eckhart 'does not
    describe an ascent [to God] through degrees, as in the Itinerary of Saint
    Bonaventure, by which the mind rises towards God. Rather, we should think of
    four determinations of existence in the here and now of the birth of the Son in
    the mind. Itinerancy is the comprehension of life which results from them.'
    Op. cit., p. 59.

8. See C-McG, pp. 241–2. Colledge agrees with Quint that the most likely source
    here is Augustine's *On True Religion*, 26.49. See ibid., p. 344, n. 11. In Sermon 84
    (Walshe, pp. 259–60), Eckhart also describes 'four steps into God.' See below,
    p. 113.

9. W 82, p. 244 (DW 8).

10. W 49, pp. 38–9 (DW 77). Cf. W 26, p. 202 (DW 57). On *Isticheit*, see also W
    96, p. 334 (DW 83).

11. W 56, p. 81–2 (DP 26).

12. W 56, p. 80 (DP 26).

13. W 84, p. 258 (DW 84). Cf. W 26, p. 202 (DW 57): 'God is something and is pure
    being, and sin is nothing and draws us away from God.' On light symbolism in
    Eckhart, see Koch, KS I, pp. 56–63.

14. W 40, p. 284 (DW 4). Cf. W 57, p. 85 (DW 12): 'All created things are nothing.'
    For Aquinas on the nothingness of creatures, see *De aeternitate mundi, Opuscula* (ed.
    Lethielleux), Vol. I, p. 25, and *Summa Theologiae*, I-II, Q. 109, a. 2 ad 2.

15. W 49, pp. 38–9 (DW 77), emphasis added. Cf. W 42, p. 293 (DW 69): 'All
    creatures God ever created or might yet create, if He wished, are little or nothing
    compared with God.'

16. See W 67, p. 154. n. 10.

17. Primarily nos. 10–13 and 20–22.

18. W 82, p. 244 (DW 75), emphasis added. The accusation was brought against him
    in the second list at Cologne, where Eckhart admitted that, baldly taken, 'This

sounds bad and wrong ...' For a similar statement, see his *Commentary on the Book of Wisdom*, 107 (LW II, p. 443): 'Note that in natural things being is always one and in the one.' Walshe observes that in this context 'Quint also notes St Thomas on the *Liber de Causis*, lect. 18: "Therefore being, which is first, is common to all things."' Walshe, II, p. 247, n. 9.

19. W 32b, p. 243 (DW 20b), emphasis added. Similarly: 'All creatures God ever created or might yet create, if He wished, are little or nothing compared with God.' W 42, p. 293 (DW 69); 'all creatures are worthless and a mere nothing compared with God.' W 49, p. 39 (DW 77).

20. Cf. John 1:18, 5:37, 6:46 and 1 John 4:20.

21. W 67, p. 151 (DW 9).

22. W 54, p. 72 (DW 23).

23. W 62, p. 115. This touches on Eckhart's notion of the purity of God's essence, its bare or 'naked' simplicity (*Luterkeit*). Cf. *Book of Divine Consolation*, op. cit., p. 210.

24. For a discussion of the tradition of the 'dark knowledge' of God, see Andrew Louth, *The Origins of the Christian Mystical Tradition*, Oxford: Clarendon Press, 1981, Denys Turner, *The Darkness of God*, Cambridge University Press, 1995, and Charles Journet, *The Dark Knowledge of God*, London: Sheed and Ward, 1948.

25. W 67, p. 150 (DW 9). 'God is not being or goodness.' Ibid., p. 151.

26. See below, p. 133, n. 10. As used here, *panentheism* does not imply any limitation of God's infinity as is the case with some contemporary uses of the term in process philosophy and theology.

27. W 49, p. 39. The allusion is to one of Eckhart's favourite citations from St Augustine, *Enarratio in Psalmum LX XIV*. Cf. *Confessions* III, 6, 11: 'Tu autem eras interior intimo meo et superior summo meo.' Cf. also W 97 (DW 21), p. 339.

28. W 18, p. 147 (DW 30). This passage is important for its evidence that Eckhart considered the ground, the abyss and the apex of the soul to be actually one and the same, the *ratio superior* of Thomistic teaching. See below, pp. 50–1.

29. Cf. *Talks of Instruction*, C-McG, p. 253; on the nearness of God, ibid., p. 266.

30. W 69, pp. 165–6 (DW 68). See above, p. 52.

31. W 13b, p. 117 (DW 5b). 'On the Ground of Being', cf. *Talks of Instruction*, C-McG, p. 268. Cf. also W 83, p. 252 (DW 51): 'God has all things hidden in Himself: not this and that in separation, but as one in unity.' The ideas of things, when they are created 'externally', nevertheless remain in God and are thus divine, for 'what is in God, is God'. This is the basis of Eckhart's much misunderstood doctrine concerning 'the uncreated something in the soul', the divine connection by which God remains in creatures and creatures in God. It is found in Augustine, Sermon 225.3, and Aquinas, *Summa Theologiae*, 1, Q. 15, a. 2. Cf. Kertz, art. cit., p. 331. Eckhart's 'mysticism of the ground' is the focal point of an especially illuminating chapter in McGinn, *The Mystical Thought of Meister Eckhart*, op. cit., pp. 35–52.

32. W 58, p. 95 (DW 26). On the identity of being and intellect in God, see Caputo, art. cit., p. 89. On 'modes' in God, see below, pp. 136, 138.

33. W 67, p. 149 (DW 9).

34. Ibid., p. 152.

35. Caputo claims that in asserting that intellectuality is God's being, Eckhart was 'striking out against the central tenets of Thomistic metaphysics, the supremacy of being (esse) ...' Art. cit., p. 90. In fact, Thomas Aquinas, like Eckhart, was well aware that being and intelligence were identical in God. Cf. *Summa Theologiae* I, Q. 14, a. 4: '... the act of God's intellect is His substance.' '... in God, intellect, and the object understood, and the intelligible species, and His act of understanding are entirely one and the same.' Cf. also I, Q. 26, a. 2.

36. LW V, p. 40. Maurer translation, p. 45.

37. W 41, p. 288 (DW 70). On Eckhart's anthropological dualism, cf. Steven Ozment, 'Eckhart and Luther: German Mysticism and Protestantism', *The Thomist* (April, 1978), pp. 263f.

38. W 54, p. 73 (DW 23).

39. See 2 Cor 4:16. Cf. *On the Noble Man*, C-McG, pp. 240–1. On interior works and exterior works, see the *Talks of Instruction*, ibid., c. 23, p. 280. On inwardness vs sensuality and the five senses, see *On Detachment*, ibid., pp. 290–1. Although considered doubtful or spurious by several recent commentators, this treatise has many Eckahrtian themes and surely emanated from Eckhart's circle if it is not from his own hand. See ibid., p. 43 and McGinn, *The Harvest of Mysticism in Medieval Germany*, op. cit., p. 525, n. 69.

40. For the human person as the image of God in the higher powers see *The Book of Divine Consolation*, C-McG, p. 211. On the powers of soul, cf. ibid.

41. W 6, p. 55 (DW 1).

42. W 92, p. 312 (DW 24). For Aquinas' teaching on the image of the Trinity *in* the soul, cf. *Summa Theologiae*, I, Q. 93, a. 5. On the human person as the image of the Trinity, see I, Q. 35, a. 2. Elsewhere Eckhart states that only Christ was made *in* the image and likeness of God; other human persons are made *to* the image and likeness of God. See below, pp. 99, 118. For Eckhart's doctrine of Christ's assumption of human nature, see *Of the Nobleman*, C-McG, p. 293. For the doctrine of Likeness, see *The Book of Divine Consolation*, ibid., pp. 221 and 227.

43. W 14b, p. 125 (DW 16b). See also p. 124.

44. W 47, pp. 27–8 (DW 46).

45. W 13b, p. 117. See also W 18, p. 147, cited above, p. 53.

46. W 61, p. 108. Cf. Eckhart's summary statement in W 93, p. 318. Cf. also W 68, pp. 158–9. McGinn interprets Eckhart's concept of the ground (*grunt*) to be the foundation and core of his mystical doctrine. See *The Mystical Thought of Meister Eckhart*, op. cit., pp. 35–52

47. W 11, p. 97.

48. W 31, p. 229. For Aquinas' doctrine, see the *Summa Theologiae*, I, Q. 79, a. 9-12; I-II, Q. 74, a. 7; II-II, Q. 53, a. 3. The turn of events by which the spark of the soul became confused with *synderesis* (or more accurately, *synteresis*) has been well-discussed by Walshe, ed. cit., I, pp. xli-xlii. Cf. W 32a, p. 238: '... the spark in the soul which is created by God and is a light, imprinted from above, and an image of the divine nature, which is always striving against whatever is ungodly, and it is not a power of the soul, as some masters would have it, and it is always inclined to

the good – even in hell it is inclined to the good. The masters say this light is so natural that it is always striving, it is called *synteresis*, which means to say a binding [to good] and a turning away from [evil].' Eckhart is closely following Aquinas here. Cf. *Summa Theologiae*, I, Q. 79, a. 12. McGinn points out that the only place Eckhart used the Latin term *scintilla animae*, however, was in his defence at Cologne. See *The Mystical Thought of Meister Eckhart*, op. cit., p. 41, n. 41.

49. (Sentence unfinished.) W 53, p. 63.

50. W 69, p. 165. Cf. also W 18, p. 147, cited above, p. 52, and W 42, p. 296, cited above, p. 51.

51. W 57, p. 85. Cf. W 24a, pp. 190–1.

52. W 42, p. 296.

53. Cf. the excellent analysis by John Caputo of this subject, art. cit.

54. W 42, p. 296.

55. W 69, pp. 165–6.

56. W 46, p. 21. Cf. W 69, p. 167: 'A man may go out into the fields and say his prayers and know God, or he may go to church and know God: but if he is more aware of God because he is in a quiet place, as is usual, that comes from his imperfection and not from God: for God is equally in all things and all places, and is equally ready to give Himself as far as in Him lies: and he knows God rightly who knows God equally (in all things).' Cf. also the *Talks of Instruction*, C-McG, p. 253.

57. W 66, p. 141. Cf. W 69, p. 169: 'If a man dwelt in a house that was beautifully adorned, another man who had never been inside it might well speak of it: but he who had been inside would *know*.'

58. W 25, p. 197.

59. W 30, p. 226. For Aquinas on the priority of intellect, see the *Summa Theologiae*, 1, Q. 82, a. 3 ad 1 and 2, and a. 4 ad 1; and II-II, 83, 3 ad 1.

60. W 4 (DP 59), pp. 40f.

61. W 4 (DP 59), p. 47.

62. W 41, p. 287.

63. W 65, p. 136. Cf. also the *Talks of Instruction*, C-McG, pp. 256–7.

64. W 59, p. 100.

65. W 72 (DW 7, DP 8), p.189.

66. Ibid., p.190.

67. W 79 (DW 43, DP 52), p. 233. Cf. also *On the Noble Man*, C-McG, p. 245. For Eckhart on divine grace, 'the indwelling and cohabiting of the soul in God', see W 79, p. 232 and W 81, p. 241.

THE PREACHER'S WAY

Now French, heavily industrialised and as famous for its goose-liver pâté as for its magnificent Rhenish cathedral, the German city of Strassburg occupied a position of signal importance in the spiritual revolution of the Middle Ages. James M. Clark observes that: 'As regards the geographical distribution of mysticism (and hence of the Friends of God), Strasbourg was undoubtedly the great centre ... Here Eckhart and Tauler preached and here (Rulwin) Merswin founded Grüner Worth. From this city influence radiated out in all directions, but especially northwards to Cologne, south to Basel, and up the Rhine Valley to Constance. This was the great highway of commerce; it was called the *Pfaffengasse*, or "parsons' alley", because it was the road to Rome, and it connected the great episcopal cities of Cologne, Strasbourg and Basel.'[1]

A free imperial city by the thirteenth century, Strassburg became staunchly Protestant during the Reformation. Seized by the troops of Louis XIV a century later, it gradually acquired its French character and spelling, made permanent by treaty in 1919.[2] But throughout the fourteenth century, this ancient port city on the Rhine was the centre of German Dominican influence, one which greatly determined its mystical character. The Friars Preachers came there in 1224 and soon acquired considerable influence because of their preaching, their learning, and their spiritual direction.[3] Soon a Dominican centre, the order built a large priory there which was dedicated in the year of Eckhart's birth on the occasion of a general chapter. There Tauler was born in 1300 and Suso would live and work. Seven Dominican women's convents, five of them founded before 1237, lay within its confines.[4] There Eckhart and Tauler would preach most of their sermons.

With the exception of Engeltal and St Catherine's, some 175 miles to the northeast near Nurnberg, most of the notable Rhineland monasteries of Dominican women also lay within a radius of ninety miles of the city. There 'some fifty miles to the south was Maria

Medingen; in Northern Switzerland there were the convents of Töss near Winterthur, Oetenbach and Zurich. There was Adelhausen near Freiburg in Breisgau, Kaisersheim in Bavaria, and finally Unterlinden at Colmar in Alsace. In all these places mystics were to be found, books were copied and written.[5] To these should be added St Katharinental near Diessenhofen, Weiler near Esslingen, Schonensteinbach in Alsace, Paradise Monastery near Soest (founded 1252) and Kirchberger. It is hardly surprising that when the Dominican Order sought eminent preachers and teachers to entrust with the supervision of the great numbers of women religious in this area, Meister Eckhart was assigned to the priory at Strassburg. There were also several houses of Beguines in the city, and it is known that both Eckhart and Tauler preached in at least three of them and corresponded with some of the *mantellatae*, 'the cloaked women', early Dominican teritaries.[6] The influence of all these women upon the friars was a source of many distinctive elements in Dominican preaching. Similarly, 'the Friends of God', a lay mystical movement instigated under the influence of Tauler by a Strassburg merchant, Rulwin Merswin, had a reciprocal influence on the Preaching Friars.

The later thirteenth and early fourteenth centuries also saw moments of extreme tension between the friars and the citizens of Strassburg over the conflict raging between Ludwig of Bavaria and the popes. From 1339 to 1343 the Dominicans were forced to quit the city because of a papal interdict. Tauler was unable to return until 1348.

The Care of Nuns

Although the 'second order' of cloistered nuns was not formally recognised as part of the order for many years after its foundation, a special relationship between the Friars Preachers and their contemplative sisters characterised the Dominican order from the beginning. St Dominic himself was placed in charge of the first convent at Prouille by Bishop Diego in 1207. Later, in Rome, Madrid and Bologna, Dominic established similar monasteries for women, many of whom were converts from Albigensianism.[7]

Among the early sisters, the memory of the courageous and blessed Diana d'Andalo is cherished by Dominicans of both sexes. Her valiant struggle from 1219 to 1223 to establish the convent of St Agnes at

Bologna against her powerful family's wishes has all the ingredients of high romance. Even more legendary was her friendship with Dominic and especially with his successor, Blessed Jordan of Saxony.[8] But there was opposition to accepting jurisdiction over houses of women contemplatives even from the friars themselves, who felt that their studies and preaching ministry were being threatened by the *cura monalium*. Such complaints would be a common refrain for many years.

By mandate of Pope Honorius III and the decision of the General Chapter of Paris in 1228, however, the affiliation of the convent of St Agnes was eventually ratified. But no new establishments were to be allowed: 'In virtue of the Holy Spirit and under pain of excommunication: we strictly prohibit any of our friars from striving or procuring, henceforth, that the care or supervision of nuns or any other women be committed to our brethren ... We also forbid anyone henceforth to tonsure, clothe in a habit, or receive the profession of any woman.'[9]

This prohibition was repeated in 1242. And in fact, no new convents were affiliated until 1245. By 1246, however, there were thirty.[10] For, as Jeanne Ancelet-Hustache observes, 'the women knew what they wanted and the obstacles gradually gave way to their pressure'.[11] By 1250, there were thirty-two monasteries in Germany alone. The total had risen by 1277 to fifty-eight monasteries, forty of them in Germany.[12] By 1300, there were approximately seventy convents in Teutonia out of ninety in all of Europe.[13] At the same time, there were only forty-six to forty-eight priories of men. (Outside of Germany, significantly, opposite proportions prevailed in the order as a whole.) By 1303 there were 141 convents of Dominican women in Europe; seventy-four to seventy-seven lay within what were now two German Provinces – sixty-five in Teutonia, and nine in the new province of Saxony, where Eckhart was now the first provincial. (Four of these convents still exist – Lienz, Regensburg, Schwyz and Spires.) The other sixty-seven convents were scattered over the continent.[14]

Who were these women who all but demanded spiritual direction of the Friars and sometimes actual incorporation into the Dominican family? Why the sudden and dramatic influx into Dominican convents in the thirteenth and early fourteenth century?

Dominican Women Mystics in the Rhineland

It has become commonplace to refer to a 'surplus' of women in this period with regard to the uncommonly large numbers of women entering Dominican monasteries in the thirteenth and early fourteenth centuries. For instance, Rufus Jones conceded that 'there was undoubtedly in the fourteenth century an unusual flowering of the feminine mind and spirit and with it the expression of a yearning for a richer and freer life.' He immediately added, however: 'There was almost everywhere an excess of women over men in the population of Europe. Then in addition there was a large class of celibate men in the Church in every city, so that there was sure to be a considerable number of women for whom there were no husbands available. Unmarried women endeavoured to find occupation in the different crafts, but most doors were closed to them. The result was that the convents and the Beguine houses were filled with women of all stations of life.'[15]

Such simple explanations cannot account, however, for the unparalleled growth of Dominican convents in comparison to those of other religious orders. (It should be noted that not only individual members but whole convents of such established institutions sought to be enrolled in the Order of Preachers at this time.)[16] The impelling cause resided more, I believe, in the spiritual aspirations of an unusually large number of women and the perceived character of the Dominican order at that time than in whatever economic and demographical forces impelled women to seek refuge in the cloister. Gieraths comments: 'Most of the nuns in Dominican convents of southwest Germany came from flourishing cities, from wealthy homes, or at least from good bourgeois environments. Consequently, they could hardly have been motivated to enter the convent by economic necessities.'[17]

Medieval Women and the Search for God

It now seems clear that the unprecedented influx of women into the Dominican houses prior to 1329 came from three distinct sources: already existing secular communities, that is, Beguines and similar groups of religiously dedicated laywomen; new foundations; and members of older orders anxious to adopt the Dominican rule. However, many of these latter, 'converted' monasteries affiliated with older orders eventually reverted to their prior affiliation, some even before 1329. These include Alzey (Augustinian until 1248; reverted 1262), Neuberg (Cistercian until 1287; reverted by 1300), and Wiederstadt (Sisters Hospitaler).[18] Further in Germany, original foundations accounted for even fewer of the new Dominican monasteries.[19] Thus, as a group, the Beguines presented the richest source of new Dominican convents. Most of the new monasteries appearing during this great period of growth were in fact of Beguine origin. The first was St Catherine's at Ammerschweir, founded by Friar Emicho of Colmar in 1220s. Then came those at Frankfurt, Adelhausen, St Katharinenthal, Engeltal, Gnadenzell, Steinheim, Diessenhoffen and Cologne. There the more famous convents at which Eckhart preached were St Maccabees and St Mariengarten. Outside of Germany, monasteries such as Metz were also Beguine foundations.[20]

In addition to the cloistered houses of nuns with Beguine origins, great numbers of lay groups of Beguines were placed under Dominican care. Hinnesbusch recounts that in the middle of the thirteenth century, 'In Cologne, thirty nine houses of Beguines near the Dominican priory, seven of them in the same street, were under the guidance of the friars'.[21] Franciscan friars were also charged with the care of penitential Beguine houses. In both cases, a considerable part of the beginnings of the 'third orders' or lay affiliations with the mendicants lies in this remarkable spiritual movement.

The Beguines

The origin of the Beguines themselves remains obscure.[22] In the medieval mind they were nominally linked with the Albigensian heresy, the name itself supposedly coming from a contraction of the term itself.[23] Generally associations of devout laywomen, early Beguines gathered into self-supporting communities for prayer and charitable service, principally care of the sick and needy. First appearing in the Low Countries in the late twelfth century this attractive spiritual movement soon spread up the Rhine valley to other European countries. St Louis IX founded a Beguinage in Paris in 1264. Like the mendicant friars, the Beguines preferred urban environment to rural settings, despite their contemplative inclinations.

Beguines possessed no common rule, mother house or superior-general. Nevertheless, during the first half of the thirteenth century, such saintly figures as Marie d'Oignies, Juliana of Cornillon and Beatrice of Nazareth received approval and encouragement from Jacques de Vitry and other church leaders.[24] Both Dominican and Franciscan friars assisted them with spiritual direction and protection from the earliest years of their apostolate. Beguines especially associated with the Dominican Order include Christine of Stommeln, Marguerite of Ypres and the incomparable Mechthild of Magdeburg.[25]

Towards the end of the thirteenth century, however, the Beguines' radical social doctrines, mysticism and sympathies with the Spiritual Franciscans led to suspicions of heresy on the part of ecclesiastical authorities. They soon found themselves accused of promoting pantheism, antinomianism and the 'Heresy of the Free Spirit', undertones of which may even be detected in the proceedings against Eckhart himself years later.[26]

After the turn of the century, the Beguines rapidly fell into even greater disrepute. In 1307, Henry of Virneburg, the powerful Archbishop of Cologne and Eckhart's eventual nemesis, convened a provincial synod against them and certain Beghards who were alleged by the Franciscans to be spreading the heresy of the Free Spirit. Wider ecclesiastical opposition culminated in the condemnation and execution at Paris in 1310 of Marguerite Porete, author of *The Mirror of Simple Souls*. Both Beghards and Beguines were also condemned, if selectively, at the Council of Vienne in 1312 under Clement V. Eventually, many Beghards accepted reform and were allowed to continue by John XXII in 1321. Many Beguines would be persecuted for over a century, however, and except for those under royal or episcopal protection had all but disappeared by the time of the Reformation. Some, however, still exist in Bruges, Ghent and elsewhere in Belgium.

Given Eckhart's perhaps surprising but momentous choice to preach in the common language of the people rather than Latin, his connection with the Beguines takes on greater significance in view of their use of vernacular in preaching and writing theological tracts. McGinn observes in this respect that 'Beguine circles and subsequently Dominican nunneries appear to have been the earliest centres for the writing down of devout letters, poems, treatises and sermons in the vernacular'.[27]

With regard to his spiritual teaching, however, the characteristically extraordinary features of Beguine mysticism – ecstasy, visions, raptures, stigmata, etc. – were decidedly not those favoured by Eckhart.[28]

What he did share with the Beguines as well as with other mystical sects of the period was a strong emphasis on the presence of God in everyday life and an emblematic stress on voluntary poverty. Herbert Grundmann notes significantly in this connection that 'Only in the movement of female piety in Germany did the idea of poverty expand in the direction of its original religious meaning, not into the organisational or the dogmatic and not into the polemical, but rather into the mystical – the striving after inward, spiritual poverty'.[29]

Free Spirits

In the thirteenth and fourteenth centuries, the terms 'Brethren' and 'Heresy' of the Free Spirit came to be employed, often indiscriminately, to refer to more or less anarchistic mystical sects including the Almaricans or Amaurians (followers of Amaury of Béne), Fraticelli, Beghards, Beguines or almost anyone who professed voluntary poverty and independence from institutional ecclesiastical authority to live in 'the freedom of the Spirit' (cf. 2 Cor 3:17). Those who in fact represented the authentic core of such a movement espoused a more or less pantheistic spirituality, wandering freely and without apparent organisation, preaching their libertarian (and frequently libertine) gospel to all and sundry. They seem to have established a kind of secret network, a medieval underground which not only threatened the integrity of the organised and visible church, but undermined the approbation of much more orthodox groups such as the Beguines, with whom they shared certain beliefs and practices.[30]

Strassburg was the scene of several attempts to eradicate the partisans of the Free Spirit. As the largest city in northern Europe, Cologne too was a favourite location for heterodox proselytising. Its formidable archbishop, Henry of Virneburg, already 'a noted opponent of heresy and of the suspect Beguines',[31] and who would soon inaugurate proceedings against Eckhart himself, convened yet another provincial synod in 1322 to deal with the 'unceasing propaganda' of the Brethren of the Free Spirit. Eventually, one of the leaders, a Dutchman named Walter, was arrested, tortured and burnt. Some fifty other suspects were also executed by drowning or burning.[32]

Such widespread spiritual agitation and ferment provides a critical background element for understanding Eckhart's indictment and condemnation. It also strongly suggests that economic and social pressures of the late Middle Ages were in themselves insufficient causes for the sudden proliferation of Dominican women's convents in Germany. While they surely existed, such forces cannot explain, to begin with, the particular and disproportionate growth of Dominican monasteries in the Rhineland, especially given the friars' disaffection at accepting more responsibility for the care of nuns. Why the disproportion? Why did Cistercian, Franciscan and Praemonstratensian convents not flourish similarly?

Given the number of women entering the monasteries and especially the vast numbers of those electing to transfer to the care of the Dominicans, it is also difficult to comprehend how mere social or economic forces could produce a truly mystical explosion instead of the tepidity, slackness and frustration found in convents elsewhere. At least the hint of an explanation for these apparent anomalies comes from two directions, one negative, the other positive.

First, in the thirteenth and early fourteenth centuries, it had become increasingly difficult and often impossible for women to enter at least Cistercian and Premonstratensian monasteries. In 1228, after half a century of growth in the numbers and strength of Cistercian abbesses, the Cistercian order had in fact resolved not to admit any new communities of women.[33] Nevertheless, ecclesiastical disapproval of unaffiliated groups of women continued to grow as the century drew on, creating a strong impetus for them to seek affiliation with an established order.

Also beginning in 1228, the Dominican friars had likewise attempted to forestall the entrance of numbers of women into the order, as noted above, but the combined pressure of the women themselves and the papacy eventually wore down the friars' resistance. To elicit such pressure, something more positive than social deprivation and relative opportunity had to attract interested well-born, well-educated women into Dominican convents, where conditions were frequently poor, stark and demanding, sometimes crushingly so.

This second, positive factor influencing women to seek entrance to the Order of Preachers involves two cardinal features of the Dominicans during this period. These are, first, the role of study and learning in general and, second, the fact that the mystical movement of early fourteenth century was largely Dominican in character, at least in Germany, where spiritual agitation was ostensibly more pronounced than elsewhere.

The Work of the Mind

Literacy had developed rapidly among lay women as well as men in the High Middle Ages, and not only among the leisured classes. Beguines and other groups of spiritual reformers valued study very highly, especially that of scripture and theology. Similarly, from the beginning, study and learning were valued within the Dominican order as the paramount work by which the ministry of preaching would be advanced. While eventually broadened to include all areas of learning, the study of scripture and theology were, ideally, the primary intellectual pursuits of both the friars and, although they did not study formally, also the nuns.

At the turn of the thirteenth century, Jeanne Ancelet-Hustache recounts, these Dominican women 'were so highly educated that, about 1289–1290, the German provincial, Hermann of Minden, recommended the choice of learned friars to preach in the Dominican convents, as befitted the culture of these religious.' She adds with fitting emphasis: 'It is in this spiritual milieu that Master Eckhart should be placed.'[34] Who indeed could have been more qualified than Eckhart, a Dominican friar who was both scholar and mystic? And not only Eckhart, but Suso, Tauler and other studious, prayerful friars sympathetic to the needs of Beguines and other devout, learned women both in and at the periphery of the order. Clark aptly if perhaps too simply summarises: 'The growth of mysticism [in the fourteenth century] was then due to the impact of scholastic philosophy on educated women in nunneries.'[35]

The Flowering of Mysticism

There were undoubtedly many other reasons why large numbers of women flocked to Dominican convents in the first decades of the fourteenth century. But not even the intellectual heritage of the order was as compelling a motive as the fact that in Germany at this time the mystical movement that catalysed the religious restlessness of a generation of both men and women was largely Dominican in character. It is thus understandable that those most strongly attracted to mystical spirituality would tend to identify with the Dominican order and most particularly its outstanding mystical theologians, Eckhart, Suso and Tauler.

Rufus Jones provides an eloquent portrait of the impact of the learned, mystical friars on the nuns:

> Meister Eckhart, as we have seen, and also Tauler and Suso, were appointed as preachers and father confessors in the Dominican convents for women, and all three of them carried on at various times a preaching mission in these convents. Many of their sermons and other writings were copied by the sisters and preserved for us through the zeal and interest of these women. These preaching mystics, all three of whom possessed contagious qualities of life, produced a profound effect upon their hearers and their confessants, and every glimpse we get into these sisterhoods of the period reveal a widespread and very intense mystical life in these groups, usually under the leadership of some signally devout woman mystic.[36]

Eckhart was particularly well known and long remembered in the convents of the Swiss Rhineland. At Töss the remarkable prioress and chronicler Elsbet Stagel asked Suso for guidance about the Meister's teaching. Their subsequent and largely epistolary friendship is one of the richest in the annals of the Order. At Ötenbach Elsbeth von Begenhofen recorded in the convent chronicle that she had sought advice from Eckhart himself concerning difficulties in the spiritual life.[37] Clark observes, similarly: 'There are some charming little anecdotes written in Strasbourg and Cologne by friars and nuns who had known Eckhart personally or by repute, which show in what regard and veneration he was held.'[38]

Content not only to preserve the teachings of their great brother Dominican mystics, the sisters put them into practice and recorded their experiences in the convent chronicles, the *Schwesternbücher* ('Sisters' Books'). They thus stabilised the vocabulary of mystical spirituality in the vernacular and also helped to maintain authentic Christian values and behaviour during an era of manic deviation in spiritual and mental health. Then, suddenly, the German mystical flowering felt the chill blast of winter.

Decline

It is readily apparent in the numbers. Even before Eckhart's condemnation, the once prodigious growth of Dominican women's convents in Germany had begun to reverse itself. By 1358, although the overall number of monasteries in Europe had risen to 157, none of the sixteen new institutions founded since 1303 were to be found in Germany. Further, many of the older convents were now under episcopal jurisdiction. Others had reverted to previous affiliations.

The reasons for the decline of the Dominican monastic movement in the later fourteenth century Rhineland are no doubt as manifold as those for its earlier growth. Among them, surely the shadows of Eckhart's trial and the catastrophic condemnation of his teachings loom very large. His living memory would in time fade even from the most faithful monasteries. But like the *Schwesternbücher*, Eckhart's sermons had been preserved in writing along with certain letters and, even if collected to be used as trial documents by his antagonists, they thus survived the oblivion of time and human mortality.

Eckhart's Spiritual Doctrine

To have aroused the suspicion, then the ire of the Archbishop of Cologne, Eckhart's teaching must have seemed too close to the doctrines of the Beguines, the Brethren of the Free Spirit and other suspect or heterodox groups for the stern old man to tolerate. The spirituality of the Dominican nuns revealed in the *Schwesternbücher* greatly resembles that of the Beguines in particular, which only stands to reason. Many of them had been Beguines. And, to be sure, the long and close connections of the Dominican friars of Cologne and Strassburg with the Beguines themselves had certainly, even necessarily coloured their preaching and spiritual direction.

Even a cursory exploration of the themes and content of the Meister's teaching reveals a pervasive similarity to Beguine spirituality and not only regarding poverty. On closer inspection, however, Eckhart's doctrine also manifests important differences not only from that but especially from the doctrines of the more radical dissenters. First of all, as we have seen, Eckhart did not only avoid but actively resisted interest in extraordinary spiritual experiences.[39] For Eckhart, God does not customarily ravish the soul with ecstatic delights or hypersensory transports, but rather communicates a loving Presence through all the events of ordinary experience, including the hierarchical elements of the cosmos *and* the Church, the body of Christ, with its Book, sacraments, preaching and authority. Second, his preaching as a whole was remarkably devoid of particular political or social commentary.[40] With regard to evangelical poverty, while Eckhart does not neglect the importance of real detachment, he concentrates on interior poverty, purity of heart. Human nobility and equality are founded for him in the Incarnation, not on natural or social right. For Eckhart, justice does not level everyone to a common, leaderless state, but elevates all to the condition of divine equanimity.

I doubt whether Eckhart skirted the borders of heterodox expression in articulating his vision of the spiritual life merely as a worthwhile but dangerous pastoral risk that backfired in the violent atmosphere of anti-heretical fervour. The beliefs, ideals and values he exhorted were in the very air itself. Eckhart could not ignore them. He could – and, I think, did – transform them, however, outmanoeuvering the heretics by revealing the orthodox intentionality of the most exciting and potentially revolutionary of these notions. His judges thought otherwise, and even altered his meaning at times to prove his complicity in holding heretical views.[41] Time's verdict, however, has increasingly challenged that decision. Eckhart remains, as Heidegger reminded us, both *Lesemeister* and *Lebemeister*.[42]

Mindful of the peril of trying to constrain the Meister in any systematic formulation, in the following chapters I shall attempt to trace in greater detail Eckhart's organic teaching on the spiritual life as it arises from the ebullient creativeness of God, through its continuation in the divine pursuit and capture of errant humanity in the net of Incarnate Wisdom, culminating in the transformation of human life and spirituality through progressive union with Christ, his Spirit and the 'unknowable Godhead'.

Because of the often overwhelming transcendence of Eckhart's vision, it will be particularly important throughout to bear in mind his constant orientation towards the Christian's work in *this* world, even after experiencing union with God in the 'second Birth'. Far from being a dreamy, speculative idler pining for some other world, Eckhart insists, as we shall see, that 'perfected' disciples, the true mystics, pass back unnoticed into the human milieu where, one in will and work with God, they energise and hallow the experience and activities of their fellow citizens and saints. Final transformation in the endless desert of the Godhead lies beyond mortal existence, he admits, but those already dead to the world of egoistic and materialistic concerns have truly risen to the first degrees of eternal life. The process can be complete only when all are One in All.

NOTES

1. James M. Clark, *The Great German Mystics*, New York: Russell and Russell, 1970 (reprint of Basil Blackwell edition, Oxford: 1949), p. 95. Cf. Phillippe Dollinger, 'Strasbourg et Colmar, foyers de la mystique rhénane (XIIIe-XIVe siècle),' *La Mystique Rhénane*, ed. cit., pp. 3–13.

2. Because the city was German in the fourteenth century, I have retained the German spelling in this book.

3. Cf. Dollinger, art.cit, p. 5.

4. St Mark (1225), St Nicholas, where Tauler died, and St Catherine's petitioned in 1370 to be removed from Dominican care but were denied. St Elizabeth burned in 1392. St Agnes, St John the Evangelist and St Mark were torn down in 1475. St Agnes' community moved to St Margaret's (founded in 1280), St Mark's to Grunenbach. Cf. Hinnebusch, I, p. 379. Cf. also Dollinger, art. cit., p. 6.

5. Clark, ibid., p. 96. Unterlinden was founded 1232, Töss in 1233. For accounts of the early spirituality of the Dominican sisters of Unterlinden, see William Hinnebusch, I, pp. 380–1, and Simon Tugwell, OP, ed. and trans., *Early Dominicans: Selected Writings*, New York: Paulist Press, 1982, pp. 387f., 417–24.

6. Cf. ibid., p. 8.

7. Cf. Hinnebusch, I, pp. 96–104 and Tugwell, op. cit., pp. 387ff. and J. Ancelet-Hustache, Master Eckhart, p. 19: 'Dominic became more explicitly the favourite saint of thousands of men and especially of women religious.'

8. Chronicles of St Agnes, *Analecta Sacris Ordinis fratrum Praedicatorum*, I, Rome, 1893–1894.

9. I Const II, 27, p. 222. (Cited by Hinnebusch, I, p. 389.)

10. Hinnebusch, I, p. 390.

11. Ancelet-Hustache, *Master Eckhart*, p. 19. Cf. Hinnebusch, I, p. 391: 'In July 1252, Pope Innocent IV exempted the Order from the affiliation of any additional convents for a period of twenty years.' However, 'After 1257 the prohibitions were practically abrogated. Clement IV's Bull of 1267 officially charged the Preachers with the direction of nuns.' Ancelet-Hustache, ibid.

11. H. Grundmann, *Religiose Bewegungen im Mittelalter*, Hildesheim, 1961, pp. 250–1; Hinnebusch, I, p. 377. Cf. also J. Ancelet-Hustache, Master Eckhart, pp. 19–20.

12. Clark, *Great German Mystics*, p. 4.

13. Hinnebusch, I, p. 379. Cf. J. Quetif and J. Echard, *Scriptores Ordinis Praedicatorum*, Paris: 1719–21, I, pp. ix–xv. According to Rufus Jones, by the middle of the

fourteenth century there were about one hundred sisters in each convent. (*The Flowering of Mysticism*, New York: Hafner Pub. Co., 1971, p. 158.) Hinnebusch suggests that the average size of the convents was just over fifty. (Hinnebusch, I, pp. 382–3.) Jeanne Ancelet-Hustache estimates the number at between eighty and one hundred (p. 21).

15. Jones, op. cit., p. 159. He notes that 'Carl Beucher points out that in Frankfurt fully 6 per cent of the female population of the town in the fourteenth century lived in houses of these types.' Ibid. The reference is to Buecher, *Die Frauenfrage im Mittelalter* (Tübingen, 1882). For a more recent discussion of the women's movement in fourteenth-century Germany, cf. Gundolf Gieraths, 'The Importance of Dominican Sisters in German Mysticism', *Cross and Crown*, 15 (1963), pp. 456–67, Grundmann, op. cit., passim, and Bernard McGinn, 'Meister Eckhart: An Introduction', *An Introduction to the Medieval Mystics of Europe*, ed. by Paul E. Szarmach, Albany: State University of New York Press, 1984, p. 241.

16. 'The already existing partly monastic, partly secular communities began to place themselves under the spiritual direction of his Friars Preachers, now known as Dominicans. Others, who belonged to the old Orders, were also anxious to come under the Dominican rule.' Ancelet-Hustache, *Master Eckhart*, p. 19.

17. Gieraths, art. cit., p. 457.

18. Hinnebusch, I, p. 378.

19. Ibid. Among the more illustrious were those of Altenhohenau near Salzburg, founded in 1235 by Count Conrad of Wassenburg, St Catherine's in Freiburg, founded by Count Egon II of Fürstenberg in 1292, and Schönensteinbach.

20. Hinnebusch, I, pp. 377f., 388, CL p. 20. For Eckhart's testimony, cf. also DW I, pp. 242, 372–3, 382, n. 4.

21. Hinnebusch, I, p. 400. On the Beguines of Cologne, cf. Southern, op. cit., pp. 319–31.

22. Cf. McGinn, 'Introduction', pp. 240, 241–4. For a comprehensive study, see Ernest W. McDonnell, *The Beguines and Beghards in Medieval Culture*, New Brunswick, NJ: Rutgers University Press, 1954.

23. For a thorough discussion of the origin of the term 'beguine', see Herbert Grundmann, *Religious Movements in the Middle Ages*, trans. by Steven Rowan, intro. by Robert E. Lerner, Notre Dame and London: University of Notre Dame Press, 1995, p. 80, nn. 26–27.

24. Cf. Vandenbroucke, art cit., p. 359.

25. Cf. Hinnebusch, I, pp. 388–9. Like Cologne, Strassburg was 'a centre for Dominican nunneries and Beguine houses'. McGinn, 'Introduction', p. 245.

26. 'Grundmann has argued that Beguine poverty was the historical foundation for the development of the distinctive "German mysticism" of which Eckhart is the most famous proponent.' McGinn, 'Introduction', p. 243. Cf. G. Leff, *Heresy in the Later Middle Ages*, New York: Barnes and Noble, 1967, I, pp. 195–230, 310–407.

27. McGinn, 'Introduction', p. 243.

28. Cf. ibid., p. 248.

29. Op. cit., p. 85. Cf. also pp. 86, 92–7. Cited by McGinn, 'Introduction', p. 243. He

adds, 'For him [Grundmann] external poverty as a part of a life of mystical prayer was dialectically lifted up or synthesized (*aufgehoben*) into a higher state of interior stripping of the spirit, and this was the historical source for Eckhart's distinctive teaching regarding detachment (*abgescheidenheit*) as the way to God.'

30. Cf. Norman Cohn, *The Pursuit of the Millennium*, New York: Oxford University Press, rev. ed., 1970, pp. 148–86, and Gordon Leff, *Heresy in the Later Middle Ages*, op. cit., I, pp. 308–407. R.E. Lerner considers the existence of the Free Spirit movement to represent something of a paranoid delusion of nervous ecclesiastics who were by that time wont to magnify the extent and influence of reformist or dissenting factions. Cf. *The Heresy of the Free Spirit in the Later Middle Ages*, Berkeley: University of California Press, 1972.

31. McGinn, 'Introduction', p. 245. 30 Cf. Cohn, op. cit., p. 165.

32. Cf. Cohn, op. cit., p. 165.

33. On the general situation of religious women at this time and the fortunes of the Cistercian abbesses in particular, cf. Southern, pp. 309–18.

34. Ancelet-Hustache, p. 21. On the role of learning and the influence of Eckhart, Dietrich of Freiburg, Tauler, Suso, the difficulty of obtaining and copying books, etc., see Hinnebusch, I, pp. 383ff.

35. Clark, *Great German Mystics*, p. 5. Cf. Gieraths, art. cit., p. 463.

36. Jones, op. cit., p. 158.

37. Cf. Clark, *Great German Mystics*, p. 2.

38. Clark, ibid., pp. 23–4, referring to Pfeiffer, ed. cit., pp. 624–7.

39. See above, p. 76 and below, pp. 107, 191ff.

40. Cf. McGinn, 'Introduction', p. 238: 'Eckhart's writings ... show no interest in the politics of the day, and surprisingly little in directly social or economic concerns.'

41. See C-McG, p. 54.

42. According to Reiner Schürmann, the origin of the expression goes back to an aphorism of Eckhart's himself (op. cit., p. 234, n. 72. The reference is to Pfeiffer, ed. cit., p. 599, 1. 19.). Cf. John Caputo, 'The Nothingness of the Intellect', *The Thomist*, 39 (1975), p. 115. Cf. also Tauler, Sermon 51, 2 (*Die Predigten Taulers*, ed. F. Vetter, Berlin, 1910, No. 45, pp. 196, 28f.), cited in Yves Congar, 'Langage des spirituels et langage des théologiens', *La Mystique Rhénane*, ed. cit., p. 29.

PART TWO
ECKHART'S SPIRITUAL
TEACHING

�֎

THE EBULLIENCE
OF GOD

For Eckhart, spirituality was not something different from theology, which no doubt is why his sermons were so characteristically doctrinal in content and intent. Similarly, the spiritual life was not by any means a way of relating the various activities of life to God, nor especially a set of practices or observances. For him, it was life itself, understood and accepted as an ascent to God, a return to the primal Source, our final and everlasting homecoming. The heart of that life, and of Eckhart's spirituality, is undeniably his teaching on the birth of the Word in the soul. This great theme is the central focus of a rich and moving theological vision, framed by the doctrine of creation and that of transformation into God as context and consequence.

Historically, Eckhart's three-dimensional mystical theology was rooted in the far-ranging synthesis begun by Albert the Great in which the Neoplatonic theme of emanation and return, especially as recast in Christian terms by Dionysius, was joined to the Augustinian theme of the conversion to God by a progressive interior ascent of the mind.[1] In the School of Cologne, these great motifs of Christian Platonism and Neoplatonism, with their emphasis on the ground of the soul, the spark of the intellect and the primarily intellectual character of union with God, were supplemented or even bound together by the Aristotelian psychology interpreted by Avicenna and Averroes and modified by Albert and Thomas Aquinas.[2]

True to this intellectual and mystical heritage, Eckhart described creation primarily as emanation – the 'external' counterpart of the divine self-effusion seething within the Godhead. Reciprocally, however, for the Meister creation '*ex nihilo*' also meant the absolute dependence of every creature upon God's constant presence, which conveys both existence and purpose. As we shall see in the following chapter, the redemptive moment in Eckhart's dialectic of *exitus* and *redditus* was similarly focused on Incarnation in a double fashion – not only on the birth of the Word in its historical moment, but perhaps even more on the eternal birth of the Word in the souls of the just. The eschatological dimension of his thought likewise had a dual intentionality – the return of all creation *to* God is simultaneously a 'breakthrough' experience in which the universe achieves its ultimate integration *in* God.

Thus, Eckhart's vision of emergence and return bridged by the Incarnate Word is not only dynamic but two-eyed, seen from the viewpoint of both time and eternity. The emanation of the Eternal Word by intellectual generation is also the conception of all things in the mind of God. The creation of the universe is a theophany. The Incarnation of the Word in time, place and corporeality is also the birth of the Word in the souls of the just. Breaking through into God in the world is also the return movement of all things back and yet ahead to their Origin and Destiny beyond time, space and matter. The emanation of the Trinity of Persons from the trackless void of the Godhead is, however, correlative to but not identical with the disappearance of all distinction and difference in union with the Godhead, where, as we shall see, even God 'unbecomes (*entwirt*)'.

Creation as Overflowing Exitus: The Doctrine of Emanation

Both of Eckhart's major themes – the reciprocal motif of Emanation-Return (*Exitus-Redditus*) and the central doctrine of the birth of the Word in the soul – derive by direct succession through Albert from the earliest Christian mystical theology. As we would expect, accordingly, both have biblical foundations as well as a mixed Middle Platonic and Neoplatonic ancestry.

This dynamic exitus-redditus theology, first found explicitly in the Middle Platonic spiritual theology of Philo and his Christian successors at the great catechetical school of Alexandria,[3] has several scriptural parallels, particularly in the gospels of John and Luke, whether in the vertical form of descent and ascent or the horizontal form of mission, that is, departure and return. Plotinus' 'Neoplatonic' version of emanation and return combined both axes and is more properly described as an expansion-contraction thematic.[4] In one place or another, Eckhart freely utilised all these motifs in developing his own doctrine.

In terms of creation, the Christian Platonism of the early Church reappears in Eckhart's writings as the famous 'boiling' metaphor used by

Plotinus. The Latin expressions he favoured are *bullitio* and *ebullitio*.[5] In the German works, he used even more dynamic language. Schürmann observes, 'The word most often used in this context is *ursprunc*. Literally it means "primitive (*ur-*) springing" (from the verb *springen*, to *spring*). Another Middle High German form, today obsolete, was *Ursprinc*, effervescence, efflorescence. The idea is always that of a kind of eruption.'[6]

Thus the expansive, living dynamism of the Godhead, the unnameable divine reality considered apart from both the distinction of persons and creation, 'springs' or 'bubbles up' (*bullitio*) as the Persons of the Trinity and 'then', in an untrammeled superabundance of being, love and goodness, 'boils over' (*ebullitio*) into creation. This 'external' manifestation of God's life and power, which is realised out of pure nothingness (another Alexandrian theme derived from the philosophical exegesis of Philo), was thus for Eckhart a continuation of the expansiveness of the Godhead, not an arbitrary act of divine will.

The Meister's favourite metaphors for this parallel burgeoning up of energy and life were those of a spring or fountain and also the growth and blossoming forth of a flower. 'I sometimes mention two springs,' he said. 'One spring, from which grace gushes forth, is where the Father begets His only-begotten Son. From that source grace arises, and there grace flows forth from that same spring. Another spring is where creatures flow out of God. This one is as far from the spring whence grace flows as heaven is from earth.'[7] In one of the Meister's most beautiful and theologically dense passages, he said, commenting on Isaiah 11:1-2: 'The tree of the Godhead blossoms in this ground [of the soul], and the Holy Ghost sprouts from its root. The flower that blossoms, delight, is the Holy Ghost. The soul, too, blossoms forth out of the Holy Ghost, who is the flower of the soul. And on that flower shall repose the spirit of the Lord. The Father and the Son rest on the Spirit, and the Spirit reposes on them as on its cause.'[8]

Eckhart saw the Trinity of Persons as a mutual and dynamic interaction of Outgoing (*Ûzganc*) and Ingoing (*Inganc*), an eternal fluxion of subsistent thought and love with its reflection in human interiority and transcendence. 'The Father is the beginning of the Godhead, for He comprehends Himself in Himself. From Him comes forth the eternal Word, yet remaining within, and the Holy Ghost proceeds from both, yet remains within, and the Father does not give birth to him, for he is the end of the Godhead, indwelling in it and in all creatures, and there is pure repose and a resting of all that ever obtained being.'[9] Further, '… the Father speaks the Son unspoken, and he remains within. I have also said before, God's outgoing is His ingoing. In proportion to my nearness to God does He speak Himself in me.'[10] Such dynamic metaphors were especially important for Eckhart's analogical understanding of the relationship of the Second Person to the First, in whose emanation as thought is contained the power and wisdom of all creation.

The Intellectual Generation of the Son as Word

Eckhart's 'cartesian revolution' with regard to the priority of understanding over being in God forms the background of two important themes in his doctrine of creation – the intellectual generation of the Son and the emanation of the external universe, including human persons, as an act of God's creative imagination. As already noted, first, Eckhart took seriously the Pauline concept of creation in and for Christ. With the generation of the Son, the utterance of the Word, all things came to be in an eternal effusion of God's own being.[11] As we have just seen, grace itself, participation in the being and life of God, also arises with the Son and at the same instant, although infinitely removed, that creatures are brought forth.

The intellectual generation of the Son had been a cardinal element in the teaching of Thomas Aquinas.[12] In most respects, Eckhart followed Thomas closely. The Trinity of Persons united in the one Godhead has consciousness as its principle (logical, not ontological) – the idea (*logos, ratio*) of God in the mind of God. This is the Eternal Word, subsistent and equally divine, the Wisdom of the Father, the Logos, who with the Father in mutual instantaneous beholding breathes forth the Holy Spirit.[13]

Like Thomas Aquinas, Eckhart often uses the example of our interior 'speaking' as a model when referring to the Word as the interior thought of God. With the Word, moreover, all creatures of whatever kind are also spoken as creative words or 'adverbs (*bîworts*)': 'The Father speaks the Son out of the fullness of His power, and all things in him. All things speak God. What my mouth does in speaking and declaring God, is likewise done by the essence of a stone, and this is understood more by works than by words.'[14]

Motherhood and God

Despite this intellectualist emphasis, however, Eckhart usually resorted to more poetic and biblical images of begetting and conceiving when describing the generation of the Second Person of the Trinity, especially in the sermons. That is, he preferred over the image of mental dialogue that of a parent begetting and bearing a child. Eckhart also affirmed that with the parental generation of the Logos, the Word and Son, all creatures are simultaneously 'begotten' and 'conceived' – not as existing beings, but as ideas, mental 'seeds' in the mind of God. Similarly, when 'externalised' in space, time and corporeality, they are 'born' out of the maternal womb of God. Eckhart, or one of his disciples, thus said: 'Where does the Father-nature have a maternal name? Where it does maternal work. Where the personal nature keeps to the unity of its nature and combines with it, there Fatherhood has a maternal name and is doing mother's work, for it is properly a mother's work to conceive [and bear]. But there, where the eternal Word arises, in the essential mind, *there* Motherhood has a paternal name and performs paternal work.'[15] Similarly, the Meister said in reference to the Word: 'In his birth all things have proceeded forth, and so great is God's pleasure in this birth that He spends His whole energy upon it.'[16]

Generation and Creation: Ideas in the Mind of God

Thus, as we have already seen above, for Eckhart as for the major line of Christian theologians since Clement of Alexandria, creatures pre-exist as 'Ideas' in the Divine Mind before they exist in actuality. Their being is thus God's being, not simply *as* God's being, the affirmation of which would entail monistic pantheism, but as an aspect or manifestation of God's being. They are nevertheless eternal, pure and perfect. Brought forth into the corporeal world of time and space, creatures (including *a fortiori* spiritual creatures) enter the finite, limited, indeed *fallen* world of nature and history. To be born into the world is thus a falling-away from oneness with God in the unfathomable bliss of mental existence in God.

But because 'Whatever is in God, is God',[17] all created things retain something of divinity about them. 'In the Father are the primal images of all creatures. This bit of wood has a rational image in God. It is not only rational, it is pure reason.'[18] Conversely, '... God is unseparated from all things, for God is in all things and is more inwardly in them than they are in themselves.'[19] Much more so the human spirit, which is capable of recognising not only its divine origin and end, but the enduring interior presence of God, the permanent impress of our preexistent state in the mind of God.

Here is the basis of Eckhart's panentheism, which in humankind is realised in mystical experience. This teaching would also end in misunderstanding and condemnation when the Meister derived from it the conclusion that the human spirit and the Word of God are one in nature as begotten: 'The Father begets His Son unceasingly, and furthermore, I say, He begets me as His Son and the same Son. I say even more: not only does He beget me as His Son, but He begets me as Himself and Himself as me, and me as His being and His nature. In the inmost spring, I well up in the Holy Ghost, where there is one life, one being and one work. All that God works is one: therefore He begets me as His Son without any difference.'[20] Here also lies the root of his initially disconcerting notion that God does not exist until creatures come to be.

To understand Eckhart correctly here is in a sense to understand all of Eckhart, for here lies the way to the heart of his mystical theology. To mistake him here, as his inquisitors evidently did, is likewise to mistake him fundamentally and completely. As we shall see in further detail later, his doctrine as a whole is fundamentally Christological and nascently Incarnational. Creation for Eckhart always means creation-in-Christ. The Word is the creative power of God reconciling all things to the Father in the ineffable unity of the Godhead. From the viewpoint of primordial creation however, its meaning in Christ is not fully revealed but awaits the rediscovery of its original glory. Hints and traces are nevertheless present in the paradoxes of time, space and corporeality.

Creating the World in the Now of Eternity

'I have often said, God is creating the whole world now this instant. Everything God made six thousand years ago and more when He made this world, God is creating now all at once.'[21]

The investigating commissions perhaps understandably balked at the notion of the simultaneity of God's creative acts, which from a creaturely viewpoint seemed to imply the eternity of the world. Here again, however, they misread Eckhart, who (correctly) pointed out that from the divine perspective, creation is eternal because God does not act under the constraints of time. Creation is therefore instantaneous. Thus also the creative ideas of all things, not merely the Son as Word, exist eternally in the mind of God, who for Eckhart was pure subsistent Intelligence. Time 'begins' when creatures are 'externalised' and thus lose their identity as divine ideas, becoming alienated, as it were, and 'trapped' in the external net of space and corporeality.

Even more alarmingly, Eckhart's critics heard him saying that by this token God too 'becomes' when creatures first exist apart from their eternal origin: 'God *becomes* when all creatures say "God" – then God comes to be,' the Meister said. 'When I subsisted in the ground, in the bottom, in the river and font of Godhead, no one asked me where I was going or what I was doing: there was no one to ask me. When I flowed forth, all creatures said "God". If anyone asked me, "Brother Eckhart, when did you leave your house?", then I must have been in there. That is how all creatures speak of God.'[22]

The Birth of God

Eckhart is saying that the divine Intelligence 'becomes' God only when creatures become creatures. Before creation, the unnameable Tri-unity was what it was within the incomprehensible 'inner', inter-personal life of Thought, Word and Love united in undifferentiated *Gottheit*. To think or utter 'God' is to admit of a differentiation which could be recognised only by the existence of that which is not essentially divine. To recognise 'God' is thus to have discovered one's creatureliness. For 'God' is a title that can only be used by what is not-God, a little-acknowledged fact clearly indicated even in the remote Indo-European origin of the word itself, which means 'to call upon or invoke'.

Thus the Father is not 'God' to the Son, nor the Son or Father 'God' to the Holy Spirit. That is how Eckhart could affirm that before creatures existed, there was no God:

> While I yet stood in my first cause, I *had* no God and was my own cause ... I was free of God and all things. But when I left my free will behind and received my created being, then I had a God. For before there were creatures, God was not 'God': He was

That which He was. But when creatures came into existence and received their created being, then God was not 'God' in Himself – He was 'God' in creatures.[23]

This daring exuberance of expression was exceeded even more jarringly by its consequence, which to conventional piety could only have seemed blasphemous or insane: 'Therefore let us pray to God that we may be free of God that we may gain the truth and enjoy it eternally ...'[24] Again, 'Therefore I pray to God to make me free of God, for my essential being is above God, *taking God as the origin of creatures*.'[25] Similarly, the Meister said with all the logical force of his mystical insight: 'I am the cause of God's being God: if I were not, then God would not be God. But you do not need to know this.'[26] And most radically, his thought culminates in the great claim that has so often brought doom upon the mystics of the West, '... I and God are one'.[27]

For Eckhart, then, to say 'God' in the vocative case (as Hocking would have put it) is to discover one's own radical dependence, one's radical *nothingness* apart from the limited being graciously lent by Being itself. But as already noted, creatures do not simply lose their primordial relationship *with-in* God when realised in concrete existence. They retain the mental impress of their divine origin and thus manifest God when truly known. As spirit, the human creature especially retains the impression of its Divine idea, and for Eckhart it is in the intellect in particular that the human soul is essentially made to the image and likeness of God. Thus, to be rid of 'God' means to return to the actual oneness within God which prevailed before creatures were 'born' into the external world. Prior to such a real return, such 'God-riddance' also signifies the overcoming of the cognitive distance between 'I' and 'God' in human consciousness through the re-cognition or dis-covery of the soul's profound and persistent unity with God in its own ground, the 'abyss'.

Obviously, the ramifications of Eckhart's theology of creation for his mystical spirituality are manifold. Because of the organic, almost cybernetic nature of his thought, tracing some of these complex branches also leads us again into his mystical anthropology and psychology, but on a higher turn of the gyre.[28] Briefly, Eckhart teaches us with Augustine that fundamental human nature possesses or retains a transcendental longing for God; it can even be *defined* as such a longing, a capacity to receive and transmit the life of God. This is only another way of saying that there exists in the human spirit a radical potential for conscious union with God. This potency is itself the real, but at first unconscious presence of God in the ground of the soul, the abyssus or *abditum mentis.*[29]

Human existence, indeed creation itself, therefore truly realises itself only as an ascent, a return (inwardly and in society) to God as origin and end. Because of the free nature of creation, especially human liberty, the ascent to God is not guaranteed of inevitable success. It is necessary, rather, to find and follow the appropriate way, the alternative being infinite loss of fulfilment, source and being. As we shall see, however, Eckhart's 'way' is an ordinary way, one accessible to men and women everywhere and at any time. For him, Jesus Christ is both the revelation of our destiny and the way to it through the birth of the Word in the souls of the just and their breakthrough back into God. Only in Christ is the meaning of human life, history and the nature of the universe fully realised.

The Grace of Christ

For Eckhart, human nature was universally one and the same; hence, because the Word adopted human nature and not a particular human person, all human beings are the Son of God, that is, all are one in Christ, and therefore in God. The begetting of the Son in eternity thus leads to the birth of the Word both in history and in the souls of the just. This birth, the central theme of all Eckhart's preaching and the subject of the following chapter, brings God into history and the human heart, leading ultimately to the rebirth of the soul into God. The mission of the Son, completed by the Holy Spirit, is to return to the Father – bringing all creation with him. For it was with and in him that all things flowed out of the creative mind of God.

Evil, Suffering and Death

Despite the worsening situation on almost every front in the early fourteenth century, including climate and agriculture, Eckhart's theology and spirituality shows a surprisingly positive, hope-filled attitude toward the world of creation.[30] As we shall see shortly, the

Meister's redemptive theology was similarly bright, focused on the Incarnation of God and the divinisation of humankind. Despite the often stark imagery of the desert of the Godhead, his emphasis on renunciation, emptiness and nothingness, he was a solar rather than nocturnal mystic, a preacher and teacher of the light.[31]

In his spiritual itinerary there are no dark nights to pass through. Images of divine darkness so beloved to the Alexandrian and Dionysian tradition are rare in his writings. When they surface, they are usually subordinated to those of light. In this respect, Eckhart more greatly resembles Clement of Alexandria and Origen than Gregory of Nyssa, Dionysius the Areopagite and Augustine. In commenting on the passage, 'Redeem the time, for the days are evil' (Eph 5:16), Eckhart said, 'Redeeming the time means the continual intellectual ascent to God, not in the diversity of images but in living intellectual truth. And 'the days are evil' should be understood thus: day presupposes night, for if there were no night, it would not be or be called day – it would all be one light. That was Paul's meaning, for a life of light is too little, being subject to spells of darkness that oppress a noble spirit and obscure eternal bliss. Hence too Christ's exhortation: 'Go on while you have the light' (Jn 12:35). For he who works in the light rises straight up to God free of all means: his light is his activity and his activity is his light.'[32]

The eschatological dimension of the Meister's thought is likewise almost wholly fixed on glory. Evil, sin and suffering, while never a dominant motif in his teaching, are nevertheless present and not unimportant. Death, too, was not neglected, but never allowed to occupy a central position in Eckhart's teaching.

The Meister's ordinary doctrine regarding sin and evil is not only orthodox, at least within the framework of Christian Neoplatonism, but almost wholly conventional.[33] But despite the balance in Eckhart's spiritual theology, especially in contrast to the preoccupations of later figures such as Thomas à Kempis, the commissioners at Cologne and Avignon found cause to condemn several of the Meister's teachings – again having first carefully isolated them from their fuller meaning-giving context.[34] Eckhart argued that if, as orthodox doctrine held, evil is nothing in itself, but rather a real privation of goodness in being, life or intelligence, then evil must ultimately be overcome by goodness and indeed be permitted in view of God's omniscience and omipotence in order that a greater good be realised. Thus, appealing to the doctrine of Thomas Aquinas, Eckhart said: 'The existence of evil is required by the perfection of the universe, and evil itself exists in what is good and is ordered to the good of the universe, which is what creation primarily and necessarily regards.'[35] The fact of sin, by logic of the *'felix culpa'* of Adam, is less an occasion for remorse than thanksgiving, in so far as human sanctity and the glory of God are much more perfectly realised by overcoming sin than would have been the case otherwise. To wish not to have sinned, consequently, would entail wishing that some perfection of the universe and therefore of God's plan not exist. Eckhart never opposed repentance or penitence, however, nor did he promote sinning in order to further the glory of God, as was occasionally and absurdly done. He counselled accepting the fact of sin as having contributed *nevertheless* to the perfection of the universe through the grace of God's forgiveness and universal providence.

Edmund Colledge has shown that, as Eckhart himself neglected to point out with sufficient force, his disputed teachings are primarily based on a little heeded but nevertheless undisputed doctrine of the fountainhead of western orthodoxy, the great Augustine himself.[36] It is hard to resist the impression in the light of such a miscarriage of theological investigation that while Eckhart may not actually have been *more* orthodox than his opponents, he was at least a better theologian. Nevertheless it is fair to say that owing probably to his own disinterest in the subject, Eckhart's treatment of the place of sin and evil is the least developed and original area of his teaching. Clearly, in his final years he seems to have lacked sufficient interest even to have mounted a spirited defence of his doctrine.

On the other hand, suffering and death were the occasion of some of Eckhart's most profound and characteristic spiritual writings, particularly in *The Book of Divine Consolation* and the *Talks of Instruction*. In general, he advocated the acceptance of suffering and death as an integral part of life, not a punishment even when a tragedy. For everyone who suffers 'from hunger, thirst, from cold or heat, or from being scorned and suffering unjustly, in whatever way God sends it, he must accept it willingly and gladly, just as if God had never created him except to endure suffering, discomfort and travail, not seeking anything for himself therein nor desiring anything in heaven or on earth, and he should consider all his suffering as trifling, as a mere drop of water compared to the raging sea.'[37] It is the same for spiritual suffering: 'all the spiritual hunger and bitterness that God permits to invade him, he shall patiently endure; and even then, having done all he can both inwardly and outwardly, he shall desire nothing.'[38]

Gently Eckhart piles argument upon persuasion, urging faith in God's love and the promise of everlasting joy to those who endure as sufficient reason willingly to endure loss and pain. More, he shows that God, too, suffers with us, joining divine compassion to human misery in order to transform us into the image of the Son of God.[39]

In his most systematic and moving treatment, *The Book of Divine Consolation*, possibly written for his friend, the grieving young Queen of Hungary, the Meister touches upon death itself only fleetingly and delicately, and, as it were, indirectly. 'If a man has lost some material possession,' he wrote, 'or a friend or a kinsman, an eye, a hand or whatever it may be, then he should be sure that if he accepts this patiently for the love of God, then by the loss he did not want to suffer he has in God's reckoning gained at least as much.'[40] He continues: 'another consolation is that probably one will find no one who does not love some living person so dearly that he would not gladly sacrifice an eye or go blind for a year, provided that he could have the eye back again, if in this way he could save his friend from death. So if a man would sacrifice his eye for year, to save from death someone who must still die in a few years' time, he ought rightly and more gladly sacrifice the ten or twenty or thirty years he might still have to live so as to make himself eternally blessed, possessing the everlasting vision of God in his divine light, seeing in God, himself and all created beings.'[41]

Eckhart's wisdom, like that of Shakespeare, bids us encounter death's darkness as a bride, not to flee from it or despise it.[42] Death is the shadowy doorway through which we must pass in order to experience the final breakthrough into God's light. Like St Francis, Eckhart seems to have regarded death less as an enemy to be feared than a sister to be welcomed. He did not simply gloss over evil, death and suffering with a patina of optimism. Rather, he counselled *Abgeschiedenheit*, as we shall see in greater detail later.[43] For only from detachment and the nothingness of the self radiate serenity, true joy and everlasting happiness.

Conclusion: All or Absolute Nothing

One of Eckhart's favorite maxims was that 'end and principle are the same'.[44] In a dense passage illustrating this insight, part of which I have already cited, Eckhart sums up much of his mystical theology:

> I have spoken before of the first beginning and the final end. The Father is the beginning of the Godhead, for He comprehends Himself in Himself. From Him comes forth the eternal Word, yet remaining within, and the Holy Ghost proceeds from both, yet remains within, and the Father does not give birth to him, for he is the end of the Godhead, indwelling in it and in all creatures, and there is pure repose and a resting of all that ever obtained being. The final end of being is the darkness or nescience of the hidden Godhead whose light illumines it, but this darkness comprehends it not.[45] Therefore Moses said: 'He who is has sent me'[46]: He who is name-less, who is a denial of all names and never had a name, wherefore the prophet said: 'Truly thou art a hidden God' (Isa 45:15), in the ground of the soul where God's ground and the soul's ground are one ground. The more we seek thee, the less we find thee. You must seek Him in such wise that you never find Him. If you do not seek Him, you will find Him.[47]

Such sentiments are at the furthest possible remove from pantheism. Rather, they point to the *coincidentia oppositorum*, the reconciliation of infinitely different realities. God pervades creation without essentially or existentially merging with it. Creatures for their part become transparent intermediaries between the divine and human. The preeminent point at which Creator and creatures meet, where the presence of God radiates through the transparency of creatures, is that spark within the human soul in which the ground of God and the ground of the soul are one ground – not confused, but united.

All of this could easily remain within the realm of abstract speculation. For Eckhart, however, as for the theologians of the Eastern Church still today, all theology is mystical theology.[48] Such ideas are only the theological expression of practical spirituality, principles to be concretised in action. Practical spirituality by the same token is the concrete historical expression of such principles.

In *life*, therefore, creatures are to be rendered transparent by the radical negation Eckhart constantly urged his hearers to practice and is so easy to misunderstand. Such a 'visual' transformation is, however, only seeing all things through the eyes of faith. Eckhart does not urge us to devalue creation, but to revalue it rightly, to 'let it be' what it truly is – nothing (which Eckhart calls *Gelassenheit or Gelâzenheit*). Nothing in itself or for itself, because it is what it is only because it manifests the creative mind of God. Nothing for us, because, as Angelus Silesius would write some centuries later:

> The rose is without why,
> it flowers because it flowers,
> it pays no heed to itself, asks not if it is seen.[49]

Here, except for the difference of theistic reference, Eckhart is truly close to the simple pointing of Zen Buddhism and even more truly echoes the Sermon on the Mount. I discover my freedom and the is-ness (*Isticheit*) of things when I refuse to subject them to my whims, desires or needs. They are not there for me. They are just there, what they are. When I 'behold' them, I recognise them as nothing for me and nothing in themselves. Then they can become transparent, revealing some facet of the infinite creativity which loans them their transient, mutable, fragile and beautiful being-there.

I, too, am such a creature. Like Catherine of Siena and the great Spanish mystics of Carmel two centuries later, Eckhart preached the nothingness of the self, but a special kind of nothingness. Nothingness in myself, for I do not give myself being, but only receive it. Like the lilies of the field, I come and go, transient, limited and fragile. It is not by denying but by accepting, even reveling in my nothingness that I extol the total being-there of God, who loans me existence. I am nothing for myself nor in truth for anyone else. No person is a thing.

When I recognise my essential no-thingness, when I escape the delusion of selfness, then I, too, can become transparent, clear, allowing the radiance of the divine splendor to shine within and through me. More than that, by becoming transparent, I rid myself of my self, that is, the veil of self-consciousness that so readily supervenes to spoil all my joys by reflexive self-preoccupation.[50]

Thus, Eckhart exhorts us to self-negation – not self-hatred or self-destruction or any of the pathological forms of spiritual masochism that counterfeit authentic mystical teaching. For the Meister, as we shall see, 'self-naughting' is not achieved by any ascetical exercises, penances, fasting and so forth. It is an achievement of intelligent insight and resolute will. It involves a wholly spiritual discipline, although manifest in the physical and mental dimensions of everyday life.

Converted into practical terms, but not 'practices', Eckhart's asceticism can be described as a progressive 'stripping' of the self – of the physical, mental and spiritual 'powers', that is, of knowledge and emotion, desire and imagination. Such radical detachment Eckhart names *Abgescheidenheit*.[51] Through it, God eventually comes to be born in us, but not until we have also become detached not only from everything that is not God, but from God as well. Eckhart thus bids us negate God as well as creatures and the self. More, he even prays that 'God will rid me of God'. As with his affirmative 'nihilism', Eckhart's 'atheism' must not be mistaken for the simple denial of God that constitutes the ultimate blindness in life. Again, Eckhart takes us to the opposite extreme from what to him would have seemed nonsense.

Sounding another favourite theme of the ancient theology, the Meister tells us that all our images of God are false because no image can truly represent God. No image, that is, except the human soul itself, which was itself made *to* the image and likeness of God. (For Eckhart, Christ alone was 'made' *in* the image and likeness of God, for the Word, the Eternal Son is the image and likeness of the Father. Our natural identity with the Son as human beings, and, much more, our spiritual (supernatural) identity with the Son as graced by adoption into Christ, conforms us *to* God with all the dynamism the word implies.)[52]

By stripping ourselves bare spiritually and psychologically in order to reveal the nothingness of our own inner transparency, we discover the abiding presence of God within us. It is thus that our radical no-thingness, the pure and receptive unself-consciousness of 'the mirror of the soul' is the truest and most creative image of God's nothingness. And that is why Eckhart tells us that when the powers of the soul have been stripped naked, when nothing can further prevent the shining-through of the eternal splendour, then God's presence can – even, he goes so far to say, *must* – be revealed in loving, conscious immediacy, for it is God's eternal will and nature to be so 'born' in the human heart. God's own fertile and dynamic nature eternally realises its creativity by this union in and with the human soul, that is, inwardly, in the now-pellucid depths of conscious being, making the virgin soul a wife and mother.

NOTES

1. Alain de Libera convincingly argues that the signal accomplishment of the Rhineland School of Dominican mystical theology was the reconciliation of these two major strands of Neoplatonic theology, op. cit., pp. 25–58, esp. pp. 43–9.

2. The Dominicans' primary innovation in this respect was the affirmation of the primarily intellectual character of mystical union with God (op. cit., p. 55), a position which intensified the debate between the 'traditionalist' Augustinian interpretation, largely Franciscan, of Bonaventure, Duns Scotus and Gonsalvo of Spain. The latter engaged Eckhart in debate at the University of Paris in 1302–1303. See Maurer, *Parisian Questions*, op. cit., and Émilie Zum Brunn et al., *Maître Eckhart a Paris: Une critique médiévale de l'ontothéologie*, Paris: Presses Universitaires de France, 1984.

3. See above, p. 51.

4. Cf. R. T. Wallis, *Neoplatonism*, London: Duckworth, 1972, pp. 61–6.

5. See Schürmann, op. cit., p. 120, esp. n. 140. Cf. Aquinas, *Summa Theologiae*, I, Q. 41, a. 5. See also Eckhart's *Commentary on the Gospel of John*, no. 43 (C-McG, p. 137) and no. 67 (ibid., p. 146) and, for commentary, ibid., p. 41.

6. Schürmann, op. cit. p. 119. For a comprehensive account of Eckhart's 'mystical vocabulary', especially see Frank Tobin, *Meister Eckhart: Thought and Language*, Philadelphia: University of Pennsylvania Press, 1986, pp. 147–83.

7. W 29, p. 221 (DW 38). Cf: W 81, p. 241 (DW 33): 'The work of grace is to make the soul quick and amenable to all divine works, for grace flows from the divine spring and is a likeness of God and tastes of God and makes the soul like God.' On 'springing up' and 'flowing out' cf. *Book of Divine Consolation*. C-McG, p. 227. For a discussion of the German meaning of these terms. see Schürmann, pp. 119–20, 247, nn. 138–40.

8. W 61, p. 108 (Pfeiffer 61, amended by Quint in 1932).

9. W 51, p. 53 (DW 15). For a fuller citation of this passage, see above, p. 89.

10. W 22, p. 177 (DW 53). For Eckhart's treatment of the Trinity, see sermons (Walshe nos.) 8, 27, 29, 33, 36, 40, 45, 50, 51, 56, 59, 60, 62, 64, 66, 76, 88, 93. Cf. also '*Deus pacis et dilectionis*', Sermon for Trinity Sunday, CL-SK, op. cit., pp. 188–91.

11. See above, pp. 43f.
12. See the *SummaTheologiae*, 1. Q. 27. a. 2; Q. 39. a. 5; Q. 41. aa. 2. 5; Q. 42. a. I. etc. For a detailed commentary and study, cf. Bernard Lonergan, SJ, *Verbum:Word and Idea in Aquinas*, University of Notre Dame Press, 1967.
13. On the intellectual generation of the Son as Word, see W 90, pp. 301–2 (Pfeiffer 103, as amended by Quint. As Walshe notes, this may be a sermon by one of Eckhart's students).
14. W 22, p. 179 (DW 53).
15. W 90, p. 301. See note 13 above. Walshe adds: 'Such a formulation is not expressly found anywhere else in Eckhart's certainly genuine works. The antithetical expression is in keeping with his style.' Note 4, p. 303.
16. W 79, p. 230 (DW 43). For other maternal imagery in Eckhart, see pp. 214, 226, 239.
17. W 2, p. 200 (DW 3).
18. W 53, p. 62 (DW 22). Cf. W 67, p. 151 (DW 9): 'In God the images of all things are alike. But they are images of unlike things.' On the doctrine of images, cf. also *The Book of Divine Consolation*, C-McG, p. 210.
19. W 49, p. 39 (DW 77). 'Unseparated' is rendered more accurately by McGinn as 'indistinct'.
20. W 65, p. 135 (DW 6). Condemned as Art. 22.
21. W 18, p. 147 (DW 30).
22. W 56, p. 81 (DP 26). Text slightly altered. See Caputo, art. cit., p. 211.
23. W 87, p. 271 (DW 52). See esp. note 7, pp. 276–7.
24. Ibid.
25. Ibid., p. 274, emphasis added.
26. Ibid., p. 275.
27. Ibid. To appreciate the full import and meaning of Eckhart's argument, this exciting sermon must be read in its entirety. Amazingly enough, it escaped citation by the inquisition.
28. Cf. Colledge, art. cit., p. 250, where he cites sermon 'Modicum et iam', W 42 (DW 69).
29. Cf. Benedict Ashley, OP, 'Three Strands in the Thought of Eckhart, the Scholastic Theologian', *TheThomist*, 42 (No. 2, April 1978), p. 236. These terms, favoured by Dietrich of Freiburg, do not differ in intention from *apex animae* or *ratio superior*. See above pp. 46, n. 28, 49–50.
30. On the disastrous changes in weather patterns at the beginning of the century, see Tuchman. op. cit., pp. 24f.
31. On light symbolism in Eckhart, cf. Koch, KS I, pp. 56–63.
32. W 9, pp. 82f (DW 86). The theme of divine darkness can be found in the following sermons (Walshe nos.): 1, 4, 51, 53, 73, 80, 83, 84 and 95.
33. On sin and evil, cf. for example W 77 (DW 63). See the discussion of Bernard McGinn in C-McG, op. cit., pp. 44f. with pertinent references.
34. Articles 4, 5, 6, 14, and 15 were condemned as heretical. McGinn judges Eckhart's defence on these points to have been weak.

35. *Commentary on the Book of Genesis*, No. 21, cited by McGinn, C-McG, p. 44. Cf. p. 90. For Thomas Aquinas' teaching, see *Summa Theologiae*, I, Q. 48, a. 2. Cf. also ibid., Q. 19, a. 9; Q. 48, aa. 1, 3-6; Q. 49, aa. 1-3; 1-11, Q. 79, a. 1, and *Summa contra Gentes*, III, 10.

36. 'Even our sins are necessary to the universal perfection which God has established.' St Augustine, *On Free Will*, 3.9. Cited by Colledge, C-McG, p. 346. n. 10. For Eckhart's teaching that sin itself and the inclination towards sin can be useful to salvation, see *The Talks of Instruction*, ibid., c. 11, p. 256 and c. 12, pp. 261–2. Cf. also McGinn's comments on p. 44.

37. W 89, p. 293 (DW 49).

38. Ibid. On evil and suffering, see 'Non simus concupiscentes malorum', sermon on the epistle for the Ninth Sunday after Trinity, CL-SK, op. cit., pp. 196–8. On suffering, see W 89, p. 293 (DW 49), *The Book of Divine Consolation*, C-McG, p. 210, and *On Detachment*, ibid., p. 294.

39. On the suffering of God, see *The Book of Divine Consolation*, ed. cit., pp. 233, 235; *The Talks of Instruction*, ed. cit., p. 260. For an insightful commentary, see Donald F. Duclow, '"My Suffering is God": Meister Eckhart's *Book of Divine Consolation*', *Theological Studies*, 44 (December, 1983), pp. 570–86.

40. *The Book of Divine Consolation*, ed. cit. p. 217.

41. Ibid., p. 219.

42. 'If I must die, / I will encounter darkness as a bride / And hug it in mine arms.' *Measure for Measure*, III, i, 82.

43. See below, pp. 107, 115–119.

44. *The Parables of Genesis*, No.165 (C-McG p. 55, No. 226: p. 121. = Sermon 15 (p. 192) = W 51.

45. Cf. John 1:5.

46. Exodus 3:14, a verse on which Eckhart expatiates in his Exodus commentary (LW II, 20-31 transl. CL-SK, pp. 225–30). Ed. note.

47. W 51, p. 53 (DW 15).

48. Cf. Vladimir Lossky, *The Mystical Theology of the Eastern Church*, Cambridge and London: James Clarke and Co., 1957, p. 7: 'the term "mystical theology" denotes no more than a spirituality which expresses a doctrinal attitude.'

49. *Die Ros' ist ohn' warum, sie blühet weil sie blühet, / Sie ach't nicht ihrer selbst, fragt nicht ob man sie siehet.* Schürmann's translation, op. cit., p. 245, n. 12. Frederick Franck renders the same lines in verse:

   She blooms because she blooms,

   the rose ...

   Does not ask why,

   nor does she preen herself

   to catch my eye.

   (*The Book of Angelus Silesius with Observations by the Ancient Zen Masters*, New York: Alfred A. Knopf, 1976, p. 66.) For Angelus Silesius as a disciple of Eckhart, see below, pp. 169–70.

50. One of the most trenchant expressions of this Eckhartian theme is found in chapter 44 of *The Cloud of Unknowing*, an anonymous English mystical work of the later fourteenth century which shows a pervasive influence of the Meister's spiritual doctrine.

51. See above, Chapter 3, p. 73, n. 27, and below, Chapter 5, pp. 99–101. For an etymological discussion of the meaning of the German term, cf. Schürmann, pp. 84–5 and Chapter 2, note 2 above.

52. On Eckhart's Christology, see Richard Woods, OP, '"I Am the Son of God": Eckhart and Aquinas on the Incarnation', *Eckhart Review*, 1 (June 1992), pp. 27–46.

THE BIRTH OF GOD
IN THE SOUL

Eckhart's teaching on the Birth of the Word of God in the soul, like that on the ebullience of God, has roots in the history of mystical theology extending back not only to the Alexandrian church and its catechetical school, but to the Hebrew and early Christian scriptures.[1] As might be expected, the relatively simple doctrine of the Psalms, Paul, John, Athanasius, Gregory of Nyssa and Ambrose, already refracted through the metaphysical yearnings of Eriugena and the spiritual concerns of the Beguines, was transformed in Eckhart's hands into a sublime and richly complex thematic.[2] The spiritual parallel of his theological doctrine of the intellectual generation of the Son, it unquestionably represents the heart of his teaching. The brilliance of the former doctrine is equalled by the poetic and even homely warmth of the latter, with its metaphors of marriage, conception and childbearing. Not surprisingly, some of his elaborations and implications brought him into open conflict with his critics in Cologne and Avignon.[3]

Preambles

As an integral element in the organic whole of the Meister's spirituality, his teaching on the birth of the Word follows on that of the divine ebullience and leads directly to his doctrine on the Return to the Source. It also presupposes certain cardinal elements of Eckhart's mystical psychology – in particular the priority of the intellect and the presence of God in the ground of the soul. For the birth of the Word of God in the heart of the just person is the sudden realisation or revelation of that presence in consciousness, that is at the apex of the mind, the spark of the soul.

Interiority of inwardness (*Innerkeit*) is, of course, the most fundamental presupposition of all spiritual growth for Eckhart: 'For whoever would enter God's ground, His inmost part, must first enter his own ground, his inmost part, for none can know God who does not first know himself. He must enter into his lowest and into God's inmost part, and must enter into his first and his highest, for there everything comes together that God can perform.'[4] McGinn comments: 'It is true that for Eckhart the internal attitude of the soul is so central that all external expressions begin to seem relatively indifferent and unimportant.'[5]

For Eckhart, the birth of God within us is first of all an 'acoustical' event, as it is in the Trinity.[6] Hearing and thus conceiving the Word in our souls precedes our untrammeled realisation of God's presence. But, Eckhart taught, our ability fully to attend to the Word within us is naturally inhibited and must be freed by the discipline of inner purification. The errant heart must become a virgin before it can be a wife and mother. 'There are three things that prevent us from hearing the eternal Word. The first is corporeality, the second is multiplicity, the third is temporality. If a man had transcended these three things, he would dwell in eternity, he would dwell in the spirit, he would dwell in unity and in the desert – and there he would hear the eternal Word.'[7]

Each of these obstacles requires remedy, and thus Eckhart identifies three qualities of spirit that must be attained in order to overcome the limitations imposed by what are, in fact, the physical coordinates of human existence separated from our Eternal Source. 'So too there are three things that favour the union of God with the soul. The first is that the soul should be simple and undivided: for if she is to be united with God, she must be simple as God is simple. Secondly, that she should dwell above herself and above all transient things and adhere to God. The third is that she should be detached from all material things and work according to her primal purity.'[8]

As a whole, Eckhart's 'ascetical' programme of simplifying consciousness, transcending the pull of the body and the demands of time, constitutes a radical *kenosis* or 'emptying' of the self so that the divine presence may rise from the depths of the soul and flood the 'God-shaped hole' within us. It begins as a negative approach, 'self-naughting' in the language of the Meister's English contemporaries. But with the 'negation of negation' entailed in achieving true freedom of heart, Eckhart's way acquires a progressively more positive character. From a human perspective, Eckhart's way is not a way *to* God, but a way *for* God, a way of self-transcendence and, as such, also the way of the cross.

The Ordinary Way

Eckhart evidently presumed that his hearers already observed the ordinary sacramental and devotional practices of medieval Christianity – he was no rebel. This is particularly clear from his *Talks of Instruction* – talks to young religious, members of his own order and beginners in the spiritual life, and also from incidental remarks in other treatises and sermons. Now Eckhart wants to lead his disciples further into the mystery of God's presence. He never proposes, however, the penances and extreme ascetical practices favoured by conventional wisdom scourgings, hair shirts, fasting, chains and the like that popular piety too easily associated with sanctity and which were so menacing to the developing spirituality of the young Henry Suso, St Elizabeth of Hungary, the Beguines and many of the Dominican nuns of the period.[9]

Rather, Eckhart deliberately leads us away from such mechanical methods of purification, showing a truer, quicker and safer route than any particular 'way': 'Indeed, if a man thinks he will get more of God by meditation, by devotion, by ecstasies or by special infusion of grace than by the fireside or in the stable – that is nothing but taking God, wrapping a cloak around His head and shoving Him under a bench. For whoever seeks God in a special way gets the way and misses God, who lies hidden in it. But whoever seeks God without any special way gets Him as He is in Himself, and that man lives with the Son, and he is life itself.'[10]

By contrast to all such spiritual 'technologies', the Meister's 'way' is simple and down-to-earth but by no means broad and easy: 'Christ fasted for forty days. Imitate him by considering what you are sure that you are most inclined and ready to do; apply yourself to this and observe yourself closely. It is often more profitable for you to refrain from these things than to go without any food. Similarly, it is sometimes harder for you to suppress one word than to keep completely silent. So it is harder at times for a man to endure one little word of contempt, which really is insignificant, when it would be easy for him to suffer a heavy blow to which he had steeled himself, and it is much harder for him to be alone in a crowd than in the desert, and it is often harder for him to abandon some little thing than a big one, harder for him to carry out a trifling enterprise than one that people would think much more important. Thus a man in his weakness can very well imitate our Lord, and he need never consider himself far off from him.'[11]

His reasoning is straightforward, blessed with the insights of Paul and Augustine, looking toward Tauler, Luther and the reformers.[12] It is not the method that works in us, but the intention. True penitence 'is a complete lifting up of the mind away from all things into God, and whatever the works may be in which you have found and still find that you can most perfectly achieve this, do them with no constraint; and if you are impeded in this by any exterior works, whether it be fasting, keeping vigil, reading or whatever else, give it up and do not be afraid that in this you may be foregoing any of your penitence, because God has no regard for what your works are, but for what your love and devotion and intention in the works are.'[13]

Eckhart's radically Christian approach recognises that true holiness is a quality of being, not doing, and that whatever good we achieve in action flows from that deeper source and not vice versa: 'People ought never to think too much about what they could do, but they ought to think about what they could be. If people and their way of life were only good, what they did might be a shining example. If you are just, then your works too are just. We ought not to think of building holiness upon action; we ought to build it upon a way of being, for it is not what we do that makes us holy, but we ought to make holy what we do. However holy the works may be, they do not, as works, make us at all holy; but, as we are holy and have being, to that extent we make all our works holy, be it eating, sleeping, keeping vigil or whatever it may be.'[14]

Radical Detachment: *Abgescheidenheit*

The initial, 'kenotic' character of Eckhart's spiritual discipline, with all its ancient Pauline roots,[15] is encompassed by the two arms of active detachment or dispossession (*Abgescheidenheit*) and its more passive complement, abandonment or 'letting go' (*Gelassenheit* or *Gelâzenheit*). Both aspects are indispensably connected and form the negative side of the Meister's 'way'. In the later spirituality of St John of the Cross, they might well be equivalent to the active and passive phases of the Dark Night of the Soul.[16]

While it would be wide of the mark to describe *Abgescheidenheit* as a method, radical detachment has a very specific meaning for Eckhart and involves every aspect of human experience: self, others, even God. Eckhart said, '… it is written: "They have become rich in all virtues." But this can never happen unless one first becomes poor in all things. This is a just bargain and an equitable exchange, as I once said long ago. Hence, as God wants to give himself and all things for our free possession, he will take away from us all property. Yes, truly, God wills on no account that we should have even as much of our own as a speck of dust in my eye. For all the gifts he has ever given us, whether gifts of grace or of nature, he never gave with another intention than that we should own nothing as our property; and in another way he has never given anything, neither to his mother nor to any man or other creature. And in order to teach us this and to keep us safe, he often takes away from us both bodily and spiritual possessions; for the honour should not belong to us but only to him. Why? Well, he himself alone wants to be altogether our own.'[17]

For Eckhart, we have become so full of ourselves, so replete with visions and desires of material gain, fame and power, that there is no room within us for the indwelling presence of God to come to birth, expand and ultimately transform us into the image of the Son. Closed off within, God calls to us from without. All creatures, the Meister insists, speak of God, urging us through their beauty, goodness, truth and integrity to empty ourselves of the images of self and things so that the Image of God, who is no-thing, may enliven our hearts and minds.

This, Eckhart preaches, is the word of disengagement or detachment in every dimension of our existence – bodily, mental, spiritual. Like all great masters and mistresses of the spiritual life, he begins with the body, urging us to dispossess ourselves of all things in order for our spirits to become free of the grasping claims of 'mineness' (*Eigenschaft*). But it is primarily in our interior stripping that spiritual freedom (no-thingness) is achieved, not so much by our own efforts, as in our abandonment of effort, our 'letting go'. God works the mystery in us when we cease not only our resistance but our struggle to cooperate, to 'help' God. And when at last the powers of the soul have been stripped, our very self must be reduced to pure emptiness. Without a trace of thingness or *Eigenschaft*, the Nothingness of God can, as it 'must', rush in to fill the vacuum. And thus the Word of God, the Unbegotten Son, is begotten and born within us.[18]

Eckhart likens the process of dispossession or spiritual impoverishment we must undergo if our souls are to become virginal to stripping or peeling off the outer (i.e. conceptual) layers of things – *all* things: the interior powers themselves, creatures, the self, even God. The interior, psychological stripping he mandates evokes echoes of both St John of the Cross and Zen Buddhism: '… if you would find this noble birth, you must leave the crowd and return to the source and ground whence you came. All the powers of the soul, and all their works – these are the crowd. Memory, understanding and will, they all diversify you, and therefore you must leave them all: sense perceptions, imagination, or whatever it may be that in which you find or seek to find yourself.'[19] Again, Eckhart said: 'Whatever belongs to the soul must be stripped away. The nobler the powers, the more they strip away. Some powers are so far above the body and so aloof that they peel off and strip off all together.'[20]

Creatures, too, must be stripped away to reveal the nothingness they are in themselves, so that they may transmit the pure image of God as we come to know them, that is, see them and deal with them in the freedom of God's true children. Thus the images of creatures in us, including our own image, must perish: 'if you want to have and to find complete joy and consolation in God, make sure you are naked of all created things, of all comfort from created things; for truly, so long as created things console you and can console you, never will you find true consolation. But when nothing but God can console you, then truly God does console you, and with him and in him everything that is joy consoles you.'[21]

Self-negation, the destruction of our own self-image, is an even more essential step toward the purity of heart necessary to conceive God's Word within: 'By putting off self we take in Christ, God, blessedness and holiness.'[22] Here, in terms as unyielding as those of the Buddha, to whose teachings his have been compared, Eckhart is in fact calling 'only' for the destruction of the self-conscious ego. Shizuteru Ueda comments, 'The "Birth of God in the soul", spoken of here in the language of the Christian doctrine of the Trinity, is the leap to realisation of his own authentic life that man experiences in "solitariness" with the surrender of the ego.'[23] By dis-covering our essential no-thingness, our radical, precarious dependence upon God, we empty ourselves of inordinate self-preoccupation, of everything in short that hinders the birth of God within.

Even our images of God must be stripped away, for all such images, in so far as they are *our* images, do not present God but only our concepts of God or those of the culture around us. Not only the unnameable One, but the Persons of the Trinity 'are strangers to goodness, truth and everything that tolerates any distinction, be it in thought or in a name, in a notion or just a shadow of a distinction.'[24]

No virtue or quality of soul is more necessary to rid the soul of dross than detachment; neither love, nor humility nor even mercy.[25] For without it, none can do their work. Its objective is the attainment of pure no-thingness – utter nakedness of spirit, total emptiness, absolute openness, the unfettered ability to conceive the Word of God.[26]

Gelassenheit: Letting Go of Everything

The voluntary self-renunciation and spiritual impoverishment of *Abgescheidenheit* are complemented for Eckhart by what he called *Gelassenheit* (or *Gelâzenheit*), 'letting go', abandonment, or in Schürmann's telling neologism, 'releasement'.[27] Such an attitude is itself an effect of radical detachment or, rather, its perfection. Here again, Eckhart does not have spiritual gymnastics in mind – no extraordinary self-inflicted sufferings, no stigmata, tears or satanic buffetings – the kind of ascetical theatrics that always attract a crowd and tend to inflate the ego. Eckhart counsels the opposite – receding entirely from the world's glance and becoming invisible, as it were, even to oneself.

As with *Abgescheidenheit*, the focus of abandonment is everything that can distract us from singlehearted receptivity to God. In more specific summary, Eckhart means:

> Letting go of things, the world, possessions: poverty
> Letting go of others: equanimity, chastity
> Letting go of self: humility, self-forgetfulness
> Letting go of emotion: 'Apatheia', self-mastery
> Letting go of willing: spiritual poverty, holy obedience
> Letting go of knowing: unknowing, meditation
> Letting go of God: Contemplation and social action.

Freeing God in Prayer

Having renounced concepts of God so that God, unmediated by any concept, can fill the empty and waiting soul with the Birth of the Word, it is also necessary to accept God's self-disappearance, God's *absence*. *Gelassenheit* means abandoning any hope of using God or acting through God for our own purposes: 'Remember, if you seek anything of your own, you will never find God, for you are not seeking God alone. You are looking for something *with* God, treating God like a candle with which to look for something; and when you have found what you were looking for, you throw the candle away. That is what you are doing: whatever you look for *with* God is nothing, whatever it might be …'[28]

Eckhart next applies *Gelassenheit* to the life of prayer, and obtains a vision of praying that set the teeth of his prosecutors on edge: 'A man should never pray for any transitory thing: but if he would pray for anything, he should pray for God's will alone and nothing else, and then he gets everything. If he prays for anything else, he will get nothing.'[29] Allied to Eckhart's injunction to live 'without why', that is, without calculating a reason for everything one does, praying for the Meister is communion with God, not (in its highest form) a wishing-well for obtaining favours: 'I never pray so well as when I pray for nothing and nobody, not for Heinrich or Konrad. Those who pray truly pray to God in truth and in spirit, that is to say, in the Holy Ghost.'[30]

The perfection of praying for Eckhart consists therefore in not-praying, that is, not in saying prayers, but simply in being open to the presence (or absence) of God. The liberated spirit at prayer knows nothing of knowing, wills nothing of loving, and from light becomes dark.[31] Eckhart is not here advocating either the abandonment of petition in prayer or of concern for others, as is evident from the rest of his teaching. He is, however, advocating the priority of pure, unselfconscious communion as the highest form of prayer, one in which the welfare of the entire world is not only included but advanced because of the universal solidarity of humankind in God through Christ.[32]

As a free 'work' of God's grace, there is nothing we can do to bring about the birth of the Word within save only ridding ourselves of obstacles that prevent it in so far as we are able and, ultimately, allowing God to remove those that inevitably lie beyond our abilities. Such self-abandonment, the abandonment of others and even of God as we have grown to 'understand' God, prepares the heart for birth by excavating the last vestiges of self-will and self-awareness. Ultimately, *Gelassenheit* marks the point at which the negative path becomes the positive path, that is, when the soul, having stripped itself of all its artificialities and particularly all self-regard, surrenders its own efforts at abandonment, leaving the final dispossession in the hands of God. For the perfection of renunciation is the renunciation of renunciation. What remains to us is attentive waiting on God: 'Just await this birth within you, and you shall experience all good and all comfort, all happiness, all being and all truth. If you miss it, you will miss all good and blessedness.'[33]

The Birth of the Word in the Soul

For Eckhart, as for the tradition he inherited, the birth of the Word of God has three moments – the eternal begetting and birth of the Word as Logos in the mind of the Father, the birth of Jesus in time, and the birth of the Word in the hearts of the just in time *and* eternity. Indeed, Eckhart refers to two births in this last regard – the birth of God's Word in the soul, and (as we shall consider in the next chapter) the birth of the soul back into God – the initial moment of return which culminates beyond death and time in the trackless desert of the Godhead: 'Why do we pray, why do we fast, why do we do all our works, why are we baptised, why (most important of all) did God become man? – I would answer, in order that God may be born in the soul and the soul be born in God. For that reason all the scriptures were written, for that reason God created the world and all angelic natures ...'[34]

Ultimately, all these births are one, like flashing facets of a single gem: '... this eternal birth occurs in the soul precisely as it does in eternity, no more and no less, for it is *one* birth, and this birth occurs in the essence and ground of the soul.'[35] In its way, the birth of the Word in the human soul is also an intellectual generation, not *by* but *in* the *abditum mentis*, just as the begetting of the Son was a radiation of God's mind. In some mysterious way, the two are one: 'As surely as the Father in his simple nature bears the Son naturally, just as surely He bears him in the inmost recesses of the spirit, and *this* is the inner world. Here God's ground is my ground and my ground is God's ground.'[36]

When, still and dark as the midnight desert, the heart has at last been prepared for the manifestation of God's Word, the Divine Presence does not leap down from heaven, but wells up from the fathomless abyss of the soul, the ground of being where God has always dwelled undetected and therefore unknown except by faith. The darkness of spiritual no-thingness is pierced by a burst of spiritual radiance, as the felt presence of God effuses the virgin soul. The Word is conceived. The Virgin has become the bride, wife and mother of God.[37] The hidden 'seed' of God has come to birth within the hearts of the just, bursting into efflorescence at the peak of the intellect, the 'spark', that uncreated power *in* (but not *of*) the soul that, at the highest point of the mind, links us beyond time, corporeality and space to our own divine origin in the eternally creative mind of God.

For Eckhart, then, we see again that ultimate beatitude does not consist in the perfection of knowledge or of love, but of co-presence in being, which grounds all the powers and acts of the soul: 'Some teachers hold that the spirit finds its beatitude in love. Some make him find it in beholding God. But I say he does not find it in love, or in *gnosis*, or in vision. But, it may be asked, has the spirit in eternal life no vision of God? Yes and no. Once born, he neither sees nor pays heed to God: but at the moment of birth, then he has a vision of God.[38] The spirit is in bliss then because it has been born, and not at being born, for *then* it lives as the Father lives, that is in the simple and naked essence.'[39]

By birth and vision, Eckhart is not referring to some esoteric mystical experience, but rather to revelation, to God's intimate self-bestowal: 'Whenever that man [who abides in God] lays bare and discloses the divine image which God has created in him by nature, then God's image in him stands revealed. Birth must here be understood in the sense of revelation of God, for when the Son is said to be born of the Father, that means that the Father paternally reveals to him His mysteries. Accordingly, the more, and the more clearly, God's image is revealed in a man, the more evidently God is born in him. Thus when it is said that God is all the time being born in him, it is to be understood that the Father lays bare the image and shines forth in him.'[40]

Thus, beyond the homely metaphors and parabolic devices, the birth of the Word in the human soul or heart has for Eckhart a truly mystical significance – the discovery of the intimate union with God in the depths and heights of human consciousness. It is, moreover, not an experience so much as it is a sudden and yet progressive realisation of presence, a union with God rooted in eternity, obscured by time, space and matter, but susceptible of being rendered conscious even in this life: '... God has ever been begetting His only-begotten Son and is giving birth to him now and eternally: and thus He lies in childbed like a woman who has given birth, in every good, outdrawn and indwelling soul. This birth is His understanding, eternally, welling forth from His paternal heart, in which lies all His joy.'[41]

Birth Effects

Clearly for Eckhart when God has been born in the soul, the effects are personally manifest. He describes them in language customarily used by mystics in their attempt to account for what has transpired in them – peace, joy, love, and perhaps most characteristically what the early mystical theologians of Alexandria called *apatheia* – not the suppression of feeling, but its transformation, equanimity: 'As long as we are not like God and are still undergoing the birth by which Christ is formed in us (Gal 4:19), like Martha (Lk 10:41) we are restless and troubled about many things. But when Christ, God's Son, has been formed in us so that "we are in his true Son" (1 Jn 5:20), and we are God's sons after every unlikeness has been cast off, "We shall be like him, for we shall see him just as he is, having been made one in him and through him" (1 Jn 3:2; Jn17:21). At that time we shall have full and perfect delight and we shall be at rest, as Augustine says …'[42]

The even-mindedness and tranquility Eckhart so often extols as the necessary quality of a healthy spirit is far from the quietism and indifference of the 'sick soul' that William James diagnoses in chapters V and VI of the *Varieties of Religious Experience*. Equanimity (which is a better way to translate *apatheia* than 'apathy', with its modern connotations of sluggish despair) does not consist in squelching emotion or suppressing passion and exuberance. Rather, it is the ability, as Kipling would someday write, to 'keep your head when all about you / Are losing theirs and blaming it on you …' ('If'.) It is the capacity to resist being overcome by emotion, dominated by passion or desire – whether fear, sorrow, rage or lust. It is the skill of remaining calm in a storm of experience, unmoved at the centre, the still point of the soul where God dwells in transparent simplicity. Such evenness does not mean impassiveness. On the contrary, it *requires* knowing feelings of joy and anger and the rest, but not being overwhelmed by that knowledge. Such *apatheia* is truly empathy – more compassion than passion, more involvement than aloofness, more divine than merely human.[43]

In a strikingly beautiful sermon, Eckhart summarises first negatively and then positively the effects of God's birth in the soul, especially the gift of equanimity: 'Do you want to know if your child is born and if he is naked – whether you have in fact become God's son? If you grieve in your heart for anything, even on account of sin, your child is not yet born. If your heart is sore you are not yet a mother – but you *are* in labour and your time is near. So do not despair if you grieve for yourself or your friend – though it is not yet born, it is near to birth. But the child is fully born when a man's heart grieves for nothing: *then* a man has the essence and the nature and the substance and the wisdom and the joy and all that God has. *Then* the very being of the son of God is ours and in us and we attain to the very essence of God.'[44] Therefore, he advises, 'cast out all grief so that perpetual joy reigns in your heart. *Thus* the child is born'.[45]

At times, Eckhart seems to be counselling a kind of Stoic reserve, a Spartan Christianity that glories in squelching sensibility to pain and pleasure: 'when you have reached the point where nothing is grievous or hard to you, and where pain is not pain to you, when everything is perfect joy to you, *then* your child has really been born.'[46] Close attention will show however, that this is in fact the opposite of his meaning, as he makes abundantly clear elsewhere: 'You may think that as long as words can move you to joy or sorrow you are imperfect. That is not so. Christ was not so … Therefore I declare that no saint ever lived or ever will attain to the state where pain cannot hurt him nor pleasure please.'[47]

Conclusion and Transition

Eckhart's way stands in sharp contrast but not opposition to that of much, perhaps most medieval spirituality, including that often associated with the Beguines. The stamp of originality is on his doctrine at every point, yet a profound awareness of ancient Christian teaching permeates it just as thoroughly. The 'ordinariness' of the Meister's spirituality may well be a manifestation of his deep roots in scripture, for at heart his doctrine is not only biblical in its force and simplicity, but also in its style and content. Moreover, that heart is Incarnational: the Birth of the Word of God in the souls of the just. This great Christological theme, with all its redolence of John and

Paul, Athanasius and Gregory of Nyssa, is indeed the centre point of his mystical theology. But as such it is neither the goal nor the final resolution. It is a prelude to a still more daring and transcendent aspect of the Meister's way – the birth of the soul into God through word and work and the completion of its journey into the mystery of the Godhead.

NOTES

1. The origin and development of this distinctive Eckhartian theme has been explored in Hugo Rahner's important article 'Die Gottesgeburt. Die Kirchenväter von der Geburt Christi im Herzen der Glaübigen', *Zeitschrift für Katholische Theologie*, 59 (1935), pp. 333–418, which was instrumental in establishing not only the consonance of Eckhart's teaching with Church doctrine, but also his rootedness in the mystical tradition of the earliest theologians of the East. Regrettably Rahner's essay has not been translated into English. Fr Karl G. Kertz, SJ, has also examined Eckhart's teaching on the Birth of the Word from a historical and theological perspective in 'Meister Eckhart's Teaching on the Birth of the Divine Word in the Soul', *Traditio*, 15 (1959), pp. 327–63. For a non-Christian viewpoint, cf. Shizuteru Ueda, *Die Gottesgeburt in der Seele und der Durchbruch zur Gottheit. Die mystische Anthropologic Meister Eckharts und ihre Konfrontation mit der Mystik des Zen-Buddhismus*, Gütersloh: Mohn, 1965, which also has not been translated into English. For more recent investigations, see the bibliography.

2. The birth of the Word in the soul appears in the following sermons, among others: (Walshe nos.) 1, 2, 3, 4, 7, 10, 12, 13b, 16, 17, 20, 24a, 29, 31, 35, 40, 43, 48, 50, 53, 59, 63, 65, 66, 68, 71, 79, 84, 88, 89, 90, and the extract from the *Commentary on the Book of Wisdom*, pp. 343–50. For scriptural sources of this theme, see Ps 44, Eph 3:17, Gal 2:20, Jn 14:23. Among the great Greek Fathers of the Church, the doctrine of the birth of the Word in the soul was most highly favoured by St Gregory of Nyssa, the first truly mystical theologian. For Gregory's teaching, cf. *From Glory to Glory: Texts from Gregory of Nyssa's Mystical Writings*, selected by Jean Daniélou, SJ, trans. and ed. by Herbert Musurillo, SJ, Crestwood, NY: St Vladimir's Seminary Press, 1979, pp. 167f. and passim.

3. The theme of the birth of the Word in the soul was the subject of condemnation in propositions 20, 21 and 22 of the papal bull *In agro Dominico*.

4. W 46, p. 21 (DW 54b). Cf. also *Talks of Instruction*, C-McG, pp. 253, 274. On inwardness vs. sensuality and the five senses, see *On Detachment*, ibid, p. 290.

5. Bernard McGinn, 'Meister Eckhart: An Introduction', art. cit., p. 249.

6. 'The Father's speaking is His giving birth, the Son's hearing is his being born.' W 12, p. 107 (DW 27). Schürmann's comment is apropos: 'It is not by chance that Meister Eckhart chose to preach. His word calls upon a hearer. The word of his judges hardened into "treatises."' Op. cit., p. 30. See also p. 31.

7. W 57, p. 83 (DW 12). The same list in reverse order appears in W 68, pp. 157ff. (DW 11), where Eckhart cites an unidentified 'writer', possibly Augustine (cf. *Confessions*, x, 41, 66). The same list appears in a different order in W 85, p. 264 (DW 85). For time, place and corporeality, cf. *On the Noble Man*, C-McG, p. 244.

8. W 85, p. 264 (DW 85). Cf. W 54, p. 72 (DW 23): 'Observe which are the three heavens. The first is detachment from all bodily things, the second is estrangement from all imagery, and the third is a bare understanding in God without intermediary.'

9. On penances and asceticism, see sermons (Walshe nos.) 4, 6, 13b, 37, 45, 52, 55, 70, 81 and 87.

10. W 13b, pp. 117–18 (DW 5b). On penitential practices and Eckhart's 'ordinary way', cf. *Talks of Instruction*, pp. 265–6.

11. *Talks of Instruction*, C-McG, c. 17, p. 268.

12. For a not entirely balanced comparison of Eckhart's mystical asceticism with Luther's attitude, cf. Steven Ozment, 'Eckhart and Luther: German Mysticism and Protestantism', *The Thomist*, vol. cit., pp. 263–5.

13. Ibid., c. 16, p. 265. In this matter, the advice of the author of *The Cloud of Unknowing* is virtually identical in two of his shorter works that show the influence of Eckhart's way: *The Epistle of Privy Counsel*, in *The Cloud of Unknowing and Other Treatises by an English Mystic of the Fourteenth Century*, ed. by Dom Justin McCann, OSB, Westminster, MD: The Newman Press, 1952, pp. 121–3, and *The Letter on Discretion in Stirrings of the Soul*, in *The Cell of Self Knowledge*, ed. by Martin Gardner, Baltimore, MD: Christian Classics, 1983. See also the translations in *The Pursuit of Wisdom and Other Works by the Author of the Cloud of Unknowing*, translated and annotated by James Walsh, SJ, New York: Paulist Press, 1988.

14. *Talks of Instruction*, C-McG, c.4, p. 250. On the difference between interior works and exterior works, cf. ibid., c. 23, p. 280.

15. Cf. Phil 2:7. The verb *kenóo* means 'to empty, destroy, or invalidate', and was used in a variety of contexts by St Paul, cf. Rom 4:14, 1 Cor 9:15, 2 Cor 9:3, etc. The adjective *kenós* connotes a specific rather than general absence of something that had been or ought to be present, cf. Lk 1:53, 20:10-11 and its parallel in Mark 12:3. On receptiveness and emptiness, see sermons (Walshe nos.) 4, 6, 34 and 37.

16. *Abgescheidenheit* figures in sermons (Walshe nos.) 1, 22, 51, 57, 63, 66, 72, 74, 88 and 96. Eckhart's doctrine of radical detachment was condemned in propositions 8 and 9 of the papal bull. For a discussion of the origin and the meaning of the German term *Abgescheidenheit*, see Reiner Schürmann, op. cit., pp. 84–5.

17. *Book of Divine Consolation*, Graef trans., Ancelet-Hustache, pp. 85–6.

18. On Eckhart's distinctive notion of 'God must', see Schürmann, p. 118.

19. W 4, p. 39 (DP 59). Cf. W 3, p. 25: 'A man cannot attain to this birth except by withdrawing his senses from all things. And that requires a mighty effort to drive back the powers of the soul and inhibit their functioning. This must be done with force, without force it cannot be done.' Quint doubts authenticity of this sermon, however: DP, p. 525. But see, as Walshe notes, the parallel Latin sermon in LW IV, p. 102.

20. W 72, p. 188 (DW 7).
21. *The Book of Divine Consolation*, C-McG, p. 220. Cf. also pp. 212, 222; *Talks of Instruction*, ibid., pp. 248–50, 253, 270; *On Detachment*, ibid., pp. 285, 291.
22. W 92, p. 311 (DW 24). On the loss of image of self, creatures cf. *The Book of Divine Consolation*, C-McG, p. 212. On the annihilation of self, cf. *Talks of Instruction*, C-McG, p. 280.
23. "*Nothingness*" in Meister Eckhart and Zen Buddhism', *The Buddha Eye: An Anthology of the Kyoto School*, ed. by Frederick Franck, trans. by James W. Heisig, New York: Crossroad, 1982 (repr. from *Tranzendenz und Immanenz: Philosophie und Theologie in der veränderten Welt*, ed. D. Papenfuss and J. Söring, Berlin: 1977), p. 157.
24. *The Book of Divine Consolation,* ibid., p. 227. On the 'stripping of God's "garments"', see sermons (Walshe nos.) 63, 67, 68 and 71.
25. Cf. *On Detachment*, ibid., pp. 285–8.
26. Cf. *On Detachment*, ibid., p. 291, *The Book of Divine Consolation*, ibid., pp. 220–2, and *The Talks of Instruction*, ibid, pp. 248–9, 270.
27. See especially pp. 16–17 in Schürmann, op. cit, for a discussion of this important German term, which was, among other things, taken by Martin Heidegger as the title of an important address. For references regarding Eckhart's influence on Heidegger, see p. 85, n. 3, 371. Clark translates *Gelassenheit* as '"resignation", or joyful endurance and patience in the face of adversity' (*Great German Mystics*, p. 59). McGinn notes that Eckhart rarely used the term himself, which becomes more common in subsequent generations. See *The Harvest of Mysticism*, op. cit., p. 166, n. 470.
28. W 40, p. 284 (DW 4).
29. W 55, p. 76 (DW 62).
30. W 70, p. 174 (DW 67). Cf. W 71, p. 179 (DW 59). Living 'without why' also appears in sermons (Walshe nos.) 6, 11, 12, 13b, 17, 43, 59, 63 and 65.
31. Cf. *On Detachment*, C-McG, p. 292. Eckhart's teaching on disinterested prayer occasioned the condemnation of proposition 7 in the papal bull. For a more contemporary description of praying evocative of Eckhart's teaching, see Rabbi Harold Kushner's now-classic work, *When Bad Things Happen to Good People*, New York: Avon Books, 1981, pp. 113–31.
32. On love for particular persons, see *The Book of Divine Consolation*, C-McG, p. 218.
33. W 2, p. 15 (DP 58).
34. W 29, p. 215 (DW 38). Cf. also W 48, pp. 33f. (DW 31): 'Such is the divine order, and where God finds the like of this order in the soul, there the Father gives birth to His Son. Then the soul must burst into light with all her power. Out of this power, out of this light springs the flame of love. Thus the soul must burst forth with all her power into the divine order.' Again, '... what would it profit me that our Father gives birth to His Son unless I bear him too? God begets His Son in a perfect soul and is brought to bed there so that she may bear Him forth again in all her works.' W 88, p. 282 (DW 75). Cf *The Book of Divine Consolation*, C-McG, p. 211.
35. W 2, p. 15 (DP 58). Cf. W 12, p. 107 (DW 27): 'Truly in that self-same birth in which the Father bears His only-begotten Son and gives him the root and all his

Godhead and all His bliss, holding nothing back, in that self-same birth He calls us His friends.' Human beings themselves, Eckhart reminds us, have a twofold birth: 'one *into* the world, and one *out of* the world, which is spiritual and into God.' W 7, p. 67 (DW 76).

36. W 13b, p. 117 (DW 76).
37. On the themes of the soul as virgin, wife and mother see sermons (Walshe nos.) 8, 24b and 90.
38. Following Quint, Walshe notes, II, p. 101: 'This is of course the mystical birth previously mentioned. When this has been achieved, God is no longer an object of contemplation.'
39. W 59, p. 100 (DW 39).
40. W 63, p. 118 (DW 40). This citation is taken from a much longer passage which should be read in its entirety to appreciate the lapidary fashion in which Eckhart develops his theme.
41. W 88, pp. 281–2 (DW 75).
42. *Commentary on the Gospel of John*, C-McG, p. 173. On 'apatheia', see sermons (Walshe nos.) 9, 45, 64, 69, 72 and 73.
43. On equanimity and equality, see sermons (Walshe nos.) 6, 12, 13b, 14b, 57, 65, 88 and 89.
44. W 7, p. 67 (DW 76).
45. Ibid. He continues in the same vein further on, '... if this child is born in you, then you have such great joy in every good deed that is done in this world that this joy becomes permanent and never changes. Therefore [Jesus] says, "None will deprive you of your joy" (Jn 16:22)'.
46. Ibid., p. 68.
47. W 9, p. 87 (DW 86).

THE RETURN TO GOD

Among philosophical systems, Neoplatonism has often been blamed for imposing a rigid, hierarchical framework on the natural and social worlds in order to understand and thereby control them. To a point, this is a valid criticism, especially of later Neoplatonism with its reliance on concepts of geometrical order and theurgical practices. But for Plotinus, the brilliant pagan mystic who represents the fountainhead of the 'new' Platonism, the dialectic of expansion and contraction best suited his temperamental and philosophical needs as a paradigm of universal process. For him, the cosmos beat like a great heart, ultimately the heart of God.

Eckhart, too, favoured the dynamic process of alternation as a model of creation, redemption and sanctification, one embracing a mystical theology both speculative and practical. For the Meister as for his brother and master, Thomas Aquinas, the origin and destiny of the universe was encompassed within a three-fold movement: first, a creative out-flow of divine energy and love, second, a mid-point or apogee at which divinity and materiality met and reversed the outward flux, initiating, third, the centripetal return of all things, united and hallowed in their Head, to their Eternal Source.

For Eckhart as for Paul, through Christ, indeed through the blood of his cross, all things were reconciled to and by God, things on earth and things in heaven (Col 1:20). The birth of the Word in the hearts of the just appropriates and ratifies that achievement for all time. It is the mid-point of cosmic history for each person and for all.

But this mystical birth, the disclosure of God's presence within the human spirit, has multiple dimensions. It effects and signifies the rectification of the soul because it is the result of grace and the indwelling Trinity. Justification does not happen all at once, however. The birth of the Word in the soul only inaugurates the return to God; continuation requires a second birth, a birth of Incarnate grace into all human works and the rectification of the world. Moreover, the soul must complete its itinerary of redemption by being borne back into God. Finally, therefore, the questing spirit breaks through into the hidden desert of the Godhead itself, where as in the beginning, it ever shall be one with its divine Source beyond all perceived distinction or difference. Eckhart described the return to God in several ways – union with God, identification with the Son, the reformation (or in-formation) of the Image of God, 'breaking through', and rebirth. Each expression conveys subtle nuances of meaning not found in the others, but all point to the same process. Several produced friction with Church authorities.[1]

The Soul's Quest for God

In an unusual passage, Eckhart identified four stages or 'steps' that the soul takes into God: 'The first is that fear, hope and desire grow in her. Again she steps on, and then fear and hope and desire are quite cut off. At the third stage she comes to a forgetfulness of all temporal things. At the fourth stage she enters into God where she will eternally dwell, reigning with God in eternity, and then she will never again think of temporal things or of herself, being fused with God and God with her. And what she then does, she does in God. May God help us to take these steps here and (thus) die, that we may rejoice with Him in eternity. Amen.'[2]

These steps, which Eckhart insists are realities of present life, represent the classical stages of spiritual progress: conversion or awakening; the purgative period of active detachment – *Abgescheidenheit*; the passive purification and illumination of the soul – *Gelassenheit*; and, finally, union with God.[3] 'Entering into God', the ultimate stage of the soul's return, itself includes three distinct but related aspects or moments for Eckhart: the birth of the Word in the soul, the mystical 'breakthrough' into God as Trinity, and the eschatological 'breakthrough' into the hidden Godhead.

Second Birth

It is abundantly evident that the Meister not only distinguished the birth of the Word in the soul from the birth of the soul into God but that he also recognised a difference between that rebirth and what he calls 'breaking through' (*durch brechen*) into God: '... the noble and humble man is not satisfied to be born as the only-begotten Son whom the Father has eternally borne, but he wants to be also the Father and to enter into the same equality of eternal paternity and to bear him, from whom I am eternally born.'[4]

Eckhart similarly alludes to the threefold character of return when he states that the human spirit 'must transcend number and break through multiplicity, and God will break through him: and just as He breaks through into me, so I break through in turn into Him. God leads this spirit into the desert and into the unity of Himself, where He is simply One and welling up in Himself. This spirit is in unity and freedom'.[5]

In rebirth, as in each moment of breaking through, God and the soul are progressively identified: 'How can a man be always being born in God? Take note: As this image is revealed in a man, so that man grows in likeness to God, for in that image the man is like the image of God as He is according to His naked essence. And the more a man lays himself bare, the more like he becomes to God, and the more like he becomes to God, the more he is made one with Him. Thus a man's being ever born in God is to be understood to mean that that man is refulgent with his image in God's image, which is God in his bare essence, with which that man is one.'[6]

Mystical union is thus a unified but not unitary event. Further, and of utmost importance for understanding the practical character of the Meister's spiritual teaching, mystical union is accomplished for Eckhart not in (or not only in) the still darkness of the great cathedrals and silent deserts of the contemplative cloister, but just as much in the marketplace and stable or the squalid hovels of the poor. Divine Justice acts wherever the unselfconscious actions of 'the Friends of God' work for earthly justice. For God is justice and the just person therefore manifests Justice. As Gerard Manley Hopkins wrote in 'As Kingfishers Catch Fire', 'The just man justices'. Similarly, divine Truth expresses itself in every human truth, divine Goodness in human goodnesses. Human justice, truth and goodness are not possessed, nor 'parts' of substantial Justice, Truth and Goodness to own as ours, but, like being itself, lent by God, borrowed and used. The less of 'me and mine' there is in such truth, justice and goodness, the more God's pure *Istikeit* shines through our works. Again, the more we become nothing in ourselves and for ourselves, the more we can let God's no-thingness transform the world into peace and perfect bliss. However, the experience of union with God is not one that leads to immobility and rest in this world, as we shall see.

Identity with God in Christ: The Transformation of Images

Eckhart's teaching on the nature of the soul's identity with God is complex and difficult to grasp, owing in some measure to the mobility of his viewpoint. Not surprisingly, some of his most serious problems with his inquisitors arose over this aspect of his theology.

It is clear, first, that Eckhart said and meant that the soul and God ultimately become one without differentiation or distinction: '... God and the soul are so entirely one that God cannot have a single distinctive feature separating Him from the soul and making Him different ...'[7] It is equally clear that he did *not* mean that the soul *became* God or that the essential and infinite distance between Creator and creature was abrogated by the infinite immediacy they shared: 'God is in the soul with His nature, with His being, and with his Godhead, and yet He is not the soul. The reflection of the soul in God is God, and yet she is what she is.'[8] Again, 'The soul, which has no nature in her ground, in that ground of love which is not yet called love – this soul must emerge from her nature, and then God lies in wait for her to lead her home into Himself. Whatever is borne into this essence comes almost to share that essence.'[9] Eckhart is not hedging with his 'almost'. He is preventing misunderstanding (for once at least) by clearly distinguishing his panentheism from what would otherwise amount to pantheism.[10] The same qualification was probably intended by Eckhart's use of the Latin neuter *unum* rather than the personal *unus* to describe the union of God and the human soul: 'The soul is one with God and not united.'[11]

In such passages Eckhart was evidently but often not too precisely attempting to describe the experience of mystical union rather than its metaphysical nature, an experience described, moreover, from God's point of view as well as that of the soul. He observes, for example, that in union with God 'Image and image are so fully one and joined, that no difference can be discerned'.[12] It is important to note his claim that the difference between divine and human images, that is the Son and the soul, cannot be *discerned*. He does not imply that there is absolutely no difference. Similarly, he states in the same place that with respect to knowledge, 'We can understand no difference between image and image. Further, [even] God in his omnipotence can understand no difference between them, for they are born together and die together'.[13]

Finally, in a passage surprisingly like a quotation from William Ernest Hocking or Martin Buber, Eckhart says, '*Ego*, the word "I", is proper to none but God in His oneness. *Vos*, this word means "you", that you are one in unity, so that *ego* and *vos*, I and you, stand for unity.'[14] One can only wonder what the Meister might have said had he the resources of language at hand that enabled Hocking to develop his final category of mystical awareness, 'consubjectivity', or 'we-consciousness'. The lack makes it even more clearly evident that for Eckhart, the 'I' and 'you' of mystical union remain metaphysically different if consciously indistinguishable *within the experience*.[15]

Without Mean or Mode

Eckhart sought to express the ineffable intimacy between the soul and God in a variety of ways, each pointing in some manner to the *immediacy* of mystical experience. Here his thought becomes almost tortuously complex as it returns upon itself with respect to the doctrine of images: 'God works without means and without images, and the freer you are from images, the more receptive you are for His inward working, and the more introverted and self-forgetful, the nearer you are to this.'[16]

One practical consequence of the requirements of divine immediacy is that images of both self and other creatures must be abandoned prior to mystical union: 'If we are to know God it must be without means, and then nothing alien can enter in. If we do see God in this light, it must be quite private and indrawn, without the intrusion of anything created. *Then* we have an immediate knowledge of eternal life.'[17]

In more direct and homely language, Eckhart explains that such relative denials safeguard not only God's transcendence, but protect us from making foolish claims about our knowledge of God and, which is worse, attempting to use God to obtain our own petty ends: 'some people want to see God with their own eyes as they see a cow, and they want to love God as they love a cow. You love a cow for her milk and her cheese and your own profit. That is what all those men do who love God for outward wealth or inward consolation and they do not truly love God, they love their own profit.'[18] It is therefore necessary to let go of all material and spiritual avarice, to become pure in heart through *Abgescheidenheit* and *Gelassenheit* in order to 'see' God: '... the natural mind can never be so noble as to be able to touch or seize God without means, unless the soul has these six things of which I have spoken: – First, to be dead to all that is unlike; second, to be well purified in light and in grace; third, to be without means; fourth, to be obedient to God's word in the inmost part; fifth, to be subject to the divine light; the sixth is what a pagan master says: blessedness is when one lives according to the highest power of the soul, which should always be striving upwards and receiving her blessedness from God. Where the Son himself receives it in the primal source, there too we should receive it from God's highest part, and so we too must keep our highest part erect towards this.'[19]

Spiritually, to be without means is to be poor, naked, stripped of all things material and mental, and thus able to be joined with God in God's own simple nakedness.[20] And, as nothing can adequately mediate God, reciprocally, God cannot become fully manifest through any mode or determination of being: 'We must take God as mode without mode, and essence without essence, for He has no modes.'[21] Eckhart is not arguing here for immediate experience as such; for him all experience is in fact mediated. All creatures are capable to some extent of being intermediaries of God: 'Once this birth has really occurred, no creatures can hinder you; instead, they will all direct you to God and this birth.'[22] Elsewhere, however, Eckhart clearly if hyperbolically denies creatures any ability to reveal God: 'All creatures are too base to be able to reveal God, they are all nothing compared to God. Therefore no creature can utter a word about God in his works.'[23] This is not a contradiction if we bear in mind that although God is present to and in all creatures, who can thus indicate something of God, no creature can *adequately* manifest God without thereby becoming God. Creatures can therefore only inadequately reveal God and can never mediate God's presence in mystical union.

There is one exception to this stricture – the true Image of God, the Son and Mediator. In fact, only identity with the Son makes union possible in Eckhart's eyes: 'In truth, to know the Father we must be the Son.'[24] Again, '... if you would know God, you must not merely be *like* the Son, you must be the Son yourself.'[25]

As the Image and Likeness of God, the Word alone adequately expresses and, in time, manifests the nature of God as Son. Elsewhere, Eckhart said that only Christ was made *in* the image and likeness of God; other human persons are made *to* the image and likeness of God.[26] The reformation of our image, distorted by forgetfulness of our ground in God and also by the fallen condition of humankind, requires by this logic a complete renovation. Our self-image must be reduced to no-thingness so that when it is devoid of all content, God's Son, *the* Image and Likeness of God, can be born within the virginal emptiness, reforming and conforming human nature to Christ's image: 'Since it is God's nature not to be *like* anyone, we have to come to the state of being *nothing* in order to enter into the same nature that He is. So, when I am able to establish myself in nothing and Nothing in myself, uprooting and casting out what is in me, *then* I can pass into the naked being of God, which is the naked being of the Spirit. All that smacks of *likeness* must be ousted that I may be transplanted into God and become one with Him: one substance, one being, one nature and the Son of God.'[27]

Being one with Christ, we can thus become one with God: 'The soul must be transfigured and impressed and moulded again in that image which is God's Son. The soul is created in God's image, but the masters say that the Son is God's image, and the Soul is created after the image of the image. But I say further: the Son is an image of God above all images, he is an image of His concealed Godhead. And from there, where the Son is an image of God, from the imprint of the Son's image, the soul receives her image.'[28]

With this all-important qualification, Eckhart seems to be arguing that a mere human creature could not be joined with God in modeless, immediate unity without effecting a hypostatic union or, quite simply, being annihilated. Both alternatives are impossible, since to annihilate any creature would contradict God's creative intent and because God is already hypostatically united to human nature in Jesus Christ. The only remaining alternative is that which Eckhart espouses: immediate union with God is possible to the soul only by virtue of identification with Christ as the Incarnate Word. Christ is neither medium nor mode, but substantially both divine and human and therefore a mediator between God and humankind. Eckhart's mystical spirituality is in essence a theology of the mystical body of Christ.

Becoming the Son of God

The transformation of the soul into God by conformity to the image of Christ is, consistently for Eckhart, a transformation of consciousness, that is, in the Meister's vocabulary, of knowing. Commenting on 1 John 3:1, Eckhart said: 'God makes us knowing Him, and His being is His knowing, and His making me know is the same as my knowing; so His knowing is mine just as in the master, what he teaches is one and the same as, in the pupil, what he is taught. And since His knowing is mine, and since His substance is His knowing and His nature and His essence, it follows that His essence and His substance and His nature are mine. And if His substance, His being and His nature are mine, then I am the Son of God.'[29]

Eckhart's radical avowal of identity with the Son of God was consonant with Christian tradition, being based on the assumption of universal human nature by the Word of God, not the particular characteristics of this or that person. In context it was certainly not pantheistic. Nevertheless, it was condemned as article 22 in the papal bull, not as heretical, but as rash and evil-sounding. It is admittedly daring: 'The Father begets His Son unceasingly, and furthermore, I say, He begets me as His Son and the same Son. I say even more: not only does He beget me as His Son, but He begets me as Himself and Himself as me, and me as His being and His nature. In the inmost spring, I well up in the Holy Ghost, where there is one life, one being and one work. All that God works is one: therefore he begets me as His Son without any difference.'[30]

Eckhart's true teaching, however, like his teaching on our unity with God, preserves the distinction between the soul and Christ considered not from *within the experience*, but as it were from a detached perspective, objectively, as can be readily grasped in the parallel passages: '... we are transformed in the Son, and so far the Son is born in us and we are born in the Son and become the one Son. Our Lord Jesus Christ is the only Son of the Father, and he alone is man and God. But there is only one Son in one essence, and that is the divine essence. Thus we are one in him, *when we have no thought but of him*.'[31]

Transformation into God

For Eckhart the entire mystery of Christ's life, death and resurrection is contained seedlike, as for Paul, in the Incarnation. The rest follows not as commentary, but as consequence. In order to express his insight into the process by which we are transformed into God through conformity to Christ's image, he is forced to invent new language: '... the eternal Word took on human nature imagelessly, therefore the Father's image, which is the eternal Son, became the image of human nature. So it is just as true to say that man became God as that God became man. Thus human nature was transformed [or 'transfigured', or 'trans-imaged' (*überbildet*)] by becoming the divine image, which is the image of the Father.'[32]

If such transformation (or transimagination) flows from or is equal to the birth of the Word in the soul, the process of return is not yet complete. Incarnation must give rise to Incorporation: '... if I have wisdom, I am not wisdom myself. I can gain wisdom, and I can also lose it. [But] Whatever is in God, is God: it cannot drop away from Him. It is implanted in the divine nature, for the divine nature is so powerful that whatever is proffered to it is either firmly implanted in it, or else it remains wholly outside. Now observe a wondrous thing! Seeing that God transforms such base things into Himself, what do you think He does with the soul, which he has dignified with His own image?'[33]

Eckhart's language grows more and more rhapsodic as he describes the higher levels of the ascent into God. As if answering his own question, the Meister develops the figure of 'the tree of the Godhead', one of the most beautiful images in all spiritual literature, commenting on Isa 11:1-2: 'There shall come forth a shoot from the stump of Jesse, and a branch shall grow out of his roots.' Eckhart said: 'The soul, which has no nature in her ground, in that ground of love which is not yet called love, – this soul must emerge from her nature, and then God lies in wait for her to lead her home into Himself. Whatever is borne into this essence comes almost to share that essence. When the bride has come home, God takes her and works with all the power He has in His ground, in the ground of the soul, in that inmost part where nothing is that does not work all together. The tree of the Godhead blossoms in this ground, and the Holy Ghost sprouts from its root. The flower that blossoms, delight, is the Holy Ghost. The soul, too, blossoms forth out of the Holy Ghost, who is the flower of the soul. And on that flower shall repose the spirit of the Lord. The Father and the Son rest on the Spirit, and the Spirit reposes on them as on its cause.'[34]

In one of his most provocative sermons, the Meister points to the biblical basis of his teaching on Incorporation into God, but chooses, as he did in his Defense, an analogy as sublime in its implications as it proved disastrous in its consequences: 'We are wholly transformed into God and changed' (2 Cor 3:18).[35] Here is an illustration. It is just the same as when in the sacrament bread is changed into Our Lord's body ... I am converted into Him in such a way that He makes me *one* with His being, not *similar*. By the living God it is true that there is no distinction.'[36]

The analogy of transubstantiation perhaps inevitably came to Eckhart's mind. We can sympathise with the intention if not the sagacity of his choice of illustrations. The point he was driving at is that the soul and God are united immediately and, *from within the experience*, substantially, without *awareness* of difference or distinction, *just as* the bread becomes Christ's body wholly and completely while retaining not only the appearance but all the physical properties of bread, including spatial-temporal multiplicity, gravity, density, etc. The bread therefore both is (really) and is not (apparently) Christ's body. Eckhart should have inverted the analogy, for, as we have seen, he elsewhere insists that the soul in union with God both is (apparently) and is not (really) substantially united to God. Unfortunately, mystical language, especially when of an ecstatic nature but also in its cooler forms, too easily conveys the impression of pantheism. It is, as Eckhart said, emphatic or (in Schürmann's insightful phrase) 'imperative', rather than indicative.

Grace

The progressive transformation of the soul into God, like the progressive incandescence of a comet as it approaches the sun, is achieved for Eckhart by the grace of God – not so much as 'work', for neither God nor grace 'work', but by *attraction*, the irresistible gravity of divine love: 'This comes from God's grace which raises the soul up to God and unites her with Him and makes her God-conformed.'[37]

Like the electromagnetic fields that pervade the universe, grace floods the soul with divine life, transforming and drawing it ever nearer: '... the grace which the Holy Ghost brings to the soul is received without distinction, provided the soul is collected into the single power that knows God. This grace springs up in the heart of the Father and flows into the Son, and in the union of both it flows out of the wisdom of the Son and pours into the goodness of the Holy Ghost, and is sent with the Holy Ghost into the soul. And this grace is a face of God and is impressed without co-operation in the soul with the Holy Ghost, and forms the soul like God. *This* work God performs alone, without co-operation.'[38]

It is grace that gives us confidence in achieving union with God, realising (as we must) that human power alone is insufficient even to acquire the detachment necessary for God to come to birth, much less to rise by its own effort to the face of Godhead: 'Often I feel afraid, when I come to speak of God, at how utterly detached the soul must be to attain to union with Him. But no one should think this impossible: nothing is impossible for the soul that possesses God's grace. Nothing was ever easier for a man than it is for the soul that has God's grace to leave all things: no creature can harm her.'[39]

Ultimately, however, not even grace can satisfy the longing of the soul. In another dangerous simile, the consequences of which Eckhart escaped by being more careful than his wont, the Meister said, 'because even grace is a creature: she [the soul] must come to a place where God works in His own nature, where the work is as noble as the craftsman, and He who is poured out and that which receives the outflowing are all one.'[40] He continued, speaking from a viewpoint *within the experience*, not 'objectively', 'Thus the soul is united and enclosed in God, and there grace slips from her: she works no longer by grace, but divinely in God. Then the soul becomes wondrously enchanted and loses herself, just as if you were to pour a drop of water into a butt of wine, so that she does not know herself and imagines she is God.'[41]

Return to the World

In Eckhart's language, when God is born in the human soul, that soul is likewise born into God, bearing the only-begotten Son back into the bosom of the Father. In another of the Meister's figures of speech, Christ, the true image of the Father, is reflected from the transparent mirror of the soul back to the Father. And, as the Holy Spirit is the love that radiates from the Son to the Father and from the Father to the Son, so, too, the Holy Spirit shines within the souls of those who bear the Eternal Word. Their loving is the Spirit's loving, their acts the Spirit's acts. And because the Spirit of God is the Spirit of Christ, it is true to say – although what Eckhart said was nevertheless condemned – that the acts of the just person, the noble person, the good person, the wifely person who has thus born the Son of God are the acts of that Son. The body of Christ is one.

Further, no self-conscious distinction now intrudes. 'God bears the Word in the soul, and the soul conceives it and passes it on to her powers in varied guise: now as desires, now as good intent, now as charity, now as gratitude, or however it may affect you. It is all His, and not yours at all. What God thus does, you must accept all that as His and not as your own, just as it is written: "The Holy Ghost makes intercession with countless mighty sighs" (Rom 8:26). He prays within us, not we ourselves.'[42]

And thus, finally, for Eckhart, when God has become united with us in us, Father, Son and Spirit with the human spirit, all our words and works are God's. 'If I am to know God without "means" and without image or likeness, then God must become practically "I", and I practically God, so wholly one that when I work with Him it is not that I work and He incites me, but that I work wholly with what is mine. I work as truly with Him as my soul works with my body.'[43] Every truly human situation thus becomes an avenue for the realisation of the Kingdom of God, for that Kingdom truly is the very self of God.

Eckhart knew, as every spiritual master or mistress does, whether from personal experience or borrowed wisdom, that contemplation is brought to perfection through loving activity in the world, in the marketplace of ordinary and sometimes extraordinary human concerns. 'As I have often said, even if a man were in a rapture like St Paul, and knew a sick man who needed some soup from him, I should think it far better you left the rapture for love and would serve the needy man in greater love.'[44] The necessary turn to action is recognised both in eastern and western forms of mysticism, as William Johnston has shown especially with regard to Zen Buddhism, a fact that supports the perceived similarity between Eckhart's doctrine and Eastern spirituality.[45]

The work of the mystic in the world is not often dramatic. It may be quite commonplace. But it is enduring and indeed recreates the world itself in the primordial image it had in God's mind: 'When the man of the soul is in true possession of his eternal bliss, when the powers [of the soul] are cut off, then that man meets with no opposition from anything. But note, you must pay heed, for such people are very hard to recognise. When others fast, they eat, when others watch, they sleep, when others pray, they are silent – in short, all their words and acts are unknown to other people; because whatever good people practise while on their way to eternal bliss, all that is quite foreign to such perfected ones. They need absolutely nothing, for they are in possession of the city of their true birthright.'[46]

The life of the transformed soul is infused with a compassion that is authentically divine – equanimous and constant, just and merciful: 'just as in human nature nothing is strange and nothing is further or nearer, so it is necessary that you should make no distinction in the family of men, not being closer to yourself than to another. You must love all men equally, and whatever happens to another, whether good or bad, must be the same as if it happened to you.'[47]

The just soul, for such would be the fitting term in Eckhart's vocabulary, has no 'why', – she acts for no ulterior motive.[48] She seeks only God and gives only love, establishes only justice. She finds God's face in all things. But even so, her spiritual itinerary is not yet finished.

Into the Desert of the Godhead

Following Gregory of Nyssa and the Alexandrian tradition of mystical exegesis, Eckhart knew that final transformation lay beyond death. He held it true that we can see the face of God in this life, but only through a glass, darkly, partially, temporarily. But *then* we shall know as we are known and the eye by which we see God will indeed be the eye by which God sees us – the reciprocal, mutual vision of Eternal Joy.

The passage through death is a transfiguration through the mystery of Christ, culminating in final union beyond the Threeness, in the Oneness of the dark and endless desert of the Godhead, 'the silent desert into which no distinction ever peeped, of Father, Son and Holy Ghost'.[49] For Eckhart, 'God leads His bride right out of all the virtues and nobility of creaturehood into a desert place in Himself, and speaks Himself in her heart, that is, He makes Her like Himself in grace.'[50]

Eckhart's bleak imagery should not deceive us. The Wasteland which beckons is only wilderness to an unreformed mind, the darkness only our ignorance of what lies beyond. Our final breakthrough into God is an entrance into our true homeland, the Eternal Source from which we took our leave into time, multiplicity and corporeality – into separate existence: 'When I return to God, if I do not remain there, my breakthrough will be far nobler than my outflowing. I alone bring all creatures out of their reason into my reason, so that they are one with me. When I enter the ground, the bottom, the river and font of the Godhead, none will ask me whence I came or where I have been. No one missed me, for there God *unbecomes* (*entwirt*).'[51]

Here Eckhart reverses the startling imagery of ebullience. God *became* 'when all creatures said "God"'.[52] Only a creature conscious of its separateness can say 'God'. When separateness no longer exists, when the soul is conscious only of the 'We' beyond 'you' and 'I', 'God' no longer exists. Only love exists; in eternal peace and perfect bliss. And then 'we' shall truly be at rest.

NOTES

1. Transformation into God was condemned in article 10; Identification with the Son in articles 11, 12, 20 and 21; Identification (Union) with God in articles 13 and 14. Sermons in which these themes are prominent include: Redditus – Return to God (Walshe nos.) 4, 6, 9, 44, 45, 51, 56, 85, 88; Reformation into God 22, 43, 47, 95; Identity with the Son 7, 11, 14b, 43, 46, 47, 53, 57, 66, 71, 89, 92; Becoming the Son 11, 43, 95; Breakthrough into God 11, 16, 48.

2. W 84, pp. 259–60 (DW 84). See also W 74, p. 202 (DW 74): 'This virtue [detachment, spiritual poverty] has four degrees. The first breaks through and makes a way for a man from all transient things. The second takes them away from a man altogether. The third not only takes them away, but causes them to be altogether forgotten as if they had never been – and this is part of the process. The fourth degree is right in God and is God Himself.'

3. Eckhart's indebtedness to another strand of ancient Christian teaching is revealed in a similar passage with its echoes of St Gregory the Great, Hugh and Richard of St Victor: 'Whoever would achieve perfection in this triple love [of Father, Son and Holy Spirit] must needs have four things. The first is true detachment from all creatures. The second, the true life of Leah, that is to say the active life which is set in motion in the ground of the soul by the touch of the Holy Ghost. The third is the true life of Rachel, the contemplative life. The fourth is an aspiring spirit.' (W 88, pp. 282–3 [DW 75].) This division of the spiritual life, which finds expression in almost all medieval writers, can also be traced back to the Alexandrian school and in particular to Evagrius of Pontus.

4. W 50, p. 46 (DW 14). Walshe comments, p. 48, n. 18, 'This seems to be the source of article 22 of the bull of 1329.' But cf. W 53, p. 64 (DW 22): God 'begets His

only begotten Son in the highest part of the soul. In the same moment that He bears His only-begotten Son into me, I bear him back into the Father.'

5. W 16, p. 136 (DW 29). For Eckhart as for Plotinus, the *exitus* or outflowing movement of the soul from its source in God is a passage from unity to multiplicity and dispersion. The reciprocal *redditus* moves from multiplicity to unity. For Eckhart at least, this is not a movement backwards, but a return *forwards*, so to speak, a true dialectical advance. For the union experienced within the Source differs from that at the Origin by a qualitative shift in consciousness. Far from a regression, it is a new realisation of integrity, cosmic in its implications.

6. W 63, p. 119 (DW 40).

7. W 49, p. 38 (DW 77).

8. W 56, p. 81 (DP 26). In his recent commentary, *The Mystical Thought of Meister Eckhart*, Bernard McGinn employs the term 'fused identity' to convey Eckhart's intention. Although I find the term problematic on philosophical grounds ('fusion' and 'confusion' are too close for comfort), it more accurately represents what the Meister had in mind than most accounts.

9. W 61, p. 108 (Pfeiffer 61, amended by Quint in 1932).

10. The term *panentheism* was coined in 1828 by K.F.C. Krause (1781–1832). It was similarly used by Friedrich von Hügel in contradistinction to pantheism to signify the presence of God in all things as opposed to the identity of God with all things. Von Hügel first mentions it, as far as I can tell, in his article 'Experience and Transcendence', *The Dublin Review*, April 1906, pp. 374–5. Cf. also *The Mystical Element of Religion*, Vol. II, London: J.M. Dent, 1961 ed., pp. 336–7. For discussion, see Joseph P. Whelen, SJ, *The Spirituality of Friedrich von Hügel*, London: Collins, 1971, pp. 112, 150–1, 174. Following Denifle's interpretation, von Hügel regrettably failed to perceive the strong panentheistic element in Eckhart's writings, however, which greatly mars his brief treatment of the Meister in *The Mystical Element of Religion*, vol. cit., pp. 317–25.

11. W 78, p. 225 (DW 64). Here Eckhart uses the simile of the containment and interpenetration of a tub of water and a stick of wood floating in it. The point is obvious that while co-present, all three remain distinct. Cf. also his remark '… for where God is, there the soul is and where the soul is, there God is.' Ibid.

12. W 42, p. 298 (DW 69).

13. Ibid. One logical consequence of such immediacy is at first glance startling, because impossible: 'if the image should perish that is formed after God, then God's image would also disappear.'

14. W 17, p. 145 (DW 28).

15. Eckhart's logic here is consistent. Following Thomas Aquinas here (*Summa Theologiae*, Ia, Q.14, a. 5), he often stated as a maxim in one form or another 'What is in God, is God'. See W 88 (DW 75). In so far as the soul has 'broken through' into God, she is as much God as she was when an idea in the mind of God before the creation of the world. Since in God, the soul 'is' God, participating unselfconsciously in God's actual being through which her actual existence derives. But the soul is neither a part of God, nor in any substantial

sense co-extensive with God. It is nevertheless true to say, as Eckhart does, that in such unity with God, where God is, the soul is. See above, n. 11. From the purely hypothetical viewpoint of some impossibly external observer, however, God remains God and the soul remains the soul, different, distinct and individual. See above, pp. 121–2.

16. W l, p. 8 (DP 57).
17. W 19, pp. 158f. (DW 71). Cf. also *The Book of Divine Consolation*, C-McG, p. 212.
18. W 14b, p. 127 (DW 16b).
19. W 30, p. 226 (DW 45).
20. For examples of *Brautmystik*, Eckhart's occasional use of erotic and bridal metaphors of union with God, see W 60, p. 61 (DW 48) and W 61, p. 112.
21. W 19, p. 160 (DW 71). Cf. W 58, p. 95 (DW 26): 'The joy of the Lord is the Lord Himself and no other, and the Lord is living, essential, actual intellect which understands itself and is living itself in itself and is *the same*. [In saying this] I have attributed no mode to Him: I have taken from Him all mode, for He is Himself modeless mode, living and rejoicing in that which he is.' In medieval philosophy and theology, 'mode' (Latin: *modus*, 'measure' or 'manner') generally referred to the proportion or measure determining the relationship of the constitutive principles of some compound thing. Since God is not composed of principles of whatever kind, God can have no mode. Cf. Thomas Aquinas, *Summa Theologiae*, 1, Q. 5, a. 5.
22. W 4, p. 45 (DP 59). The example he seizes on here is lightning.
23. W 32b, p. 243 (DW 20b).
24. W 11, p. 100 (DW 26).
25. W 14b, p. 127 (DW 16b).
26. See above, p. 57, n. 42 and p. 91, n. 52.
27. W 7, p. 66 (DW 76).
28. W 95, p. 326 (DW 72). On becoming the Son of God, see *On the Noble Man*, C-McG, p. 243. On the human soul as the image of God in its higher powers, see *The Book of Divine Consolation*, C-McG, p. 211.
29. W 7, pp. 65–6 (DW 76). Cf. also W 17, p. 145 (DW 28): '... we are that very Son, and His birth is His indwelling and His indwelling is His birth. It remains ever the One, that continually wells up in itself.' See Woods, '"I am the Son of God": Eckhart and Aquinas on the Incarnation', art. cit.
30. W 65, p. 135 (DW 6).
31. W 43, p. 5 (DW 41). Italics added. Cf. also W 53, p. 63 (DW 22); '... if you ask me, since I am an only son whom the heavenly Father has eternally begotten, whether I have eternally been that son in God, my answer is Yes and No. Yes, a son in that the Father has eternally begotten me, not a son by way of being unborn.'
32. W 47, pp. 27–8 (DW 46). Walshe's note. McGinn observes in this respect, 'If "God became man so that man might become God", the ancient Christian adage at the centre of Eckhart's view of redemption, then his teaching on the *grunt* must be seen as Christological at its core.' *The Mystical Thought of Meister Eckhart*, op. cit., p. 51.
33. W 25, p. 200 (DW 3).

34. W 61, p. W8 (Pfeiffer 61, amended by Quint in 1932).

35. The *Revised Standard Version* reads, 'And we all, with unveiled faces, beholding the glory of the Lord, are being changed into His likeness from one degree of glory into another; for this comes from the Lord who is the Spirit.'

36. W 65, pp. 135–6 (DW 6). Condemned as article 12 in the bull of John XXII.

37. W 62, p. 114 (DW 82). The term Eckhart uses is *Gotvar*, 'God-coloured'. Walshe, p. 116, n. 10. Eckhart's teaching on works, seemingly ambiguous, is in fact characteristically two-dimensional. For him God and grace both work and do not work. 'God works, the Godhead does no work: there is nothing for it to do, there is no activity in it. It never peeped at any work. God and Godhead are distinguished by working and not-working.' (W 56, pp. 81–2.) Thus God works by mercy and love: 'God works mercy in the highest and purest acts that God is capable of.' (W 72, p. 189. Cf. also W 92, p. 312 and W 61, p. 108.) Regarding 'work' as agency, Eckhart had said, 'Grace performs no works, it is too delicate for this, work is as far from grace as heaven is from earth. An indwelling, an attachment and a union with God, – *that* is grace, and God is "with" that, for there immediately follows: "God be with you" – and there the birth occurs. Let no one think this is beyond him. What matters the hardship to me, if He does the work?' (W 29, p. 221.) Similarly, 'Grace never did any virtuous work: it has never done any work at all, though it flows forth in the doing of good works. Grace does not unify by works. Grace is the indwelling and cohabiting of the soul in God.' (W 79, p. 232. Cf. also W 68 for same doctrine.) The reversal of the conventional definition of indwelling or sanctifying grace is notable. Eckhart was not unaware that grace had real effects, however, and in that sense 'worked': 'The work of grace is to make the soul quick and amenable to all divine works, for grace flows from the divine spring and is a likeness of God and tastes of God and makes the soul like God.' (W 81, p. 241.)

38. W 64, p. 125 (DW 81). See also previous note.

39. W 73, p. 196 (DW 73).

40. W 62, p. 114 (D W 82).

41. Ibid., pp. 114–15.

42. W 3, p. 33. (Although Quint doubted the authenticity of this sermon, its parallel exists in LW IV, 102. Walshe, I, p. 36, n. 1.) Cf. below. For Eckhart's teaching on the transformation of the powers of the soul into the image of God, see *The Book of Divine Consolation*, C-McG, p. 211.

43. W 41, p. 289 (DW 70).

44. *Talks of Instruction*, trans. Hilda Graef, Ancelet-Hustache, p. 79. This fact of religious history is the major thesis of William Ernest Hocking's philosophical study of mysticism, *The Meaning of God in Human Experience*, New Haven: Yale University Press, 1963 ed.

45. Cf. William Johnston, SJ, *Silent Music*, New York: Harper and Row, 1974, pp. 82–91. Cf. Also Shizuteru Ueda, 'Nothingness', art. cit., p. 159, William Johnston, SJ, *The Still Point*, New York: Fordham University Press, 1970, Claude Geffré and Gustavo Gutierrez, eds, *The Mystical and Political Dimensions of the Christian Faith*, New York: Herder and Herder, 1974 (Concilium, vol. 96).

46. W 37, pp. 270–1 (not included in Quint). The 'man of the soul' here means the spiritually perfected person. In this sermon and elsewhere, the 'man *in* the soul' means the intellect. It should be noted that in this passage Eckhart, far from advocating some form of Quietism, says that the good works of those well-advanced in spiritual perfection appear so ordinary as to pass unnoticed. They have, moreover, no further use for the 'practices' of devotion that characterise the way of beginners. Their contemplation of God is habitual and overflows in works of love. Cf. Mt 6:1-6.

47. W 13a, p. 110 (DW 5a). Surely there is echoed here Terence's great dictum, *Homo sum, humani nil a me alienum puto.* (*Heauton Timoroumenos*, 1. 77.) Cf. also W 44, p. 282 (DW 58) on works of justice and love, and *The Book of Divine Consolation,* C-McG, p. 218 on the love of particular persons.

48. On the theme 'Without Why', see above, p. 103, and W 11, p. 98 (DW 26).

49. W 60, p. 105 (DW 48).

50. W 64, p. 126 (DW 81).

51. W 56, p. 82 (DP 26).

52. See above, pp. 83–4.

PART THREE
JUDGEMENT

❋

UNWILLING HERETIC

Eckhart's testimony at the inquisitions in Cologne and Avignon and, according to the bull of condemnation, his dying words themselves forever repudiate any effort to cast him in the role of a religious rebel. His loyalty to the Church was final. Nevertheless, Eckhart was no less clearly perceived by his persecutors as rebellious, even heretical, a dangerous man who led simple people along paths of destruction.

Why was this faithful teacher and preacher so feared and hated? Was it only because, as the legend has it of John Scottus Eriugena, that 'he made us think'? Or were there other, more insidious reasons for his condemnation? Was Eckhart a scapegoat, as has been alleged, or the victim of the jealousy, envy and spite of lesser men? Or did his efforts to explore the nether limits of the human experience of God unintentionally go beyond the pale of orthodoxy?

Such questions are difficult, perhaps impossible to answer, especially with limited access to all the pertinent records and the inexact or incomplete character of many of Eckhart's works. By examining those that have survived, however, particularly those documents that have come to light in only relatively recent times, it is possible to attempt at least a provisional evaluation of the last, difficult years of the Meister's life.

The involvement of at least two Friars Minor in the attack on Eckhart has not unreasonably prompted many historians to suggest that enmity between the orders, which had reached a crisis point at this time, lay behind the whole affair. This thesis was strongly advanced in the last century by Wilhelm Preger. Otto Karrer similarly argued that Scotist Franciscans engineered the condemnation of Eckhart as 'expiation' for the canonisation of Thomas Aquinas in 1323.[1] William of Ockham's invidious complaints about Eckhart's theological misprisions and his comparatively favourable treatment at Avignon seem to support such a contention, as does the complaint against Eckhart and Nicholas of Strassburg in the *Great Appeal* of the Franciscan Minister General, Michael of Cesena, dated 18 September 1328.[2]

Eckhart himself, however, made no such charges against the Friars Minor either individually or as a whole. Although scorning the intellectual pretensions of the commissioners in Cologne, he also referred to the archbishop in terms of deference and respect. His statement that fame and the envy of false brethren had brought him before the commission most probably refers to the machinations of William of Nidecken and Hermann de Summo, two Dominicans who had come against Eckhart as witnesses and who seem to have drawn up lists of suspect statements.[3]

In recent times, an increasing number of Eckhart scholars have concluded that there is no real evidence of prejudice in the proceedings against Eckhart.[4] However, the relentless antagonism of Henry of Virneburg toward Eckhart cannot be simply explained away as an instance of misplaced episcopal zeal. Unless Eckhart's teachings were in fact heretical, which modern scholarship has also seriously questioned, reasons for his trial and condemnation must be sought elsewhere. Moreover, the fact that fifty years of growing tension between the Franciscan and Dominican orders reached a crisis state just as accusations were brought against Eckhart cannot be considered a negligible factor. While these bitter disputes may not have provided the immediate occasion for the process against him, they undoubtedly contributed to the ambience of distrust and hostility that impelled not only Eckhart, but William of Ockham, Michael of Cesena, Marsiglio of Padua, John of Jandun and others to their various unhappy fates.

The Mendicants: Fraternal Rivalry in the Fourteenth Century

The two great mendicant orders of the Middle Ages were virtual twins, born in the early decades of the thirteenth century in response to declining spiritual and institutional vitality in the Church. This was particularly the case with regard to the emerging demands of urban expansion with its new democratic sentiment, the proliferation of radical and mystical sects outside the organisational structure of the Church, and the corrupting influence of a rapidly developing money economy.[5] Despite fundamental similarities, especially the emphasis on personal and corporate poverty in the orders, from the beginning the Friars Minor and Friars Preachers were distinguished by their attitudes toward the place of academic study, the clerical character of their orders, and principles of organisation and government.

Intellectually, Franciscans such as Bonaventure, Roger Bacon and Duns Scotus, while not entirely closed to the new Aristotelian outlook introduced by contact with Islamic culture, remained stubbornly and conservatively Augustinian. The Dominicans, although indebted to the Augustinian tradition according to their rule and temperament, more wholeheartedly embraced the new 'pagan' doctrines, especially under the commanding influence of Albert the Great and Thomas Aquinas.[6] Soon, the two orders were pitted against each other in a philosophical and spiritual conflict that would last for over a century: whether the spiritual faculty of intellect and its proper act of understanding were superior to those of will and love. Many (but not all) influential Dominicans, including Eckhart, championed the new Aristotelian, intellectualist position, while the Franciscans, adhering to the more Platonic Augustinian tradition, defended the voluntarist position. Positions on the nature and degree of apostolic poverty also divided them sharply.

Jeanne Ancelet-Hustache refers to a 'new offensive' of Franciscans and other conservative Augustinians that sought to reaffirm the older tradition towards the end of the thirteenth century. This effort probably began with the appointment of the secular priest Henry of Ghent to a chair of theology at Paris which he occupied from 1276–1292. Eckhart's public debates there in 1302–1303 with Gonsalvo of Spain clearly centred on the priority of intellect vs. will. At Oxford the situation was even more reactionary. There Roger Bacon, although the author of extensive Aristotelian commentaries when a student at Paris, now railed against Albert and Thomas Aquinas. There Dominicans, too, actively resisted the innovations of 'Averroists' such as Thomas Aquinas. Robert Kilwardby, the Dominican Archbishop of Canterbury, himself expressly condemned the 'Averroist' teachings of Thomas Aquinas at Oxford in 1277, only eleven days after the Paris condemnation. And from Oxford in 1305 the great Franciscan John Duns Scotus was sent to Paris where he lectured until 1307. Eckhart himself may well have been returned to Paris by his superiors in 1311 as part of a Dominican 'counter-offensive' against the Franciscan intellectual attack. (Duns Scotus had already been sent on to Cologne in 1307, however, where he died the following year.)

Dominican Reaction and Counter-reaction

Sentiment within the Dominican order against the intellectualist position of Albert and Thomas was not limited to Oxford. After a number of propositions from the teachings of Thomas and Siger of Brabant were condemned at Paris in 1277 for their 'Averroism', some members of the Order openly rejected major aspects of Thomas' doctrine, notably James of Metz and Durandus of Saint-Pourçain, a celebrated professor who developed a form of early nominalism.[7]

Such deviations so antagonised the major party in the Order that at chapters in 1278 and 1279 and again in 1309 and 1313, at least passive adoption of Thomas' teaching was enjoined upon every Dominican. That is, while it was forbidden to deny Thomas' positions on critical issues, freedom was provided for different interpretations and limited internal disagreement. As we have seen, Eckhart himself freely departed from Thomas' teaching on a number of important points. Durandus, known later as 'Doctor Modernus', rejected Thomism far more radically and was ultimately investigated by both Dominican and papal commissions. Having become a bishop in 1317, he only narrowly escaped censure by virtue of episcopal immunity. Ultimately, he was cleared of all charges under one of his former investigators, Jacques Fournier, by then Pope Benedict XII. (Fournier was also one of the theological experts consulted in the process against Eckhart.)

Franciscan conservatives, buoyed up by the condemnations at Paris and Oxford, soon offered corrections of 'Brother Thomas' at Oxford and elsewhere. In at least one case, that of Richard Knapwell, charges of false doctrine were pressed against a Thomistic Dominican.[8] In the meantime, radicals such as William of Ockham so elevated the will, particularly the Divine will, that to Thomists such as Eckhart the necessary relationship between faith and reason must have seemed fundamentally abrogated. The vital link between the human mind and God's mind through the intelligibility of universal species was, in effect, denied. Reciprocally, in so far as Eckhart's intellectualist mysticism emphatically reinstated the connection between human and divine intelligence through the world of ideas, his teaching would understandably have earned the antagonism of Ockham and other early nominalists such as Durandus of Saint-Pourçain.[9]

The Problem of Poverty

Differences regarding more practical matters widened the rift between the great mendicant orders. While they had originally shared a common vision of the necessity of radical poverty, it was over this issue that the most bitter disputes would be fought, including those that raged just prior to and following the condemnation of Meister Eckhart. A closely related area, one of extreme tension between Dominicans and Franciscans, involved the violent power struggle between the papacy and the Holy Roman Empire. Antagonism toward the papacy for the suppression of the Spirituals had fostered a political alliance between the radical Franciscans, including their General, Michael of Cesena, and the chief opponent of papal policies, Ludwig of Bavaria, the Holy Roman Emperor. The Dominicans, on the other hand, consistently sided with the popes.[10] The situation reached desperate proportions in 1327, the year of Eckhart's trial, when Ludwig invaded Rome and in 1328 installed a Spiritual Franciscan, Pietro Rainalducci, as anti-pope under the name Nicholas V. (Rainalducci eventually submitted to John XXII, was absolved and imprisoned at Avignon for the remainder of his life, which ended in 1333.)

Dissension had appeared very early in Franciscan history over whether radical poverty was an absolute or modifiable character of the order and, indeed, of the Church.[11] The Spirituals, sometimes known as Zealots and, after 1317, *Fraticelli*, took the name in order to distinguish themselves from 'Conventual' Franciscans, the followers of Elias of Cortona, St Francis' successor, who attempted to mitigate the primitive rule and remodel the order. Internal arguments grew more violent under the more extreme apocalyptic influence of the Calabrian abbot Joachim of Fiore (d. 1202), whose *Eternal Gospel* was published and interpreted in 1254 by a young Franciscan, Gerard of Borgo San Donnino.

Within a few years, some of the Spirituals led by Angelo of Clareno in the March of Ancona, Ubertino of Casale in Avignon, and Peter John Olivi (Pierre Olieu) in Provence began seizing Conventual houses and possessions by force. The new pope, John XXII, replied with vigour, issuing bulls of condemnation in 1317 and 1318. Also in the latter year, 'Twenty-seven members of a particularly stubborn group of Spiritual Franciscans of Provence were tried by the Inquisition and four of them burned at the stake at Marseilles in 1318.'[12]

In 1321 the debate over apostolic poverty flared anew, threatening schism in the order and even in the Church, especially with the active involvement of the emperor and his academic allies, William of Ockham and Marsiglio of Padua. Particularly heated discussions with Dominicans ensued, continuing through the trial and condemnation of Meister Eckhart.

It would be a mistake, however, to assume that relations between the two mendicant orders had the character of unremitting antagonism during the late thirteenth and early fourteenth centuries. Like real siblings, their deeper bond survived the years of surface conflict between ideas and attitudes. Friars met together in moments of rare affection just as they became formidable allies when opposed by a common enemy such as the secular masters at Paris and Oxford who attempted repeatedly to strip the mendicant students and professors of their academic rights and exemptions. Even despite the conflict over philosophical and theological champions, one of the most touching events in mendicant relations involved the Friars Minor who attended the death of Thomas Aquinas and his eventual canonisation.[13] It would not be until the darkening years of the late fourteenth century, however, that the major tensions between Dominican and Franciscans would begin to be resolved and, given the bitter disputes over Eckhart's teaching in earlier decades, in a most surprising way.

Crises of Spirituality and Politics

Franciscan complaints that Beghards and Beguines were advocating the heresy of the Free Spirit had instigated Henry of Virneburg's first inquisition in 1307. (Another, more bloody purge had been carried out as recently as 1322.)[14] Nothing suggests, however, that the Friars Minor played such a role in Eckhart's case. The fact that two of his inquisitors were Franciscans indicates only that members of their order had been entrusted with the duty of assuring doctrinal orthodoxy in the archdiocese. Nor, despite Eckhart's scathing remarks about the incompetence of his prosecutors, should we dismiss their abilities too lightly. Further, while Eckhart more or less successfully defended himself from the charges brought against his doctrine at Cologne, many of the suspect propositions were later condemned by the papal commission in Avignon.

Earthquake: The Trial in Cologne

The actual accusation of promoting heresy came as a shock not only to Eckhart, but to the Dominicans and Cologne itself. He was, after all, a trusted and justly famous Church figure – a Master of Sacred Theology, twice occupant of the prestigious chair for externs at the University of Paris, several times prior, provincial and vicar, and the most noted preacher of his day.

There had been distant rumblings before the earthquake struck. Disturbed by their involvement in the dispute between the emperor and the pope, in 1325 the Dominican General Chapter of Venice warned the friars of the province of Teutonia to avoid political feuds in their preaching. The prior of Ratisbon (Regensburg) was removed from office. And on 1 August of that year, Pope John XXII named Friars Nicholas of Strassburg and Benedict of Asinago-in-Como, both Masters of Theology, as papal visitators to admonish the erring and to restore good order.[15] Benedict either did not fulfil his part of the mission or concluded his duties quickly. In any event, Nicholas arrived alone in Cologne as the ground began to shift beneath his former master's feet.

Nicholas had served as lector under Eckhart some years before but in the intervening years had distinguished himself by the strength of his commitment to the teachings of Thomas Aquinas, who had been canonised barely three years earlier. Nicholas' presence in Cologne during the next two turbulent years would provide Eckhart with important reserves of moral and legal strength. His major task seems to have involved disciplining the two troublesome Dominicans, William of Nidecken and especially Hermann of Summo, who had evidently distributed some slanderous pamphlets and was gravely suspect on both moral and doctrinal grounds. Both later came forth as witnesses against Eckhart.

Alerted by rumours that the episcopal investigation was under way, in late 1325 or early 1326 Nicholas subjected Eckhart's writings and teachings to a preemptive review and declared them free of false doctrine. Eckhart, moreover, was clearly innocent of any political partisanship. Nevertheless, sometime that summer the commissioners delivered their first list of suspect articles, summoning Eckhart to appear before the archbishop's tribunal.

Henry of Virneburg had appointed two theologians to the task of examining the teaching of Cologne's most illustrious professor – Master Reiner Friso, a canon of the cathedral, and Peter of Estate, a former head of the Franciscan custody in Cologne, who was later replaced by another Franciscan, the lector Albert of Milan. The archbishop's investigators had been thorough, not only assembling Eckhart's Latin works and the German treatises, but collecting copies of the vernacular sermons as well. Their initial *rotulus* or list of articles included forty-nine propositions taken from Eckhart's written works, both Latin and German: *The Book of Divine Consolation*, the commentaries on Genesis and Exodus and a number of vernacular sermons.[16] No doubt some copies of the latter had been circulated from convent to convent, but it may well have been necessary to obtain others from as far away as Switzerland. That the process seemed to drag on interminably, as Eckhart finally complained, may indicate a fairly massive search, especially after the first *rotulus* was submitted and received Eckhart's response.[17]

Eckhart delivered his thunderous formal reply on 26 September, observing that 'if I were less famous among the people and less zealous for justice, I am certain that such attempts would not be made against me by the envious', a possible reference to William of Nidecken and Hermann de Summo.[18] He protested at once that the proceedings against him were illicit because of his order's exemption from episcopal jurisdiction. He had, in addition, already been found innocent by the inquiry of Nicholas of Strassburg, the papal visitor. These facts would become the basis, later, of his and Nicholas' appeals to the Pope.

The most difficult limitation under which Eckhart laboured, both at Cologne and Avignon, especially given his propensity for colourful and daring expression, was having to defend propositions taken *prout sonant*, that is, out of context. Nevertheless, despite Koch's disparaging remarks about Eckhart's presentation of his case, the ageing Meister seems to have successfully refuted many of the charges against him, arguing point by point, sometimes acknowledging apparent error, at others insisting on the truth of the statement under question as it stood.[19] The commissioners responded with new *rotulus* containing fifty-nine articles taken wholly from Eckhart's vernacular sermons. Once again, the Meister prepared a detailed reply, taking occasion to remark on the 'certain malice or crass ignorance' of his interrogators, their 'imbecilic ... coarse and truncated intelligence'.[20]

The situation exploded in early January 1327, when Nicholas of Strassburg was cited by the commission for obstruction with regard to the two troublesome Dominicans, William and Hermann, who were attempting to come forward under episcopal protection to testify against Eckhart. Nicholas rejoined with three strong protests, the first on 14 January, and two the following day, appealing for letters of dismissal in order to take the case to the papal court at Avignon. On 24 January, Eckhart made the same appeal. On 13 February, Eckhart mounted the pulpit in the Dominican church. He preached. Then in a lengthy Latin statement read by his secretary, Conrad of Halberstadt, which he translated into German himself, sentence by sentence, Eckhart argued his innocence before the people of Cologne.[21]

On 22 February, the appeals to the pope were denied as frivolous. This, however, was a formality; once the appeals had been lodged, referral was automatic. Thus in late spring, accompanied by his provincial, Henry of Cigno, and three lectors, Eckhart left for Avignon. Nicholas of Strassburg may have walked with them. In early summer, surely no later than July, the party arrived in Avignon.

At the Court of the Pope

The Dominicans apparently expected the Meister to be vindicated. 'Indeed the chief motive of his famous teaching assistant, Nicholas of Strassburg, ... in intervening was to ensure that the renegade Dominican Hermann de Summo, who seems to have acted throughout as Eckhart's enemy, was suitably punished.'[22] Apparently, Nicholas, acting in his capacity as papal visitator, had imprisoned Hermann for a time in Cologne. The archbishop retaliated by sending the culprit to Avignon as his emissary. There, however, the Dominicans at least succeeded in preventing both Hermann and William of Nidecken from testifying against Eckhart.

The reigning pontiff to whom Eckhart and Nicholas appealed, John XXII (Jacques Duèse), was a well-informed, energetic and able administrator and jurist, now in his seventy-eighth year.[23] During the first eleven years of his pontificate, he had enlarged and restored the papal curia, established church finances on a sound footing by imposing a new system of taxes, and strengthened the hierarchical institution by establishing new dioceses and redefining the boundaries of older ones.

At his election in 1316, Jacques Duèse had been the candidate of Robert of Anjou and as pope quickly fell under the sway of Philip IV and his successors. This earned him the lasting suspicion and ill-will of the German monarchs as well as the resentment of the Italians. In 1314 Germanic distrust was ignited into active conflict upon the double election of Ludwig of Bavaria and Frederick of Hapsburg in which Henry of Virneburg had played so conspicuous a role. In such cases, it fell to the pope to decide the issue. Jeanne Ancelet-Hustache relates: 'John XXII therefore asked Louis of Bavaria to present himself before him and lay down his crown. Louis replied by convoking a General Council. Thereupon the Pope excommunicated him (1324). Louis in his turn accused the Pope of heresy and demanded his deposition. The rumour spread that John intended to elevate the King of France, Charles IV, to the imperial dignity. Louis now approached his old enemy, Frederick of Austria, went to Italy where he had himself crowned Emperor in the name of the people by Scierra Colonna and confronted John with his anti-pope (18 April 1328).'[24]

Within two years, however, the anti-pope had submitted to John and Ludwig himself was forced to seek reconciliation. But the truce was only temporary. Papal power would soon be curtailed again by popular as well as various royal encroachments. However, radical imperial attempts to limit papal power had also begun to lose their driving force. Nevertheless, the opposition between the pope and the emperor and its repercussions in the activities of the two great mendicant orders would by then already have come to a tragic conclusion in the trials of Eckhart and the leading Spiritual Franciscans.

Although reputedly the composer of the prayer *Anima Christi* later used and popularised by St Ignatius of Loyola, the pope's theological skills unfortunately lagged rather significantly behind his administrative abilities. His most famous opinion (c. 1333) occasioned charges of heresy from Ockham, Michael of Cesena and others, not least of them being the King of France, Philip VI, to whom the matter was of particularly pressing concern.[25] The Spiritual Franciscans' motives were surely political, but not wholly so; they had already fled to Ludwig of Bavaria for protection against their hated adversary, who had attempted to dissolve them utterly in 1317 and again in 1323. There was also the matter of the execution of the four Spirituals in 1318 and in 1326 the pope's posthumous condemnation of the teachings of Peter John Olivi, one of the Spirituals' foremost theologians.

The papal opinion now at issue concerned the seemingly obscure question of whether the souls of the just enjoyed the beatific vision immediately upon death (presuming no faults remained to be expiated) or, as John preferred, only after the final judgement. Here, the pope's views, which he conceded he was willing to retract if proved erroneous, clearly conflicted with the majority theological opinion and, indeed, the Church's traditional teaching. Sage advice fortunately prevented the pope from imposing his view in an apostolic constitution. After his death, his unorthodox views were diplomatically laid to rest by his theologically more astute successor, Benedict XII, who as Cardinal Fournier, had functioned with misgivings as theological expert during the investigations of the writings of Olivi, Durandus of Saint-Pourçain, Ockham, and most significantly for our concern, Eckhart.

The Inquisitor of Montaillou

In Eckhart's case, two commissions were set up to examine his teachings, one of theologians, the other of cardinals. Among the latter, Jacques Fournier was a Cistercian abbot and bishop whom John had created cardinal only in 1327. Much younger than Eckhart, Fournier was born some time after 1280 at Saverdun in the northern part of the Comté de Foix, a region now part of Ariège.[26]

In 1317 he was created Bishop of Pamiers. A shrewd financial administrator, he soon increased agricultural tithes, a move which caused considerable local dissension. He also distinguished himself 'by his inquisitorial pursuit of heretics and other deviants in the region around Montaillou'[27] and thus quickly attracted the attention of Pope John XXII.

Fournier's Inquisition lasted from 1318 until 1325. True to his own meticulous character, and to the enormous benefit of later historians, he caused the depositions made to the courts to be recorded in detail.[28] Significantly in view of his later reputation, Fournier was considered by the accused as 'a very devil of an Inquisitor ...'[29]

In 1326, Fournier was promoted to the diocese of Mirepoix, having made himself unpopular in Pamiers, according to Ladurie, by his 'obsessional, fanatical and competent pursuit of all kinds of suspects'.[30] On 18 December 1327, he was made cardinal and was called to Avignon to serve as theological advisor to Pope John XXII.[31] In that capacity, the most important cases concerning which he was called on for advice were the four posthumous questions against Peter John Olivi in 1326,[32] the proceedings against Michael of Cesena and William of Ockham; and those against two Dominicans – the anti-Thomist Durandus of Saint-Pourçain and Meister Eckhart.[33] In this task he was joined by another influential cardinal, himself a Dominican, one whose involvement decisively altered the course of Eckhart's fate.

The Friend at Court

Like Eckhart, Cardinal William Peter of Godin was born in 1260.[34] Also like Eckhart, he entered the Dominican order in 1276 or 1277. An exemplar of the long years of training entailed in becoming a

Master of Theology, he incepted at Beziers in 1279 and, following the academic custom of the time, taught philosophy and theology for over seven years. From 1292 to 1296, he studied at St Jacques in Paris, and was then assigned to Toulouse to lecture on the *Sentences* of Peter Lombard. In 1304, he was declared Magister at the University of Paris, and in 1306 was called to lecture on theology at the papal curia, 'the next Dominican after Albert to lecture in the papal household'.[35]

In 1312, William Peter was named cardinal and from 1320 to 1324 served as papal legate in Castille. Returning to Avignon, he was almost immediately involved in the posthumous process concerning the *Postilla super Apocalypsim* of Peter John Olivi, which was condemned by John XXII in 1326. The condemnation of Olivi's doctrine only a year before Eckhart's trial began must have added fire to an already overheated situation, especially since the charges against Olivi had been preferred by a Dominican prelate.[36] Ockham was already in Avignon, labouring under 'house arrest' much as that under which Eckhart himself would soon be placed. Michael of Cesena had also been summoned to Avignon in 1327 and was by then en route to the papal court.

The Trial in Avignon

Eckhart's appeal of 24 January 1327 brought before John XXII as many as five lists of at least 109 articles denounced as heretical by the Inquisition of Archbishop Henry of Virneburg. Their reduction to the more modest twenty-eight was apparently the work of Cardinal William Peter. Fournier, however, 'was entrusted with presenting the commissioners' findings, and his own, on Eckhart's theology ...'[37] From his notes relative to the case of Durandus of Saint-Pourçain, it is clear that Fournier was unhappy over the defects of the system used to evaluate suspect propositions. He may have had such reservations about Eckhart's treatment as well. Similarly, Cardinal William Peter 'was unwilling to condemn propositions without judging them according to their context and Eckhart's intentions'.[38]

Fournier's later reminiscences and the report of the theological commission provide some insight into how the investigators reached a final verdict. Eckhart was allowed to defend himself, and did so vigorously if not always successfully. In surprisingly strong language, the Dominican scholars Koch and Théry held that the Meister's handling of his case was inept.[39] Hinnebusch concedes that Eckhart, now sixty-seven and possibly ailing, made a poor defence. Other scholars, notably Dempf, Ancelet-Hustache and McGinn, disagree.[40] In the end, however, both Fournier and the commission concluded that each of the twenty-eight propositions was 'hereticus, prout sonat,' that is, 'heretical as stated' which is to say, of course, out of context.

Apparently Fournier felt that Eckhart had drifted into a form of Sabellianism,[41] subordinating the Son and the Holy Spirit to the Father. He was particularly unflattering with respect to Eckhart's purported statements in articles 22 and 23 of the 'votum theologicum' (12 and 13 in the bull of condemnation), which he referred to as 'blasphemous and insane', and 'worthy of laughter among all intelligent persons'. The rest, particularly articles 17 through 21, and 24 to 26 (nos. 20, 21, 22, 10 and 11 and 23–25 in the bull) Fournier declared to be merely 'wrong and heretical'.

Eckhart's Death and Condemnation

Sometime after Fournier rendered his opinion but well before the pope issued the bull of condemnation, Meister Eckhart died, probably in Avignon, perhaps en route back to his homeland. The date is not certain, although it occurred before 30 April 1328, when John wrote to Henry of Virneburg advising patience at the length of time the process was taking.[42] In passing, the pope remarks that Eckhart is already dead. The Chronicle of Johannes Meyer, OP, claims that the Meister died in 1327 after barely a single month in Avignon.[43] If that early a date is unlikely, we can at least estimate Eckhart's death to have occurred between July 1327 and April 1328. Recent research suggests that based on a memorial found in a seventeenth-century source, he died on 28 January 1328, a day now observed as the Feast of St Thomas Aquinas.[44] His final place of earthly rest has never been discovered.

Even before the bull of condemnation was promulgated, reaction was swift. In 1328, the Dominican general chapter meeting at Toulouse cautioned friars against preaching 'subtle' truths.[45] Some commentators believe that this was aimed at Eckhart. But if Eckhart died on 28 January 1328, then the reprimand of the Chapter of Toulouse, issued on 28 May 1328 would not have applied to him, since the capitulars would have surely known by then that he was dead. It seems logical to conclude that as this was a reiteration of previous reprimands, those, too, were unlikely to have been directed at Eckhart, who had already been cleared from suspicion of teaching false doctrine by a preemptive investigation conducted by Nicholas of Strassburg, the papal representative, in 1326, well after the investigation of the Cologne archdiocesan tribunal had commenced. Given the large number of Dominican preachers in Germany at the time, the earlier reprimand may have been directed at any number of friars. To assert that Eckhart was specifically intended goes beyond the evidence. But on 27 March 1329, Pope John issued the bull *In agro Dominico* – the title of which might well have been an ironical jibe at the Dominican order. Its promulgation was officially intended for the jurisdiction of the Archbishop of Cologne.[46] But news of the death and condemnation of so famous a preacher and scholar must have sent waves of perplexity through Eckhart's community and the citizens there and would have soon travelled far and wide. If so, the reports have been swallowed up in the disasters that followed, as the Black Death reached the ports of Europe and Germany descended into a maelstrom of petty civil wars.

With three exceptions, nos. 11, 13 and 20, the sources of the condemned propositions have now been identified.[47] Any number of alternative sources would have rendered approximately the same reading. What distinguishes the particular form in which the propositions appear in the bull is their conciseness and boldness. By the same token, that force and clarity is made to appear in greater relief by being removed from context, both particularly and as a whole, where their appropriate sense and reference would have substantially weakened the case of the prosecution.

Another perplexing difficulty arises in that the division and description of the articles in the bull itself does not accurately reflect the minutes of the commission, the opinion of Fournier and perhaps of the pope as well. As is evident from the text, only articles 1 through 15 – all described as authentically Eckhart's – are condemned as heretical. However, the eleven articles from no. 16–26 are not so condemned, although they are severely reproved as 'evil-sounding, rash and suspect of heresy'. The two final articles, nos. 27 and 28, while also condemned as heretical, are only alleged to have been Eckhart's authentic teaching (even though adequate textual evidence exists that in fact they were).

After an exhaustive study of the relevant documents and various opinions, Josef Koch came to the conclusion that neither Jacques Fournier nor Pope John was responsible for the alterations in the bull. Koch's own conjecture is that the reformulation was the work of Cardinal William Peter of Godin, who had also exercised a moderating influence during the two processes against Olivi.[48] Whatever the case, it is also important to observe, as Colledge insists, that the condemnation of *In agro Dominico* pertains only to certain of Eckhart's propositions and the works which contain them. Unlike the cases of the Beghards and Beguines, William of Ockham, Marsiglio of Padua, and John of Jandun, the man himself is not condemned.[49] Eckhart himself, moreover, is described in the concluding paragraph of the bull as having retracted anything that could have generated a heretical opinion in the minds of the faithful 'or one erroneous and hostile to the true faith'.[50] Significantly and consistently, however, Eckhart carefully avoided to the end any admission that his teaching had in fact been proved heretical, unshakeably insisting that because heresy is fundamentally a matter of the will, he remained innocent. In Hinnebusch's view, Eckhart's 'errors' were merely verbal and he remained 'unquestioningly loyal to the Church and its doctrine'.[51]

Final Accounts

From the vantage point of more than six hundred and fifty years of hindsight, it seems evident that the condemnation of Eckhart's teachings resulted from a violent confluence of complex spiritual and worldly concerns far broader and more deadly than the religious rivalry of the Dominican and Franciscan orders. An examination of the trials in light of the final tragedy indicates, as Alain de Libera has argued, that the principal motivating factors were in fact primarily political rather than religious.

Grounds for suspicion of heresy did exist. In Cologne, a centre of dissent and agitation, numerous tracts attributed to Eckhart had been circulated by heterodox groups under cover of the Meister's name and reputation. At his trial Eckhart repeatedly and apparently successfully insisted that they were spurious.[52] But it is arguable that not even the content of suspect propositions authentically his warranted the persecution Eckhart received nor especially anathematisation. Other factors were surely involved, and hardly theological issues.

By the time of Eckhart's trial, Henry of Virneburg, who had elected Frederick of Hapsburg in 1314, had become a supporter of Ludwig of Bavaria, following the latter's reconciliation with Frederick in 1325 prior to his invasion of Rome. As a whole, the Dominican order continued to support the pope. The archbishop, already irritated by the zeal and success of the Dominican preachers in his diocese, no doubt also smarted because of their exemption from episcopal jurisdiction. He seems to have been especially stung by the preemptive intervention of Nicholas of Strassburg, the papal representative but also a Dominican, which exonerated Eckhart of teaching false doctrine. Thus, Henry of Virneburg appears to have decided to set an example once for all by striking the Preaching Friars at the top.[53] In addition to summoning Eckhart before his Inquisition, he also cited Nicholas. At a stroke he served warning to the Dominicans and the pope, reasserted control over his diocese at the expense of an exempt religious order, deprived the Beguines of their most eloquent advocate and stripped from the radical dissenters the cover of respect and authority they had assumed. That both Eckhart and Nicholas should have fared badly in Henry of Virneburg's court is therefore not surprising. Eckhart's fate in Avignon, however, cannot be accounted for so easily.

The condemnation of fifteen propositions taken from his teachings despite the efforts of his provincial, Nicholas of Strassburg, the Procurator General of the Dominicans and Cardinal William Peter of Godin to defend him resulted, I think, from a fatal combination of factors. To begin with, the theological abilities of many of his examiners were neither particularly well-developed nor patient of diversity. Jacques Fournier, an obvious exception, was a Master of Theology but at least tacitly supported the rebellious anti-Thomistic faction among the Dominicans. Moreover, the tenor of his comments displays not only an inability, even an unwillingness to comprehend Eckhart's meaning, but also an intellectual arrogance that bridled at the German master's homely metaphors and daring analogies. Conversely, and also exceptionally, William Peter of Godin and even Nicholas of Strassburg, while sympathetic to Eckhart as a Dominican, adhered to the stricter Thomistic school. Eckhart and his interrogators were like men speaking different languages.[54] Most of all, although it seems evident that the commissioners relied on Eckhart's good faith and had anticipated his retraction, the fact of his death in advance of the final verdict removed the last threat of determined refutation from the most likely source.

Pope John XXII did not condemn Eckhart's teachings in order to mortgage his canonisation of Thomas Aquinas. Faced with armed opposition from the emperor, who had occupied Rome and set up an anti-pope, as well as the Spiritual Franciscans, who had just mounted a fierce verbal attack from the safety of Munich, the pope could not risk reversing the opinion of his commissioners and further alienating the powerful Archbishop of Cologne. Quite simply, beleaguered as a ruler as well as a theologian and even under accusation of heresy himself, John XXII sacrificed Eckhart, who was not a heretic but was at least safely dead, as an act of political expedience.

Aftermath

Two additional letters of John XXII to Henry of Virneburg exist in the Vatican archives. The first, of 15 April 1329, instructs the archbishop to publish the condemnation of Eckhart's propositions in the region of his authority.[55] The other, of 11 April 1331, concerns the process against Nicholas of Strassburg, which to the considerable displeasure of the archbishop had not prevented him from serving as definitor at the General Chapter of Perpignan in 1327 among other things. The charges were quietly laid aside.[56]

Archbishop Henry of Virneburg died the following year.

On the death of John XXII at the age of eighty-five in 1334, Jacques Fournier was elected Pope at Avignon, taking the name Benedict XII. In his 1336 bull, *Benedictus Deus*, the new pope ended the controversy over the beatific vision that had so agitated the previous pontificate. In itself, this hardly abated the Spiritual

Franciscans' hostility, however, which flared up intermittently until the death of William of Ockham in 1347.[57]

As pope, Fournier inaugurated several significant religious reforms, many of which were reinstituted two centuries later by the Council of Trent. Politically, Benedict XII was less successful. Like his predecessors, he was partial to the French King, Philip VI. Moreover, his conciliatory attitude toward Ludwig of Bavaria was interpreted as weakness, which led the Electors at Rense to adopt many of the anti-papal positions advocated by William of Ockham and Marsiglio of Padua, further debilitating papal prerogatives.

As if to worsen matters, the Hundred Years War between England and France erupted during Benedict's pontificate, effectively forestalling his plans for another crusade. Finally, and despite his hopes to return the papal see to Rome, Benedict effectively ensured the papacy a long stay in France. 'It was Fournier who initiated the building of the Palace of the Popes in Avignon, and he who invited Simone Martini there to paint the frescoes.'[58] And there in 1342 died the Inquisitor of Montaillou.

Tension between the Dominican and Franciscan orders remained acute for several years. A diatribe against Eckhart and Nicholas was lodged, as noted before, as part of Michael of Cesena's *Great Appeal* of 18 September 1328. Between 26–28 May in that year, Michael, William of Ockham and several other Spiritual Franciscans had escaped from Avignon and fled to the court of Ludwig of Bavaria in Munich. There they joined Marsiglio of Padua and perhaps John of Jandun, who died that year. Writs of excommunication followed. In 1331, William was expelled from his order and sentenced to perpetual imprisonment. After the accession of Benedict XII, William of Ockham and the others continued their attacks on the papacy. Marsiglio of Padua died in 1342, William of Ockham in 1347. The death of Ludwig in the same year effectively ended the anti-papal designs of the imperium. The spiritual movement that the 'Michaelites' or Fraticelli had represented in an extreme form survived, however, and found eventual expression among the Friars of Strict Observance. In 1415, the *Osservanti* received approval at the Council of Constance and in 1517 separated from the conventual friars as 'the true order of St Francis'.

On the part of the Dominicans, strenuous denunciations of Ludwig, Michael of Cesena and the Spirituals are found in the Acts of the general chapter of 1330 and the Chronicles of the order.[59] Gradually, however, as Clark relates, 'The hostility between the two great Mendicant Orders which was so painfully evident at Eckhart's trial largely subsided'.[60] Following the revival of Franciscan mysticism between 1340 and 1350, even 'the great Dominican mystics were regarded as worthy models to be followed in Franciscan friaries and nunneries'.[61]

One of the most prominent of later fourteenth century Franciscan spiritual writers, Marquart von Lindau, drew heavily on works of both Tauler and Eckhart, particularly the latter's *Commentary on the Gospel of John*.[62] It may well be the case, as Clark maintains, that by the time of Marquart the creative period of German mysticism had run its course. If so, his teaching nevertheless suggests a fitting resolution of the bitter struggle between the two great medieval orders. For, as Clark tells us, except for the influence of Duns Scotus and Bonaventure, 'his mysticism is entirely Dominican ...'[63]

NOTES

1. Cf. Koch, KS, I, pp. 320–3; McGinn, 'Condemnation', p. 393. Cf. Blakney, 'Introduction', pp. xviii, xxiii. Jeanne Ancelet-Hustache argued similarly in her 1957 book, cf. pp. 122–3.

2. A fragment from the Appeal was published by M.H. Laurent, OP, 'Autour du procès de Maître Eckhart', *Divus Thomas*, 39 (Piacenza, 1936), pp. 446–7. Hereafter, 'Laurent'. Also cf. Koch, KS, I, p. 320.

3. See McGinn, 'Condemnation', p. 392, Ancelet-Hustache, p. 121, and especially McGinn, *The Mystical Thought of Meister Eckhart*, op. cit., p. 15.

4. Koch, KS, I, p. 321, Hinnebusch, II, p. 308, and McGinn, 'Condemnation', p. 393. The most incisive treatment of this question is that of Ingeborg Degenhardt, *Studien zum Wandel des Ekhartsbildes*, Leiden: Brill, 1967, pp. 13–15.

5. Cf. Lester K. Little, *Religious Poverty and the Profit Economy in Medieval Europe*, Ithaca, NY: Cornell University Press, 1978, esp. pp. 146–69.

6. Cf. Weisheipl, op. cit., pp. 280, 286.

7. On Durandus, cf. Koch, KS, II, pp. 7–168, Hinnebusch, II, pp. 156–62, and Weisheipl, pp. 342f.

8. Hinnebusch, II, pp. 150–4, and Weisheipl, p. 340. On the Franciscan archbishop John Pecham and his prosecution of Knapwell, cf. Hinnebusch, II, pp. 150–2, 155, 164f. and Weisheipl, pp. 285–6, 288–9, 341–2.

9. Yet another philosophical quarrel which divided Dominicans and Franciscans concerned the unicity vs. multiplicity of form, a technical philosophical problem entailed in conflicting interpretations of Aristotle. In this, too, Eckhart remained a loyal follower of Thomas and an opponent of the Franciscan school.

10. The intense friction between Dominicans and Franciscans resulting from these controversies forms the background for Umberto Eco's philosophical murder-mystery *The Name of the Rose* (New York and London: Harcourt, Brace and Jovanovich, 1983). Eco assumes the viewpoint of the Spiritual Franciscans and accordingly, an anti-Dominican bias which, from a historical perspective, unbalances his otherwise fascinating novel and the film based on it.

11. Cf. M.D. Lambert, *Franciscan Poverty: The Doctrine of the Absolute Poverty of Christ and the Apostles in the Franciscan Order*, 1210–1323, St Bonaventure, NY: Franciscan Institute Publications, 1998 (London: SPCK, 1961).

12. Tuchman, op. cit., pp. 36–7.

13. Several Franciscans, having learned that the great Dominican theologian lay ill at Maenza (the castle of his niece, Francesca), visited him there along with Dominicans and Cistercian monks from the nearby abbey of Fossanova. When he lay dying at Fossanova a few weeks later, Franciscans were also among those who had come to keep vigil. Cf. Weisheipl, pp. 325–6 and especially p. 327. When Thomas was canonised in 1323, moreover, Friars Minor were again among his ardent supporters. Cf. Weisheipl, ibid., p. 348.

14. On Henry of Virneburg as 'a noted opponent of heresy and of the suspect Beguines', see McGinn, 'Introduction', p. 245, Norman Cohn, op. cit., p. 165, and Clark, *Great German Mystics*, p. 15. Cf. also Johannes Vitoduranus, *Chronicon*, in *Thesaurus Historiae Helveticae* (Tiguri: 1735), p. 36.

15. Cf. *Acta Capitulorum Generalium Ordinis Praedicatorum*, ed. by Fr. Andreas Frühwirth, Rome: 1899, Vol. II (MOPH, Vol. IV), pp. 160–1, esp. n. 1. It is not possible to determine from the documents themselves whether Eckhart was himself one of those with whom the chapter was concerned. Many modern scholars, following Koch, tend to think he was not. Cf. also Laurent, p. 334, n. 6. On Nicholas of Strassburg, cf. Alain de Libera, pp. 18–19, Rudi Imbach, 'Nicholas de Strasbourg', *Dictionnaire du Spiritualité*, 1981, cols. 301–2, and M.-M. Gorce, 'Nicolas de Strasbourg', *Dictionnaire de théologie catholique*, Vol. XI, Paris, 1931, col. 633.

16. Cf. Koch, KS, I, pp. 324–6, 11, p. 423. Fifty-eight separate points were taken from the various works. The critical edition of the Cologne Process, edited by Loris Sturlese, is now published in the final volume of the Latin Works (LW 5: 197–226).

17. Despite the occasional false '*reportaciones*' and mistakes the Meister rejected during the processes at Cologne and Avignon, it can be assumed that the vernacular sermons accurately reflected not only Eckhart's actual teaching, but at least some of the daring, original and often poetic form of his language as well. The *ars memorativa*, a now-lost element fostered in ancient and medieval culture, was especially developed in Dominican spirituality. For a fascinating

ECKHART'S WAY

study of the *ars memorativa* in medieval and renaissance culture, see Frances
Yates, *The Art of Memory*, Chicago: The University of Chicago Press, 1966.
18. Théry, art. cit., p. 185. Cf. C-McG, p. 71.
19. Cf. Koch, KS, I, pp. 333ff. For translated texts see C-McG, pp. 71–6, Clark, op.
    cit., pp. 251–8, and Blakney, op. cit., pp. 258–82.
20. Théry, art. cit., p. 196. See C-McG, pp. 76–7 and Blakney, op. cit.,
    pp. 282–305. The second *rotulus* contained sixty-eight separate points.
21. See footnote 19 above.
22. Colledge, art. cit., p. 251. The official grievance of Gerard of Podahns, acting
    for William Dulcin, the Vice Procurator of the order, against William of
    Nidecken and Hermann de Summo in the Vatican Archives was published by
    Laurent, pp. 430–5.
23. Ancelet-Hustache, p. 43. Southern similarly describes the pope as a capable
    administrator, 'able and clear-sighted', op. cit., p. 45. He was also industrious;
    his yearly average of letters was 3,646, as compared, for instance, to Sylvester
    II (999–1003), who averaged only ten per year. Cf. also Weisheipl, p. 344. John
    XXII was the first pope to have graduated from the University of Paris.
24. Ancelet-Hustache, pp. 42f.
25. Cf. Tuchman, pp. 45–6.
26. Emmanuel LeRoy Ladurie, *Montaillou: The Promised Land of Error*, trans. by
    Barbara Bray, New York: George Braziller, Inc., 1978, p. xi.
27. Ladurie, p. xi.
28. Cf. Ladurie, p. vii.
29. Ibid.
30. Ladurie, pp. xi–xii. Cf. Koch, KS, II, pp. 367–8.
31. Koch, ibid. Cf. Colledge, p. 243.
32. Koch, KS, II, pp. 369, 374–7. On Olivi and the condemnations of the Council
    of Vienne, see also pp. 143–4.
33. Fournier's full response to Eckhart's propositions is lost, but fragments of it
    were found in the *Sentence Commentary* and *Ten Responses* of John Hitalinger of
    Basel. Cf. Koch, KS, II, p. 370, McGinn, 'Condemnation', p. 397, and C-McG,
    p. 12. On Olivi and Ockham, see also pp. 143–4, Koch, KS, II, pp. 377–81, and
    Ladurie, p. xii. On Durandus, see also pp. 143–5 and Colledge, pp. 245–7,
    C-McG, pp. 11–13.
34. For a capsule biography, cf. Hinnebusch, II, pp. 62–3, 309. As he was almost an
    exact contemporary of Eckhart, it is highly unlikely that he was ever a student
    of the Meister as McGinn suggests. See *The Mystical Thought of Meister Eckhart*,
    p. 17 and *The Harvest of Mysticism*, pp. 105–6.
35. Hinnebusch, II, p. 43.
36. This was Cardinal Bishop Nicholas Ostia, OP, who proposed eighty-four
    articles, later reduced to sixty. Only four questions, those eventually
    condemned, were addressed by Fournier.
37. Colledge, 'Times and Writings', p. 245. The opinion of the commission against
    Eckhart was discovered in the Vatican archives by Cardinal Mercati, Prefect of the

Vatican, and edited by Franz Pelster in 1935: *Articuli contra Fratrem Aychardum Alamannum*, Vat. lat. 3899, f. 123r–130v, published by Pelster in 'Ein Gutachten aus dem Eckehart-Prozess in Avignon', *Aus der Geiste welt des Mittelalters. Festgabe Martin Grabmann* (Beiträge Supplement III) Munster, 1935, pp. 1099–124. Cf. Koch, KS, I, p. 312 and McGinn, 'Eckhart's Condemnation Reconsidered', p. 397, n. 34.

38. Hinnebusch, II, p. 309. Cf. also Colledge, ibid., p. 245.
39. McGinn considers Koch's pronouncement to have been 'peremptory and gratuitous'. 'Eckhart's Condemnation Reconsidered', p. 396. On the procedures and stages of the investigation, cf. Koch, KS, I, pp. 205–8, 312–313.
40. Cf. McGinn, 'Condemnation', pp. 391, 411–414.
41. Cf. Koch, KS, I, p. 339 and II, p. 384.
42. Koch, KS, I, p. 345. The text of the somewhat mutilated letter was published by Thomas Kaeppeli, 'Kurze Mitteilungen über mittelalterliche Dominikanerschriftsteller', AFP (Vol. X, 1940), pp. 293–4.
43. Koch, ibid.
44. See above, p. 37, n. 21.
45. Cf. *Acta*, op. cit., p. 180.
46. Koch, KS, I, p. 344. Copies of the Bull have been found elsewhere in Germany, however, indicating that the condemnation had a wider orbit. See Robert E. Lerner, 'New Evidence for the Condemnation of Meister Eckhart', *Speculum*, 72 (1997), pp. 347–66. For the Latin text of the Bull and the pope's letter of authorisation to Archbishop Henry of Virneburg, see Laurent, pp. 435–44. For the English translation of *In agro Dominico*, see C-McG, pp. 77–81. The critical edition of the papal bull will be published in the final volume of the LW.
47. See appendix B. Cf. Koch, KS, I, pp. 325–7, C-McG, pp. 316f., nn. 2–28; and Laurent, pp. 436–43, nn. 74–102.
48. Koch, I, pp. 343–4 and Hinnebusch, II, p. 309. Colledge remains of the opinion that Fournier mitigated the Bull. (C-McG, p. 13. Cf. also Colledge, 'Times and Writings', p. 248.)
49. See Colledge, 'Times and Writings', p. 253.
50. Cf. C-McG, pp. 15 and 81, and McGinn, 'Condemnation', p. 400.
51. Hinnebusch, II, p. 310.
52. Many, not all of which were heretical in intent, have survived, including Schwester Katrei (cf. Quint, DP, pp. 441–9). See the English translation by Elvira Borgstädt, 'The Sister Catherine Treatise', in *Meister Eckhart: Teacher and Preacher*, op. cit., pp. 347ff. Cf. E. Weber, 'Mystique parce que théologien: Maître Eckhart', *La vie spirituelle*, 652 (1982), p. 734.
53. Cf. Alain de Libera, op. cit., p. 234.
54. This impasse of language has been commented upon by Ancelet-Hustache, Schürmann, McGinn and others and warrants closer examination. Cf. especially Yves Congar, 'Langage des spirituels et langage des théologiens', *La Mystique Rhénane*, op. cit., pp. 15–34.
55. Laurent, pp. 444–5.
56. Laurent, pp. 445–6.

57. Writings: Cod. Vat. lat. 4006, 'De statu animarum sanctarum ante generale judicium', and 'Decem questionnes in Durandum'. On the document found in the papal library at the time of Gregory XI (1375) and edited by Franz Ehrle, cf. Koch, KS, II, p. 368. On the responses between 1325–30 concerning Michael of Cesena, William of Ockham and Peter John Olivi concerning the beatific vision, and those regarding Eckhart, see Koch, KS, II, pp. 370–3.

58. Ladurie, p. xii.

59. *Acta Capitulorum Generalium OP*, op. cit., pp. 197, 201; *Cronica Ordinis* for 1324, p. 22.

60. Clark, *Great German Mystics*, p. 104.

61. Ibid., p. 107.

62. Marquart, considered by many to be the greatest Franciscan mystic of the later fourteenth century, flourished after 1379 and died at Constance in 1392. Cf. Clark, *Great German Mystics*, esp. pp. 107ff. Clark relates, 'I have shown elsewhere that Marquart quotes Eckhart and Tauler in his *Exodus*. (*Modern Language Review*, Vol. XXXIV [1939], pp. 73–8; see also Vol. XLII [1947], pp. 246–51.) In his *Commentary on the Gospel of St John* he borrows largely from Eckhart's work on the same subject. We find imbedded in his writings some of the most beautiful passages of these great mystics. Neither of them is named; in the case of Eckhart this is natural enough, nor need we be surprised at the omission of Tauler's name. It is common medieval practice only to mention by name those authors who were of unquestionable authority, such as the Fathers of the Church or the founders of Scholasticism.' Ibid., pp. 107–8.

63. Ibid., p. 109.

THE LEGACY

Eckhart's name finds no mention in the chronicle of the Order of Preachers for the grim years between 1325 and 1330.[1] Nor is there any mention of the former prior of Erfurt, vicar of Thuringia and Bohemia, provincial of Saxony and regent master of Paris in the earlier, less difficult years.

But if Eckhart's fame and teachings fell into official disrepute after his posthumous condemnation in 1329, their impact in Germany launched a spiritual tidal wave that for a time swept everything before it. Even Franciscan spirituality acquired a Dominican cast. And if the Meister's name, like those of disgraced kings in ancient lands, was effaced from the official records of his time, the same was not true of his most devoted disciples, Heinrich Suso and Johann Tauler.

Nor was the living memory of their beloved Meister forgotten by the extraordinary Dominican women of the southern Rhineland, whose spirituality had been entrusted to his care and that of his brethren and disciples. Eckhart's colleagues at Cologne likewise preserved not only his memory but over five hundred Latin excerpts of his teachings and commentaries as Thomas Kaeppeli discovered in a hitherto unknown manuscript in 1960. Other manuscripts were also carefully preserved, such as that found in the library of Cardinal Nicholas of Cusa a century later.

Largely through Tauler's preaching and direction, Eckhart's spirituality influenced Rulwin Merswin at Grüner Wörth in Strassburg and the wider mystical movement known as the Friends of God. The Meister's doctrine was known for instance to Jan van Ruysbroeck and Gerard Groote in the Netherlands, to the author of The Cloud of Unknowing and indirectly through the Dominican sisters to Margery Kempe in England[2] and, again through the sermons of Tauler, even to Luther himself.

In the seventeenth century the Rhineland tradition of the mysterious Meister Eckhart resurfaced in the mystical doctrine of Jacob Boehme and Angelus Silesius. Rediscovered by poets in the eighteenth century, Eckhart's teaching touched philosophers in the nineteenth. By the end of that era, scholars had begun the process of textual reconstruction that would make the authentic teachings known to the entire world in the twentieth century.

Eckhart's Sons

The synthesis of speculative and mystical elements begun at Cologne by Albert the Great culminated in the preaching and teaching of his last student, Meister Eckhart. It also effectively ended with it. Heinrich Suso and Johann Tauler were mystics and preachers as well as teachers, but although students of Eckhart's at Cologne and proponents of his mystical doctrine, they did not continue his philosophical and theological pursuits.[3] Conversely, the scholarly interest of Berthold of Moosberg (d. c. 1361), the most Neoplatonic of the later members of the Rhineland school, differed considerably from the Meister's bold flights of metaphysical and mystical imagination.[4]

The Meistersinger

Heinrich Suso has been called the lyric poet among the mystics, the last of the Minnesingers – the German representatives of the romantic tradition of the French troubadours and trouvères. For he was from Swabia, renowned for its courtly love, chivalry, music and poetry, echoes of which can be found in all his writings. He was born in Constance in 1295, the son of Count Heinrich Von Berg, 'a worldly-minded, perverse, difficult man'.[5] Small wonder that when he entered the Dominicans, young Heinrich retained his mother's family name, Süs or Seuse (rendered awkwardly as 'Suso' in English), for she was everything that his noble father was not – religious, sensitive, tender-hearted.

He entered religious life at the very young age of thirteen. As Clark relates: 'Apparently a substantial donation from the Von Berg family secured the necessary permission for entry two years before the prescribed age was attained.'[6] This departure from custom soon proved to be a major source of anxiety for the sensitive youth, however. 'In later years Suso's conscience was troubled by the circumstances of his admission. He believed himself to be guilty of the mortal sin of simony and destined to be damned eternally, until Eckhart comforted him and restored his peace of mind.[7]

As a student friar, Suso lived at Strassburg and it is possible that it was there he first met both Eckhart and his younger confrere of that city, Johann Tauler. In any event, they were both at the studium in Cologne from 1323–1325, just as Eckhart himself arrived from Strassburg. Toward the end of Suso's studies, the first accusations against his teaching master were pressed. Courageous and loyal, Heinrich composed his first book at least partially as a defence, *The Little Book of Truth*. In it, he distinguished Eckhart's doctrines from those of the proponents of the Free Spirit. He also thereby denied that Eckhart was guilty of the heretical interpretation laid upon his teachings. Soon circulating widely, *The Little Book of Truth* was duly brought to the attention of higher authorities and a severe censure of the young friar resulted.

As the trial of Meister Eckhart dragged on in Avignon in 1327–1328, Suso finished his studies and returned to Constance as lector in the priory there. He also began to preach and minister to the nuns of the region. Somehow he also found time to write another work, *The Little Book of EternalWisdom*. Before the manuscript could be circulated, however, he was summoned before a Dominican chapter, probably at Antwerp in 1327, which reprimanded him for promoting false doctrine and he was deprived of his teaching position.

Suso managed to retain the confidence of his brethren, however. During the calamitous period of the papal interdict against Ludwig of Bavaria, the Dominicans of Constance were forced into exile in various places. In 1343, Suso found himself elected prior of one such group which had taken refuge outside the city in the Scottish Cloister. Throughout this time he also preached widely and gave spiritual instruction to the Dominican sisters and lay mystics who were already calling themselves the Friends of God. He became a close friend of Elsbet Stagel, the Dominican prioress of Töss in Switzerland, with whom he corresponded for some time. Also the convent chronicler and a woman of uncommonly good sense as well as holiness, she managed to preserve his letters and in effect served as his amanuensis for the autobiographical *Life of the Servant*.

Sometime after 1334, Suso composed his only Latin work, the *Horologium Sapientiae* (Clock of Wisdom). By then he had earned the order's benediction and was even granted permission to publish *The Little Book of Eternal Wisdom*, which Denifle accounted 'the finest fruit of German mysticism'.[8] In fact, the *Horologium Sapientiae* is largely a paraphrase and further development of the earlier work.

Although Suso gave up writing and teaching at the age of forty, towards the end of his life he apparently consented to edit his earlier works together with a prologue and two books of letters into a single volume, the *Exemplar*. *The Life of the Servant*, although written by Elsbet Stagel, was also edited by Suso himself for inclusion in that edition.[9] Many scholars consider the collection of letters of Suso and Stagel to be the finest of its kind from the Middle Ages.

A writer of lyrical genius, Suso's contribution to German literature is as great in many respects as that of Eckhart himself. In addition to the rhapsodic prose of his exhortations, letters and biography, he was also capable of more scholarly enterprises and flights of speculation. These, however, must have failed to interest him much. Not without reason was he called the last Minnesinger.

After a career of stinging humiliations and quiet triumphs, Suso died in Ulm on 25 January 1366. His unflagging loyalty to his beloved Meister was eventually rewarded by full exoneration within his lifetime. As we have seen, his name is mentioned with pride in the Chronicles of the Order along with that of Tauler. Four hundred and sixty-five years later, he was beatified and his cult approved by Pope Gregory XVI.

Suso's fundamental teaching is based on Eckhart's twin themes of *Abgescheidenheit* and *Gelassenheit*.[10] *The Little Book of Truth* is more theoretical than his later works. In it, he considers questions concerning God's being, life and transcendence; creation; the divine presence in the soul; redemption and mystical union, which like Eckhart he maintained against pantheistic interpretations did not abrogate individual identity but only conscious self-preoccupation.[11] His themes include the nothingness of God and creatures, God's ground, the fathomless abyss, the naked Godhead and the existence of eternal ideas in the mind of God. The mystical afterglow of Rhineland Neoplatonism lingers throughout.

The Little Book of Eternal Wisdom is much more practical, homely and simple although by no means naive. Again, Suso stresses self-abandonment, conformity to the image of Christ, especially as the crucified Saviour, and the true way of Christian living. Evidently he wrote out of personal conviction based not only on sound doctrine, but his own experience. Hinnebusch observes: 'The elements of his spiritual doctrines are constantly illustrated by reference to his own experience. Though scattered throughout his works, they form a consistent whole and represent in essence a milder form of Eckhart's speculative mysticism.'[12] The imprint of Eckhart is in fact everywhere apparent, but nowhere obtrusive. Suso, like his younger friend and confrere, Tauler, parroted no one.

The Preachers' Preacher

Johann Tauler was born in Strassburg of a patrician family about the year 1300.[13] Destined to become one of the greatest preachers of his time, he entered the order dedicated to that ministry when about sixteen. (Tauler's sister also became a Dominican at the monastery of St Nicolas, where Johann himself died on 16 June 1361.)[14] Eckhart would have been in Strassburg at that time, now at the peak of his intellectual and administrative abilities as lector, preacher and spiritual director of the sisters of Alsace and Switzerland. Suso may still have been a student there as well. In 1325, Tauler was sent for further studies to Cologne, where Eckhart was now resident and Suso had preceded him. There he probably fell even more under the sway of the Meister's mystical teaching.

The impact of Eckhart's accusations, trials, death and condemnation must have been as much a source of profound suffering for the young friar as it was for his older confrere. Shortly afterwards, he returned to Strassburg as lector and remained there until the community was forced to leave the city for Basel during the struggle between the pope and Ludwig of Bavaria. In 1343 the Dominicans returned to the city, but Tauler remained behind for three more years. It was at Basel apparently that he made contact with the informal network of mystics which came to be known by the term Tauler himself would popularise, 'the Friends of God'.[15] After his return to Strassburg in 1347, the year the Emperor Ludwig died, he remained there until his death at the age of sixty or sixty-one. Always a popular preacher, Tauler further endeared himself to the citizens of Strassburg during the outbreak of the Black Death in 1348 by devoting himself completely to the care of the sick and dying. Tauler's career was exemplary. Following in the way of his Meister, he taught, preached and offered spiritual direction to the many convents of Dominican women in the region. Eighty-one of his sermons, transcribed from memory by his audiences, have been preserved.[16] He mentions Eckhart by name only once, but there are many allusions and his sermons largely continue the fundamental themes of the Meister's preaching – the reciprocal nothingness of God and creatures, the presence of God in the ground of the soul, *Abgescheidenheit*, the birth of the Word in the soul, and the soul's union with God.[17] Like his master, he discouraged ascetical extremes. His manner was warm and engaging. His preaching was also doctrinally profound, but unlike Eckhart, Tauler avoided entanglement in the webs of theological controversy. He rarely mentions the spark of the soul. He is likewise careful to affirm the distinctions between Creator and creatures and between soul and God in mystical union as well as the role of grace in effecting that union.

After his return to Strassburg in 1347, he became confessor to a wealthy merchant, Rulman Merswin, who for a time was of some influence among the Friends of God. On learning of Merswin's austere penitential practices, Tauler typically ordered him to cease. (Equally typically, the headstrong merchant returned to them as soon as the time limit Tauler imposed had expired.) Tauler was also a confidant of the saintly Margaret Ebner, the Dominican prioress of Maria Medigen, whom he visited in 1347 or 1348. He was likewise close to the priest-mystic Henry of Nördlingen, the friend of both Suso and Margaret Ebner, who wrote of Tauler in a letter to her, 'he teaches the truth as wholeheartedly as any teacher I know'.[18]

The influence of Tauler's sermons on subsequent German spirituality was enormous. But as was the case with Eckhart and Suso, not only were spurious works attributed to him in later years, but fantastic accounts of his life were written and circulated, many of them surviving to the present. Partially as a result, and partially because of the real merits of his authentic writings, he became a favourite among Protestant reformers in the sixteenth and seventeenth centuries, especially Luther.[19] Two centuries of controversy followed. Both Tauler and the

'Pseudo-Tauler' had some impact on the early German Romantics. He was read by Brentano, Von Baader and Hegel as well. Also like Eckhart, only in the nineteenth century were the authentic outlines of his story and teaching freed from the accretions of legend and propaganda.[20]

Eckhart's Daughters: Dominican Women Mystics of the Rhineland

Among other disciples who remained faithful to Eckhart's way, preeminence belongs to the Dominican women of the Rhineland whose communities were assigned to the Meister's care early in his career and to whom he primarily directed his ministry of preaching and guidance. This remarkable host of women includes not only the cloistered nuns but the lay sisters or *mantellatae*, generally Beguines, who had attached themselves to Dominican care and protection.

After the first and second generation of friars, including Dominic himself, Jordan of Saxony, Humbert of Romans, and Albert the Great, the influence of Eckhart, Suso and Tauler on the Dominican Sisters of the Rhineland was undeniably pervasive and most influential. Many other friars shared the honour and burden of guiding the spiritual development of these devout and energetic women – Peter of Dacia, Henry of Halle and Dietrich of Freiburg among them.

The sisters' spiritual direction (other than from their own by no means negligible resources) was not limited to the friars, however. Diocesan priests such as Henry of Nördlingen attended to the regular care of their life of faith. Other early and important influences on their spirituality included the writings of Mechthild of Magdeburg (c. 1207–1282), herself a Beguine and one of the first mystics to write in German. Similarly, *The Messenger of Divine Love* by St Gertrude the Great (1256–1302) and *The Book of Special Grace* by St Mechthild of Hackeborn (1241–1299), both nuns of Helfta and disciples of Mechthild of Magdeburg, exercised a powerful influence on Dominicans of both sexes.[21]

Several outstanding figures among the sisters are known to us from this period – Mechtilt von Stans and Jutzi Schultasin of Töss, Elsbet von Beggenhofen of Ötenbach, Anna von Ranswag of St Katherinental, Else von der Nüwenstatt of Adelhausen and many others. Of Christina Ebnerin (1277–1356), the prioress and chronicler of Engeltal, Rufus Jones has written that she 'seems to me to have been one of the purest

and noblest of the women mystics of this period in Germany'.[22] Toward
the end of her life, Christina Ebnerin like Elsbet Stagel came to know
Henry of Nördlingen. Through his direction, she discovered the
teachings of Tauler, which influenced her profoundly.

Bl. Margaret Ebner (1291–1351), who was most probably not
related to Christina, was the daughter of an important noble family of
Donauwörth. A woman of outstanding sanctity, the cause of her
canonisation is well underway at present.[23] Another remarkable
Dominican mystic among these women was Elsbet Stagel (d. 1360),
thanks to whose shrewdness and foresight the life history and letters of
Heinrich Suso were preserved for posterity. Jones is unsparing in
attributing to her a 'trained and well-ordered mind, a seasoned and
disciplined life …' She was a 'wise and inspiring guide' possessing
'distinct literary gifts', richly endowed with the 'beauty of holiness …'[24]

The Sisters' Books

The original writings of the sisters take the form of personal revelations
and occasional letters. In contrast to the Franciscan convents of the time,
in almost all the Dominican convents, chronicles or *Schwesternbücher*
detailing the lives and spiritual experiences of their most illustrious
member were also kept and preserved. Although stereotypical in many
respects and often intended to extol the former virtues of convent life
during a period of perceived decline, these chronicles nevertheless contain
original and striking evidence of genuine spiritual development as well as
apparent artifice and even hysterical delusions common to the age. Most
of these materials also represent important contributions to vernacular
literature during the formative period of the German language as well as
a rich treasury of hundreds of religious case histories.[25]

The spiritual doctrine in the *Schwesternbücher* does not differ in most
respects from that of Eckhart, Suso and Tauler, although much greater
emphasis is placed on actual experience, especially ecstatic experience,
as well as ascetical practices and bodily mortification. Here, the
influence of the Beguines is surely evident. A frequent counter-theme,
however, concerns their directors' advice or even a heavenly warning to
the sisters to relax these austerities – a traditional tension between the
friars and their sisters from the time of Jordan of Saxony, Dominic's
successor.

As many commentators have observed, the German Dominican women were, more than their brethren, practical rather than speculative mystics. Yet the often-detailed records of their lives include sufficient information concerning their experiences, despite the occasional stereo-typology, to construct at least a rudimentary account of the nature and meaning of their experiences. Fundamentally, the character of the sisters' teaching can be summarised under the following points: the necessity of self-renunciation; the action of the Holy Spirit in all believers; the possibility of mystical union with God; the essential equality before God of lay persons and religious, women and men, aristocrats and serfs; fidelity to the visible Church in belief and practice and the spiritual preeminence of the mixed life of action and contemplation.[26]

On the basis of her study of the chronicles of six major convents, Hester R. Gehring catalogued the varieties of virtues and experiences emphasised by the sisters according to the traditional division of medieval spirituality into the active, contemplative and mixed forms of life and also the three 'ages' or 'ways' of the spiritual life: purgative, illuminative and unitive. This was a natural choice, as the categories were familiar to the sisters themselves, although they did not attempt to organise their accounts according to them any more than Eckhart did with respect to his doctrine.

As Valerie Lagorio maintains, self-renunciation was preeminent among the fundamental virtues of the purgative way – obedience, humility, constancy and zeal, self-denial and abstinence, mortification (*Abtôtung*), and the desire for suffering. The nuns, she remarks, 'were entirely untouched by the fear of death'.[27] The way of enlightenment was characterised by mystical experiences more typical of contemplative life – visions and revelations of both a sensory (or quasi-sensory) nature and a more purely intellectual nature. Revelations, as might be expected, were most often aural, including voices both speaking and singing as well as music. Experiences of suprasensory taste and smell were also recorded. So also, however, were many instances of inner, intellectual communications devoid of sensory elements.

The unitive way was marked by ecstasies and rapturous states to a degree far greater than the teachings of Eckhart and his male disciples would have countenanced. It thus represents the sisters' most obvious difference from the friars' spirituality as well as their most manifest debt to the Beguines: 'Christine Ebner of Engeltal, speaking of a certain sister, remarked ingenuously: "She was the only one in our convent who never had ecstasies, and yet she was a very holy religious".'[28] Overall, however, momentary experiences of mystical union were ultimately given less prominence than an awareness of the abiding presence of God, a clear echo of Eckhart's 'middle way'. But there is also a greater emphasis than in the Meister's writings on 'mystical betrothal' and 'marriage', terms which are perhaps more characteristic of women's spirituality in an expressly patriarchal era. (The same can be said, roughly, of the differences and similarities between the teachings of St Teresa of Avila and St John of the Cross in the Carmelite tradition.)

Appraisal

In the invigorating dawn-light of psychiatric and especially psychoanalytic theory a few writers did not hesitate to label some of the sisters hysterics and their experiences pathological expressions of thwarted sexuality and social stress.[29] As might be expected, opinion was sharply divided even then. Rufus Jones himself admitted that some, even many of the sisters were outstanding representatives of balance and religious depth.

But even by contemporary standards, much of the reported life and especially the asceticism of the German Dominican sisters appears grim and even morbid. As we have seen, however, the severity of some of the sisters' voluntary practices was mitigated either by order of their spiritual directors such as Suso, or by a direct revelation from God, the Virgin Mary or another heaven-sent messenger. And if the sisters' lives were a willing struggle to the death (*Abtôtung*) with the forces of sin in and around them, not only were their lives also blessed with transcendent joy, but their deaths were sometimes occasions of holy merriment and even laughter.[30]

Gehring's intensive study of the language of the *Schwesternbücher* reveals not only the influence of the great Dominican mystics, Eckhart, Suso and Tauler but also the sisters' role in articulating and stabilising a mystical vocabulary as nearly capable as one can be of describing the nature of their experiences. Accomplishing such a task during the formative phase of a national language seems to have been the function of mystics at this period in England, Italy and the Low Countries as well as in Scandinavia, Germany and Switzerland. The South German Dominican women are perhaps unequalled in this regard, especially in light of the doctrinal contributions of their spiritual advisers and their own great numbers. Their intention, however, was primarily to witness before a less ardent generation to the felt presence and activity of God in their midst. And so their language becomes a key to understanding something of the nature of mystical experience itself. It is here that the lasting contribution of the German sisters ultimately lies and here that we find a common ground where the reports of their experiences and those of contemporary mystics may be compared and evaluated.

The Friends of God
Much has been written about the mystical network of the later fourteenth century known as 'the Friends of God', whom Clark characterises as an informal association of 'persons with strong mystical tendencies and interests, and in particular those who had attained union with God, the highest stage of the contemplative life'.[31] Religious and diocesan priests, nuns and laypersons of both sexes were all represented. The leadership was strongly Dominican – Suso's name is mentioned, but more especially that of Tauler, along with Christina Ebnerin and Margareta Ebner, John of Tomback, Dietrich of Colmar, John of Sterngassen and Nicholas of Strassburg.[32] Henry of Nördlingen and Jan van Ruysbroeck were also linked with the Dominicans and other members of the group.

Not surprisingly, Eckhart's influence upon this loose-knit band was definite, especially as channeled through the preaching and guidance of Suso and Tauler. Already, however, the *Lebemeister* had acquired an umbra of legend, looming not only larger than life as the years went on, but in an increasingly distorted form. This is particularly evident in the writings of an influential citizen of Strassburg, Rulwin Merswin (1307–1382), whose mysterious correspondent, the 'Friend of God from the Oberland' was established as a pious (or not-so-pious) fraud by Heinrich Denifle in 1880.[33] Nevertheless Merswin remains an important if lesser and slightly comic figure in the gloaming of the Rhineland mystical tradition.

Eckhart's influence on Franciscan spirituality, especially in the writings of the greatest of the fourteenth century mystics of that order, Marquart of Lindau, has been mentioned previously.[34] The impact of Eckhart's doctrine on the spirituality of the Low Countries is also clear, although in the case of Jan van Ruysbroeck at Groenendael, his disciple Gerard Groote of Deventer, and Jan Van Leeuwen, their attitude was always critically discerning with regard to authentic and spurious doctrine. It was in the Netherlands that the important distinction between 'true' and 'false' Friends of God was made and applied, for there were still partisans of the Free Spirit who appropriated the spiritual authority not only of Eckhart but of his disciples. It is not without significance that Rulman Merswin's successor as leader at Grüner Wörth, Nicholas of Basel, was burnt as a heretic at Vienna in 1409.

Later in the fifteenth century, the brilliant polymath Cardinal Nicholas von Kues (Cusa) esteemed Eckhart greatly. A valuable copy of parts of the *Opus Tripartitum* with cautionary marginal notations was preserved in his library. His development of the doctrine of 'learned ignorance', his fondness for paradox, his fascination with the reconciliation of opposites, and his Neoplatonic mysticism all hail back to the Rhineland tradition of Albert and Eckhart.[35]

The Later Tradition

Also as noted before, Eckhart's influence on Luther and the early Reformers in the following century has been much debated over the past several years. Clearly, Luther had read and been deeply impressed by Tauler's sermons, some editions of which included Eckhartian excerpts. The Dominicans' resistance to ascetical practices and penances as unproductive exterior 'works' naturally appealed to him. His dalliance with this aspect of Rhineland teaching may have delayed the emergence of his final theological position, however. And in other areas, as Ozment has shown, Luther was either unaffected or even misunderstood the earlier doctrines. In any event, his use of the Rhineland mystics was highly selective and, in later centuries, generally overestimated by both Protestant and Catholic writers.[36] Nonetheless, Sebastian Franck, Valentin Weigel, Johann Arndt and other radical Lutherans were to varying degrees indebted to Eckhart and his legend. In one way or another, the Meister's influence was also felt by the Spiritualists, Anabaptists, Hutterites and eventually the Pietists. It is present in works such as *The Temple of Souls* and the writings of Daniel Sudermann. Similarly, Jacob Boehme manifests some degree of influence by the medieval German Dominicans.[37]

Thus, although a dimming reflection of its former brightness, Eckhart's teaching continued to influence German religious thought in the sixteenth and seventeenth centuries. Among the various interpreters of Eckhart's teaching during the post-Reformation period, pride of place should doubtless go to Johannes Scheffler (Angelus Silesius), whose great poem, *'Der cherubinischer Wändersmann'* ('The Cherubic Wanderer') remains a monument of German mystical theology as well as an amazingly accurate rendering of the Meister's doctrine.[38]

Scheffler was born in 1624, the son of an immigrant Lutheran Polish nobleman who had settled in Breslau, Silesia. After his parents' death, Johannes entered the University of Strassburg in 1643 to study medicine. He transferred to the University of Leyden, Holland, where he came into contact with a circle of religiously sensitive refugees, including another Silesian, Abraham von Franckenberg, the disciple, editor and biographer of Jacob Boehme.

Scheffler finished his medical studies and graduated at the University of Padua, where he again came into contact with Catholicism. At the age of twenty-three, he returned to Silesia, where in 1649 he was appointed court physician to the Duke of Öls. His mentor Franckenberg lived in seclusion on a nearby estate, regarded with suspicion by the Lutheran clergy of the area. After Franckenberg's death in 1652, Scheffler found himself increasingly alienated from his Lutheran countrymen. Finding greater acceptance among Catholics, he was cultivated by the Jesuits. He soon lost his position at court and was received into the Catholic Church in 1653. His adopted name was symbolic, 'the Silesian Angel', or 'God's Silesian Messenger'. In 1661, he was ordained a priest, and devoted his remaining years to disputation and controversy with other Christian groups. He died in 1677.

'The Cherubic Wanderer', first published in 1657 under another title, consists of 302 verses composed during four days of ecstatic inspiration and represents the height of Schleffler's poetic accomplishments. Frederick Franck claims that Scheffler's short verses resemble in form and theme the gnomic verse of the great Zen masters. While deeply influenced by the language of Boehme and especially of Meister Eckhart, the contents reflect Scheffler's own mystical experience. As a whole, his spirituality is marked by a deep and pervasive love of nature and a special tenderness for animal and plant life:

> The rose that
> with my mortal eye I see
> flowers in God
> through all eternity.[39]

The German Enlightenment: Romanticism, Idealism and Criticism

Although shadowed, the tradition of the old Lebemeister survived during the centuries that followed – not, unfortunately, without further distortions and exaggerations. Eckhart but also Suso and Tauler were thus known in varying degrees of accuracy to the writers of the late eighteenth century rebirth of critical scholarship, but hardly outside of Germany. At one time or another Schlegel, Herder, Görres, Schopenhauer, Fichte and the great Hegel fell briefly under the spell of the mysterious Meister.[40]

The critical rediscovery of Eckhart and the beginning of true Eckhart scholarship began early in the nineteenth century with the initial efforts of Carl Schmidt and his disciple Auguste Jundt to rescue the Meister from the speculative webs of Hegelian idealism. In 1857 Franz Pfeiffer collected and edited all the Meister's known writings – including many now known to be spurious. These he published in two volumes.[41] A circle of Eckhart scholars quickly formed, including Wilhelm Preger, and H. J. Denzinger. More and more articles and textual recensions appeared in a flood of publishing enthusiasm.

Then in 1880 the Dominican scholar Heinrich Denifle, already disconcerted by what he considered to be the excessively Protestant and uncritical views developing among the majority of Eckhart's new students, including Otto Karrer, Spamer and others, discovered in the library at Erfurt a collection of Latin fragments ascribed to the Meister. These, he learned, were heretofore missing elements of the great *Opus*

Tripartitum, the ambitious and unfinished product of Eckhart's scholarly abilities and interests.[42] With the publication of the Latin works, a new and sometimes stormy epoch of Eckhart studies opened.

The Twentieth Century

In the early part of the new century, however, along with works by Paracelsus, Boehme and Fichte, Eckhart's German writings were pressed into service in the literary canon of the pre-Nazi Völkisch sects such as O.S. Reuter's *Deutsche Orden*. The pronounced anti-Christian bias of these neo-pagan groups makes their interest in Eckhart particularly odd.[43] Their interest resulted later in the reputed connection between Eckhart and Nazism, a movement which in fact despised the neo-pagan cults as politically ineffective.

Fortunately, as the Meister's doctrine was retrieved by textual criticism from this perversion and the spurious accretions of centuries of similar misunderstanding, details of his life and especially the condemnation of 1329 were also slowly uncovered by painstaking historical sleuthing. More critical texts were discovered. In 1923, Dom Augustine Daniels, OSB, edited and published Eckhart's *Rechtfertigungsschrift*, his written response to the charges brought against him at Cologne. These texts were re-edited by Fr Gustave Théry, OP, in 1926.[44]

About this time Cardinal Franz von Ehrle, SJ, discovered documents in papal archives from time of Gregory XI (1375) containing responses of Jacques Fournier (Benedict XII) on Eckhart, Durandus, Michael of Cesena, William of Ockham, and Peter John Olivi written between 1325 and 1330.[45] Similarly, *the votum* or theological opinion against Eckhart of the commission established by John XXII was found by Cardinal Giovanni Mercati (d. 1957), also Prefect of the Vatican Library, and was published by Franz Pelster, SJ, in 1935.[46] The following year, M.H. Laurent, OP, published a still more accurate version of the relevant documents from the Vatican archives concerning Eckhart's trials in Cologne and Avignon.

Textual scholarship had advanced sufficiently by the mid-thirties for two ambitious projects to be undertaken which proposed to publish all the authentic Latin and German works of Meister Eckhart. The interest of Nazi officials in Eckhart for propaganda purposes resulted in the eventual cessation of the Santa Sabina project begun in Rome by

Klibansky and Théry. Fortunately, the German project managed to survive Nazi interference and the Second World War under the editorial leadership of two remarkable scholars, Josef Quint and Josef Koch, OP. It is now virtually complete except for the concluding volume of indices.

East Meets West

The rediscovery of Meister Eckhart in the late nineteenth and early twentieth centuries also rendered his teaching accessible to comparative evaluation with Asian religious traditions and, in some cases, by eastern authorities themselves. One of the earliest efforts to understand Eckhart in light of the east was that by Rudolf Otto, who compared the Meister's doctrine with that of the monistic theism of Shankara.[47]

Not only has Eckhart's doctrine also been compared to Buddhist teachings, it has been studied by Buddhist scholars themselves, notably Shizuteru Ueda and Daisetz Suzuki. Ueda, for instance, comments with regard to the theme of the birth of the Word in the soul: '... Eckhart stands very close to Mahayana Buddhism, the philosophical base of Zen Buddhism. A more deep-reaching spiritual kinship appears when Eckhart speaks of a "breakthrough to the nothingness of the godhead".'[48] Suzuki devoted great energy to demonstrating the Zen-like character of much of Eckhart's doctrine, although his interpretation, like that of Ueda, must always be considered from the viewpoint of their own tradition rather than that of Christian belief, in regard to which they are understandably not so well versed as was, for instance, Otto.[49]

Among western scholars, Reiner Schürmann and John Caputo have also discussed the fascinating parallels between Eckhart's thought and Zen Buddhism.[50] Similarly, as we have already seen, Frederick Franck has compared Angelus Silesius' interpretation of Eckhart with classical Asian aphorisms, aptly illustrating the fundamental unity of human wisdom without violating its irreducible pluralism of expression in different cultures.

Eckhart was of course no more an Advaita Vedantist or Zen Master than he was a Lutheran, a Hegelian or a Volkisch proto-Nazi. Nevertheless, his spirituality remains comprehensible in the east as well as the west, not, I believe, because it is uncomplicated and superficially malleable, but because it is profoundly, sometimes indecipherably simple

– as all great spiritual teachings are. It can accordingly be usurped and misused, like the teachings of Jesus themselves. But Eckhart's vision not only survives the systems that attempt to appropriate his spirituality, it emerges from such encounters more itself in our eyes than it had seemed previously.

The Continuing Search for Meister Eckhart

Thus, although Eckhart's memory was not completely disfigured, much less obliterated, by the condemnation of 1329 and subsequent centuries of misunderstanding, he is more our contemporary today than he was to writers of the nineteenth and early twentieth centuries. For, thanks to their cumulative work, his spirituality and theological doctrine are not only more accessible than at any time since the fourteenth century, but more comprehensible to disciples of both the east and west, now themselves more attuned by decades of comparative studies to the subtle nuances of speculative mysticism and its practical implications. In this, the Meister has at last taken the rightful place long denied him by Christianity alongside many of the world's great masters and mistresses of the inner life.

Today, after 650 years of largely silent waiting, from Cologne and Strasbourg to Kyoto, the voice of the Master is being heard again in more than a dozen languages. Widely disparate thinkers from Martin Heidegger to Daisetz Suzuki have returned to the old Meister as a source of spiritual and intellectual inspiration. In many respects, despite the condemnation of 1329 and the cloud of forgetting that at first engulfed his memory, Eckhart's influence has grown rather than diminished over the centuries, being greater now than at any time in the past.

Perhaps we will learn more of him in the years to come. Thomas Kaeppeli's 'sensational' discovery in 1960 of 592 excerpts from his Latin writings serves to remind us that lost and forgotten works are not necessarily gone forever. Moreover, questions about the man and his doctrine linger to haunt us, even as we temporarily rest the case regarding the importance and meaning of his preaching: was he a mystic and was he a heretic?

NOTES

1. *Chronica et Chronicorum Excerpts*, ed. by Benedictus Maria Reichert, OP, MOPH, Vol. 7, Rome: 1904, pp. 19–22.

2. Cf. Sanford Brown Meech and Hope Emily Allen, *The Book of Margery Kempe*, Vol. I (Early English Text Society, No. 212), London: Oxford University Press, 1940, pp. 376–8.

3. Clark observes: 'The condemnation of Meister Eckhart had put an end to speculation. Henceforth, mysticism was confined to safer channels. It is not surprising that Tauler is practical in tendency.' *Great German Mystics*, p. 45.

4. Berthold largely continued the more scientific inquiries and philosophical speculations of Dietrich of Freiburg and Ulrich of Strassburg. Cf. Alain de Libera, op. cit., pp. 315–423 and Hinnebusch, II, pp. 156, 300.

5. Hinnebusch, II, p. 312.

6. Clark, *Great German* Mystics, p. 56.

7. Ibid.

8. Cited in Hinnebusch, II, p. 316.

9. The standard reference is Karl Bihlmeyer, *Heinrich Seuse, Deutsche Schriften*, Stuttgart: Kohlhammer, 1907, and Frankfurt, 1961. Cf. also Melchior Diepenbrock, *Heinrich Susos Leben und Schriften*, Ratisbon: Mainz, 1884, and the modern German translation of the *Exemplar* edition by Nikolas Heller, 1926. Heller's edition with its introduction and notes was translated by Sr M. Ann Edward, OP, *The Exemplar*, 2 vols., Dubuque, Iowa: The Priory Press, 1962. Cf. also James M. Clark, trans. and intro., *The Little Book of Eternal Wisdom* and *The Little Book of Truth*, London: Faber and Faber, 1953, and C.H. McKenna, OP, trans., *The Little Book of Eternal Wisdom*, London: Washbourne, 1910. The best and most complete English edition is *Henry Suso: The Exemplar with Two German Sermons*, trans., ed. and intro. by Frank Tobin, preface by Bernard McGinn, New York: Paulist Press, 1989.

10. For a detailed recent discussion of Suso's life and teaching, see Frank Tobin, trans., ed. and commentary, *The Exemplar*, ed. cit., pp. 1–51, and Bernard McGinn, *The Harvest of Mysticism*, pp. 195–239.

11. Cf. Clark, ed. cit., p. 29.

12. Hinnebusch, II, p. 318.

13. Cf. Clark, *Great German Mystics*, pp. 36–54, Hinnebusch, II, pp. 310–12 and Richard Kieckhefer, 'John Tauler', *An Introduction to the Medieval Mystics of Europe*, ed. cit., pp. 259–72, and Ancelet-Hustache, pp. 146–55. For a recent study of Tauler's life and teaching, see McGinn, *The Harvest of Mysticism*, pp. 240–96.

14. Hinnebusch erroneously lists his death as 6 June, op. cit., p. 311.

15. Although of biblical provenance and found in the writings of Clement of Alexandria, John Chrysostom and Thomas Aquinas, as well as in those of Mechthild of Magdeburg and Eckhart himself, the term became one of Tauler's characteristic expressions. The measure of his influence is seen in that 'From about 1340 onwards it becomes part of the ordinary vocabulary of the mystics'. Clark, *Great German Mystics*, p. 92.

16. A collection of twenty-three of Tauler's sermons has been translated by Maria Shrady, *Johannes Tauler Sermons*, New York: Paulist Press, 1987. The standard reference is Ferdinand Vetter, *Die Predigten Taulers* (Deutsche Texte des Mittelalters, 11) Berlin: 1910. Cf. also Georg Hofmann, trans., *Johannes Tauler: Predigten, Freiburg*, 1961 and Einsiedeln, 1979, and Louise Gnädinger, ed. and commentary, *Johannes Tauler: Gotteserfahrung und Weg in die Welt*, Olten und Frieburg-im-Breisgau: Walter Verlag, 1983. Other English translations: John Tauler, *Spiritual Conferences*, trans. and ed. by Eric Colledge and M. Jane Colledge, Rockford, Ill.: TAN Books, 1979, and *Signposts to Perfection: A Selection from the Sermons of Johann Tauler*, ed. and trans. by Elizabeth Strakosch, St Louis and London, 1958. A short excerpt can be found in *The Varieties of Mystic Experience*, ed. by Elmer O'Brien, SJ, New York: New American Library, 1965, pp. 139–42.

17. For Eckhart references, see Vetter, ed. cit., sermon nos. 15 and 64 (Hofmann, nos. 15a and 33).

18. Clark, *Great German Mystics*, p. 39. On Tauler and Ruysbroeck, cf. ibid.

19. Cf. ibid., pp. 48f. For a critical appraisal see Steven Ozment, *Homo spiritualis: A Comparative Study of the Anthropology of J. Tauler, J. Gerson and M. Luther (1509–16) in the Context of their Theological Thought*, Leiden: Studies in Medieval and Reformation Thought, Vol. 6, 1969, and 'Eckhart and Luther: German Mysticism and Protestantism', *The Thomist*, 42 (1978), pp. 259–80.

20. See Clark, ibid., pp. 50–2.

21. Cf. Ancelet-Hustache, pp. 17–18. For a thorough discussion of the spirituality of the Dominican nuns there, see Leonard Hindsley, *The Mystics of Engelthal: Writings from a Medieval Monastery*, New York: St Martin's Press, 1998. Cf. also *The True Prayers of St Gertrude and St Mechtilde*, Canon John Gray, trans., New York: Sheed and Ward, 1936.

22. Jones, op. cit., p. 160. Cf. Hinnebusch, I, pp. 311f., 321. The text of her writings has been edited by G. W.K. Lochner, *Leben und Geschichte der Christina Ebnerin, Klosterfrau zu Engelthal*, Nurnberg, 1872.

23. Cf. Sacra Congregatio pro Causes Sanctorum, *Decretum Augustan Vindelicorum seu Ordinis Praedicatorum Confirmationis Cultis ab Immemorabili Tempore Praestiti Servae Dei Margaritae Ebner, Moniali professae Ordinis S Dominici 'Beatae' Nuncupatae*, Rome, 24 February 1979. Her *Revelations* were edited by Strauch in 1882. See Leonard Hindsley, OP, ed. and trans., *Margaret Ebner: Major Works*, intro. by Leonard Hindsley, OP, and Margot Schmidt, New York: Paulist Press, 1993. Cf. also H. Wilms, OP, *Der seligen Margareta Ebner Offenbarungen und Breife. Übertragen und eingeleitet*, Vechta in Oldenburg, 1928, and Hinnebusch, II, pp. 311f., 320.

24. Jones, op. cit., p. 171. The eminent Quaker scholar was not always so generous in his estimation. Of Adelheid Langmann (d. 1375) he found 'very little of importance to tell', considering her a 'seriously distraught person', 'plainly pathological' and 'hysterical ...' Jones, op. cit., pp. 168–9. Cf. Hinnebusch, II, pp. 313–315, 321. Cf. also Jeanne Ancelet-Hustache, *La vie mystique d'un monastère de Dominicaines au moyen âge desprès la chronique de Töss*, Paris, 1928; Ferdinand Vetter, ed., *Das Leben*

des Schwestern zu Töss beschrieben von Elsbet Stagel samt der Vorrede von Johannes Meier und dem Leben der Prinzessin Elisabet von Ungarn, Deutsche Texte des Mittelalters, Vol. VI, Berlin: Weidmann, 1906, and Hieronymus Wilms, OP, *Das Beten der Mystikerinnen dargestellt nach den Chroniken der Dominikanerinnenklöstere zu Adelhausen, Diessenhoffen, Engeltal, Kirchberg, Oetenbach*, Töss und Unterlinden, revised ed. (Quellen und Forschungen, Vol. II) Freiburg im Breisgau, 1932. Jones, op. cit., pp. 168–9. Cf. Hinnebusch, II, p. 321.

25. 'At Freiburg in Breisgau the biographies of no less than thirty-six nuns were written about 1318. At Engeltal Christina Ebnerin recorded information about the lives of fifty inmates of her convent. Elsbet Stagel narrates the lives of thirty sisters at Töss.' (Clark, *Great German Mystics*, op. cit., p. 106.) In addition, 'the Chronicle of Ötenbach relates in great detail the lives of three sisters and deals more briefly with four others. The Chronicle of Weiler has twenty-seven life histories, the Adelhausen Chronicle thirty-four, the Töss Chronicle forty; the Engeltal and St Katharinental texts each have fifty-four.' (Hester Reed Gehring, *The Language of Mysticism in the South German Dominican Convent Chronicles of the Fourteenth Century*, Ph.D. Dissertation, University of Michigan, 1957, Ann Arbor: University Microfilms, 1984, p. 15.) Hundreds more are to be found in other chronicles, most of which exist in German editions but have not been translated into English. See Leonard Hindsley, *The Mystics of Engelthal*, op. cit. For excerpts from the Latin chronicles of the sisters of Unterlinden, see Tugwell, op. cit., pp. 417–24.

26. See Valerie Lagorio, 'The Medieval Continental Women Mystics: An Introduction', *An Introduction to the Medieval Mystics of Europe*, ed. cit., p. 172.

27. Gehring, op. cit., p. 192.

28. Felix Vernet, 'The Dominicans', *Mediaeval Spirituality*, trans. by the Benedictines of Talacre, St Louis, MO: B. Herder Book Co., 1930, p. 61.

29. Cf. Rufus Jones, op. cit., pp. 158–75, especially pp. 163–9 where he cites 'a large factor of hysteria and abnormality in evidence ... a trail of superstition and of self-torture ...'. On Adelheid Langmann, see above, p. 174, n. 24. Cf. also Anna Groh Seeholtz, *Friends of God: Practical Mystics of the Fourteenth Century*, New York: Columbia University Press, 1934, pp. 123–6, where she speaks of the sisters as 'hysterical,' 'pathological,' 'repressed' and 'uninspired'. Zoepf and other critics were sometimes even less reserved.

30. Gehring, op. cit., pp. 210ff.

31. Clark, *Great German Mystics*, p. 92.

32. See Thomas S. Kepler, ed. and interp., *Mystical Writings of Rulman Merswin*, Philadelphia: Westminster Press, 1960, p. 16. For a recent and very thorough commentary, see Bernard McGinn, *The Harvest of Mysticism in Medieval Germany (1300–1500)*, New York: Crossroad Publishing Co., 2005, pp. 414–31. Cf. also Ancelet-Hustache, pp. 142–4, Clark, *Great German Mystics*, pp. 91–6, Hinnebusch, II, pp. 320–1 and Jones, op. cit., pp. 104–38.

33. Cf. Clark, ibid., pp. 84–6. But also see Kepler, ed. cit., pp. 23–6.

34. See Clark, ibid., and above, pp. 151ff.

35. See especially McGinn, *Harvest of Mysticism*, op. cit., pp. 432–83. Cf. also Clark, *Great German Mystics*, p. 24, McGinn, 'Introduction', pp. 255, n. 85, Ancelet-Hustache, pp. 167–70, and the collection of essays by Koch, KS, I, pp. 457–623. Cf. also Herbert Wackerzapp, *De Einfluss Meister Eckharts auf die ersten philosophischen Schriften des Nikolaus von Kues*, Munster: Aschendorff, 1962.
36. Cf. Ozment, 'Eckhart and Luther', art. cit., and *Homo spiritualis*, op. cit., passim.
37. Cf. Ozment, art. cit., pp. 272ff. Cf. also Henry L. Finch, 'A Note on Two Traditions in Western Mysticism: Meister Eckhart and Jacob Boehme', *Centerpoint*, 3 (No. 1, 1978), pp. 41–50.
38. The standard reference is the critical edition by J. Schwabe, Basel, 1955. Works: H.L. Held, ed., 3 vols. Munich: 1921, 1924; cf. also the edition of G. Ellinger, 2 vols., Berlin: 1924. English translations: Angelus Silesius, *The Cherubic Wanderer*, trans. by Maria Shrady, New York: Paulist Press, 1986; Angelus Silesius (Johannes Scheffler), *Cherubic Wanderer* (selections), tr. and intro. by J.E. Flitch, CT: Hyperion (Library of World Literature Series), 1978 (1932). A recent translation of selections from the poem has been charmingly rendered in calligraphic form together with appropriate Zen sayings by Frederick Franck, trans. and ed., *The Book of Angelus Silesius with Observations by the Ancient Zen Masters*, New York: Alfred A. Knopf, 1976. One of the many merits of Reiner Schürmann's penetrating commentary on eight of Eckhart's sermons is his frequent citation of Scheffler's poetic version of the Meister's teaching. The French subtitle of Schürmann's book, *La joie errante*, cleverly captures the mood of the poetic form as it also reflects Scheffler's title. And, like Franck, Schürmann draws striking comparisons to Zen Buddhist teachings, not, however, with regard to the poems of Angelus Silesius, but to Eckhart's doctrine itself. See below, pp. 201f.
39. Ibid., p. 42.
40. Cf. Clark, pp. 26–8, Maurer, p. 7 and Schürmann, p. 245, n. 111.
41. Franz Pfeiffer, *Deutsche Mystiker des 14. Jahrhunderts*, II: Meister Eckhart, Leipzig, 1857 (repr. by Aalen, 1962). Translation by Evans, ed. cit. Cf. also: Franz Pfeiffer, ed., *Meister Eckhart*, 2 vols., Gordon Press, 1977. The history of Eckhart scholarship has itself been investigated critically by Ingeborg Degenhart, cf. C-McG, p. 312, n. 1.
42. See M.D. Knowles, 'Denifle and Ehrle', *History*, 54 (1969), pp. 1–12. For a brief account of the work of Denifle as well as Schmidt, Jundt, Preger, Strauch, Spamer, Jostes and Pahncke, see Clark, *Great German Mystics*, pp. 27–35 and C-McG, p. 312, n. 3.
43. Cf. Clark, *Great German Mystics*, pp. 34–5. Cf. also Ancelet-Hustache, pp. 172–3 and esp. pp. 177–8.
44. See the bibliography for references. A brief survey of this period of Eckhart scholarship can be found in Clark, *Great German Mystics*, pp. 31–5 and C-McG, pp. 62–4.
45. *De statu animarum sanctorum ante generale judicium, Decem questiones in Durandum*, Cod. Vat. lat. 4006. Cf. Koch, KS, II, pp. 368, 373 and Colledge, art. cit., pp. 246–7.

46. See bibliography. Cf. Koch, KS, I, p. 312 and McGinn, 'Eckhart's Condemnation Reconsidered', p. 397, n. 34.

47. Rudolf Otto, *Mysticism East and West*, translated by Bertha Bracey and Richenda Payne, New York: The Macmillan Co. 1960 (1933), pp. 183–282. Cf. also C-McG, pp. 49, 208.

48. Ueda, 'Nothingness', art. cit., p. 158. Cf. *Die Gottesgeburt*, pp. 99–139.

49. See D.T. Suzuki, 'Meister Eckhart and Buddhism', in *Mysticism Christian and Buddhist*, New York: Harper and Row, 1971, pp. 3–38 and passim. For a more recent evaluation, see Brian J. Pierce, OP, *WeWalk the Path Together: Learning from Thich Nhat Hanh and Meister Eckhart*, New York: Orbis Books, 2007.

50. Cf. Schürmann, op. cit., appendix, 'Meister Eckhart and Zen Buddhism', pp. 221–6, nn. 40–1, p. 250 and passim, and 'The Loss of Origin in Soto Zen and Meister Eckhart', *The Thomist*, 42 (April, 1978), pp. 281–312, and Caputo, 'Heidegger, Eckhart and Zen Buddhism', op. cit., pp. 203–17.

TIME'S VERDICT

Odd as it might seem to anyone with some acquaintance with the history of Christian spirituality, even recent opinion has been sharply divided about whether Eckhart, one of the fountainheads of fourteenth century mysticism, was himself a mystic. C.F. Kelley claimed, for instance, that Eckhart was a metaphysician and preacher using mystical themes for didactic and homiletic purposes: 'If detached intellection or pure metaphysics, in terms of which Eckhart expounds the doctrine of Divine Knowledge, is not to be confounded with ontology, neither is it to be identified with any contingent form of mysticism.'[1]

Needless to say, Eckhart has found many to champion the cause of his own mystical character. The resulting dispute between those who affirm and those who deny that Eckhart was a mystic, while academic to a great degree, is not pointless. For since it is experience – although reformed or transformed experience – to which Eckhart directs his hearers' attention and efforts, the authenticity of his teaching and preaching hangs in large measure upon the outcome. Was Eckhart merely a finger pointing directions or was he a scout returned to lead others along ways he had explored himself? Had Eckhart experienced directly, at first hand, the truth of the message he preached?

Unfortunately, scant information exists about Eckhart's own 'inner life' on which to base a conclusion. The more we seem to learn of the Meister's doctrine, the less we know about the person and his own experience. And, as might be expected, Eckhart never used the word 'mystic' to describe himself or, to my knowledge, anyone else. As far as I can tell, he never used it at all.

Such reticence has provided past support for those who doubt or deny that Eckhart was in fact a mystic. Gustave Théry, for instance, one of the Meister's Dominican commentators earlier in this century, inclined towards that position.[2] More recently, Maurice O'C. Walshe, the most recent major translator of Eckhart's German works as well as a student of German mysticism, noted that 'It might have seemed unnecessary to have to state categorically that Eckhart is a mystic – indeed one of the greatest of Christian mystics. But in 1960 Heribert Fischer[3] claimed that this designation was the invention of literary scholars, and Fischer's view is echoed by John Margetts in *Die Satzstruktur bei Meister Eckhart*.[4][5] A similar position was espoused by Kurt Flasch.[6]

Every argument from silence is precarious. With respect to the mystics, it is even more so, for the very word comes from the Greek root *múein*, which means 'to be silent'. And, overall, scholarly consensus as well as the long tradition of western mysticism affirms that Eckhart was himself in truth a mystic. Walshe observes, for instance, that a 'crushing rejoinder' to Fischer's contention 'was given by the greatest of all Eckhart specialists, Josef Quint.'[7][8] In addition to Quint, and it is surely safe to add Koch, Eckhart has been deemed a mystic by a host of modern scholars including Jeanne Ancelet-Hustache, James M. Clark, Edmund Colledge, Alain de Libera, Richard Kieckhefer,[9] Bernard McGinn, Dietmar Mieth, Rudolf Otto,[10] Reiner Schürmann and others.

It is hardly conceivable that Eckhart, however brilliant a philosopher or persuasive a preacher, would have spellbound so many of the bonafide mystics of his own time (including Suso, Tauler, Margareta Ebner and Elsbet Stagel), much less those of the intervening centuries, had he not known from the immediacy of his own experience the truth of his teaching.

But if the Meister was truly a mystic, one who had come to an experimental knowledge of God, we know virtually nothing about that experience. For, like many mystics, the Meister hardly grants us so much as a glancing peek at his inner life. Walshe maintains, however, that one such glimpse may be found in an indirect allusion, something like St Paul's oblique self-reference in 2 Cor 12:2ff: 'It appeared to a man as in a dream it was a waking dream that he became pregnant with Nothing like a woman with child, and in that Nothing God was born, He was the fruit of Nothing. God was born in the Nothing.'[11] Walshe comments: 'in view of Eckhart's frequent references to the birth of the Son in the soul, we may well assume that he is here telling us of a personal experience.'[12]

Whether or not this was a personal reminiscence, as I am inclined to think it was, Eckhart certainly taught, as we have seen, that the birth of the Word in the Soul was ingredient within personal experience, the moment of perceived revelation in the spirit which flowers eventually into ever more conscious union with God. Whether Eckhart lived to savour the full florescence of that experience in his mortal life we cannot know. Again, however, the authority with which he describes it, especially in terms of contemplative union with God in ordinary life experience rather than ecstasy and rapture, strongly suggests that he knew from personal experience what he was talking about.

Ecstasy and Contemplative Action

Even so, as we have also seen, Eckhart's teaching on union with God is not easy to understand nor to summarise, not least because his statements on the subject seem to surface without regard to systematic organisation in a great many of his sermons and treatises. Not surprisingly, in this regard opinion has also been mixed. In a perceptive essay, Richard Kieckhefer therefore examined Eckhart's teaching on mystical experience to determine whether, as some commentators have held, the Meister promoted an ideal of ecstatic union with God incompatible with ordinary life events or, as others claim, he encouraged his listeners to cultivate a habitual awareness of God continuous and compatible with ordinary experience in the world.[13] He concluded that although Eckhart occasionally referred to ecstatic states, usually in an academic rather than hortatory fashion, he was not much interested in discussing them. Further, 'Eckhart did not view ecstasy or abstractive union with God as integral to the life of the soul, or even as a goal to be sought or particularly treasured'.[14] More positively expressed, Eckhart urged his disciples to cultivate a mystical spirituality that expressed itself actively in the world as Reiner Schürmann, Friedrich-Wilhelm Wentzlaff-Eggebert and Dietmar Mieth have argued against Hermann Kunisch and James Clark.[15]

It was as clear for Eckhart as for the greater tradition of Christian mystical spirituality that 'God is present within the human soul and within creation generally, and that the moral task incumbent upon human beings is to heighten their awareness of God's indwelling so that they may better manifest it in their lives'.[16] Indeed, as Mieth would have it, 'Eckhart sees the contemplative life as imperfect and immature until it has blossomed forth in activity'.[17] But, in arguing (correctly, I believe) that Eckhart's authentic teaching stressed non-abstractive contemplative union with God compatible with ordinary life activities, has Kieckhefer thereby undercut the experiential aspect of the birth of the Word and the progressive 'breakthroughs' back into Godhead?

It can be argued, for instance, that one does not have an experience of the 'spark of the soul' or even of *Gelassenheit* or *Abgescheidenheit*. These are structures of the spiritual life and forms of activity as well as structural elements of Eckhart's doctrine. As abstract concepts and inferred categories, they are not experiences. But one does know tranquility of soul; one feels anger; one strives and wills; and even, it may be argued, one experiences the presence of God. But how does one experience the birth of the Word in the soul? Or is that phrase Eckhart's way of explaining (or, rather, describing) in poetic form a profound but subliminal transformation of spirit which manifests itself in certain activities?

Is it thus true, as Kieckhefer suggests, that one cannot experience that birth in oneself at all, but can only detect it inferentially in others?[18] Is the birth of the Word in the soul a spiritual renewal like baptism or the eucharist, concealed within the mystery of word and matter? Similarly, does one experience 'breakthrough into God' (or the Godhead) in any sense that can be meaningfully described or can it, too, only be inferred and alluded to? Is 'breakthrough' merely a general if characteristic way of pointing to the ultimate transformation of the human spirit beyond human consciousness?

It seems to me from the very exuberance of his language that for Eckhart the birth of the Word and, *a fortiori*, the consequent 'breakthroughs' into God constitute a recognisable shift in consciousness, a concrete mystical experience.[19] (Ueda and others have compared the former to Zen satori, a form of enlightenment.) Such a shift in attention from the objects of experience to the Field which grounds them and in whose light they stand revealed need not abstract one from ordinary life, of course, nor need it be relegated to the realm of inference or reasoned interpretation. Interpretation is ingredient in every experience, as the American philosophers William Hocking, John Dewey, John E. Smith and others have argued. However, experience and interpretation are not by that congruence identical nor indistinguishable in their moment nor synonymous in their meaning.

Thus, while accurate and convincing in most respects, especially regarding Eckhart's insistence on the priority of contemplation in action, I believe that Kieckhefer fails to distinguish adequately between Eckhart's speculative teaching about the nature and character of the soul, of God, of the structures of existence and the world which are either presupposed by or consequent to the experience of God's presence, and his pragmatic description of that experience. He fails, that is, to discern the difference as well as the similarity between Eckhart the indicative theologian and Eckhart the mystic, the imperative preacher and the spiritual guide. As a result, he too easily identifies the experiences of the birth of the Word in the soul, re-birth into God, and final Breakthrough into the Godhead with the reflexive interpretation or re-interpretation of those experiences. He mistakes the map for the journey.

Similarly, Eckhart's insistent emphasis on the 'Godhead' beyond the 'God' of Persons, the 'silent darkness into which no distinction or image ever peeped', the 'trackless wasteland, the hidden desert', does not, I think, point in the direction of essential tension or polarisation in his doctrine between the Trinity and Unity of God. Rather, Eckhart's doctrine concerns the experience of union with God in oneness of being beyond all distinctions of Persons and certainly beyond all theological analysis.

It also reminds us with uncommon and needed force that the doctrine of the Trinity remains a mystery, not an explanation (as if one were possible), nor even a description (as if one could be adequate). It thus preserves the mystery of divine unicity against tritheism, perhaps the most common of all popular Christian theological illusions. Similarly, it avoids simple unitarianism, which dissolves the richness of God into the rigid monarchical homogeneity of absolute idealism – even without the philosophical underpinning. But Eckhart's teaching does not aim primarily or only at conceptual precision or elucidation. His interest as a preacher and spiritual guide lay, rather, in the mystery of union between God and the human spirit. Such a mystical bond, while transcending all efforts to fathom or describe it, was for Eckhart not only a possibility, but the supreme goal and real objective of all human existence and, it may be added, all theology.

In one form, he tells us, such spiritual union lies proleptically within the orbit of everyday human experience. The other opens out beyond life (and death) to an infinite realm of blessedness, joy and peace. It fell to Eckhart to attempt and in great measure to succeed in delineating a way leading to both the provisional and the fully realised union – a way of selflessness beyond self-abnegation, a way of service beyond activism, a way of deliverance beyond freedom. To the extent he failed, and every mystic eventually fails, Eckhart's cartography does not so much disappoint us, much less mislead us. Rather, like a Zen master, he challenges us to transcend the limitations of all such human efforts to describe the indescribable, 'to eff the ineffable', not by devising new terms and categories and far less by rigorously defending those of the past, but by inviting us to live the mystery to which he points.

For Eckhart, as for every Christian mystic, all human persons at all times are directly and immediately experiencing the presence of God – whether they recognise it or not. The birth of the Word in the soul therefore means, among other things, at least this: becoming focally aware of God's presence, not as any 'thing', but as 'no-thing', the ground of our existence, the field of all experience itself. Further, it means that this underlying and overarching 'Field of all Fields' (in Hocking's pregnant phrase) is a living presence – not merely the One, but Someone.

Was Eckhart a Heretic?

Much has been written in the previous pages about Eckhart's fundamental orthodoxy – too much, it might seem at this point. Yet to understand Eckhart fully, one must understand him truthfully as well as wonderfully. Orthodoxy is not a fetish or a badge of merit. It is a quality of teaching and belief subject to judgement by the people of God, the recognition of fidelity. Eckhart was by no means infallible and he expressed ready willingness to retract any statement that could be shown to be in error. He did in fact err and admitted it freely at Cologne.[20] But he did not err with respect to his commitment to the faith of the Church as a whole. Further, according to a growing consensus of scholars, he was particularly innocent of heresy regarding the fifteen articles taken out of context from his writings and sermons.

If anywhere, Eckhart's heterodoxy lay in being creative in an era in which theological creativity had become suspect, in being a preacher of daring expression in an age in which strange doctrines could be heard on any street corner, in being unafraid to expose and espouse the elements of truth and wisdom to be found even in strange doctrines as well as those of the Beguines which were not so much strange as they were threatening to the clerical and noble estates.

To the narrow mind of Archbishop Henry of Virneburg, Eckhart must have appeared demonic. To the inquisitorial mind of Jacques Fournier and the papal commission at Avignon, he in fact seemed mad. But to those who knew him well, his brethren and sisters at Cologne and throughout Germany, and in particular his provincial, Henry of Cigno, the papal visitator, Nicholas of Strassburg, and young Henry Suso, Eckhart remained 'the Meister'.

The verdict against fifteen of Eckhart's propositions and two others associated with his teaching seems to have gone officially unchallenged until recent times, although, as we have seen, there is bountiful evidence that his memory and teachings were preserved not only by Suso, Tauler, the sisters, and Nicholas of Cusa, but by his Dominican brethren in Cologne who had transcribed almost six hundred excerpts from his Latin writings.[21] Critical but conservative scholars such as the Dominicans Denifle and Koch suggest that Eckhart was more incautious in his expression than heretical, although Denifle was wont to think the worst at times. More recently, John Loeschen has concluded from the perspective of process thought that Eckhart was driven by the force of his own logic to a heretical position like that ascribed to Gilbert of Poitiers involving a fundamental difference between the divine essence (Godhead) and the divine persons.[22]

While Loeschen appears to second Eckhart's alleged doctrinal heterodoxy for his own purposes, non-Christian authors seem to affirm Eckhart's 'heresies' without much concern. For instance, the Japanese Zen scholar Daisetz Suzuki, while conceding that Eckhart was 'an extraordinary "Christian"', considers that 'his God is not at all like the God conceived by most Christians'.[23] Among Eckhart's 'heresies', he mentions in particular 'his pantheistic tendency'.[24] Similarly, Shizuteru Ueda concludes that Eckhart's doctrine of the birth of the Word in the soul departs considerably from orthodox Christian doctrine.

Christian theologians, however, have on the basis of a far deeper penetration of Eckhart's sources come to the contrary conclusion. The great Jesuit scholar, Hugo Rahner, was one of the first to propose after a meticulous study of Eckhart's writings and his sources that the Meister was not only a loyal and Catholic Christian, but unexceptionally orthodox in his teaching when it was viewed as a whole.[25] Similarly, Karl G. Kertz, SJ, after subjecting Eckhart's doctrine of the birth of God in the Soul to painstaking scrutiny, concluded that his treatment was 'perfectly sound Catholic doctrine'.[26]

Bernard McGinn has also analysed in considerable detail both the charges against Eckhart and his responses.[27] After sifting through the distinctions and counter-distinctions, he concludes that while many of the condemned propositions seem to conflict with traditional Church teaching when taken out of context, they, like the eleven articles deplored but not condemned in the bull, can also be interpreted in a fundamentally orthodox sense.[28] McGinn also argues that in fact the eleven 'deplorable' propositions are no less (or more) heretical than the other seventeen articles. And in the case of propositions 26 and 28, he observes, one is condemned, the other deplored, even though both are traditional statements of Christian 'negative' theology.[29] Such proved inconsistency can only strengthen the case for an ecclesiastical re-airing of the whole process, such as that proposed by the Dominican General Chapters of Walberberg, Avila and Mexico City in 1980, 1986 and 1992.

If McGinn leaves the door of orthodoxy cautiously open for Eckhart, other scholars have been far more willing to concede the Meister's innocence. Jeanne Ancelet-Hustache has argued strenuously for his basic consonance with the Faith.[30] From a strictly historical perspective, M.D. Knowles observes almost in passing that 'There is still room for debate as to whether Eckhart was a mystic using scholastic terminology, or a theologian adopting a Neoplatonist outlook, but of his radical traditionalism and orthodoxy there is no longer any doubt'.[31]

While not concerned to show that Eckhart was fundamentally orthodox in his teaching, Reiner Schürmann incidentally suggests as much by showing that the objections of his prosecutors missed the point of the Meister's teaching, which is deeply rooted in the mystical theology of the eastern Church.[32] Schürmann similarly corrects Suzuki's claim that Eckhart was a pantheist and related misprisions of the Zen master.[33]

While Edmund Colledge acknowledges Eckhart's orthodoxy, he also cites with approval the caution of Cardinal Nicholas of Cusa, who believed it prudent to 'keep his writings out of the hands of the uninstructed, who will not understand what he teaches, so wholly different from what they are accustomed to'.[34] Of course, the lack of fundamental instruction in spiritual development was in itself a large part of the problem of medieval Catholicism, just as it is today. Restricting the books and sermons of Meister Eckhart to the dusty shelves of theological libraries will not solve that problem today, however, any more than did relegating his works to the flames six hundred years ago. Eckhart is not for beginners, but then, neither is *The Cloud of Unknowing* nor the works of St Teresa of Avila.

But, as I have suggested earlier, Eckhart's propositions were condemned not so much because they were heretical, nor because of petty or serious antagonism between Dominican and Franciscan theoreticians, nor because of their conflicting allegiances to pope and emperor, nor even because of ineptitude on the part of his inquisitors – several of them keen enough scholars and masters of theology such as Jacques Fournier. Nor do I think it was because Eckhart botched his own defence, as Josef Koch at times implies.[35] If anything, as Kertz has shown, Eckhart handled the defence well, perhaps even brilliantly on occasion.

More even than the combination of these factors – all of which were entailed to some extent in the circumstances of the case – the crucial factor involved in bringing the calamitous farce to its bitter end was a missing of minds. Eckhart may have understood his interrogators better than they understood him – and they surely failed to understand him, not merely his scholarly analysis, his evangelical zeal, loyalty to the Church, or apostolic intentions. It was the poetry they could not appreciate, the daring excesses of speech and flights of imagination by which the great scholar transcended the arid limitations of the learned disquisition and dispute, seeking to move his listeners by the art of preaching.[36] For Eckhart was an artist and they – it is not less than fair if anachronistic to say – were bureaucrats.[37]

Even then, even after his bureaucratically convenient death, Eckhart's reputation might have been saved by the intervention of the pope. Unfortunately John XXII was neither immune to the imperatives of institutional necessity nor capable of sufficient theological or spiritual discernment to perceive the true significance of Eckhart's doctrine. And thus, whether mitigated by his own hand (which is unlikely) or that of Cardinal William Peter of Godin, the bull went forth.

Eckhart's Revolution

It has been proposed in recent years by various writers that Eckhart was a social revolutionary, a sort of pre-Marxist spokesman for the poor, oppressed and alienated masses of medieval Europe.[38] He has even been characterised as leading the attack on the authority of the Church, state and the feudal system.[39]

To be sure, the late Middle Ages were rife with antinomian, anticlerical and populist views. The Brethren of the Free Spirit and Beghards roamed the continent; the Poor Men of Lyon, Fraticelli and Spiritual Franciscans preached absolute poverty in the face of ecclesiastical pomp and luxury; peasant revolts such as that of the Pastoreaux ensanguinated the soil of France, Germany and, later, England. It is likewise true that Eckhart was a champion of evangelical poverty. One of his most trenchant remarks comes at the end of a difficult sermon: 'I say humanity is as perfect in the poorest and most wretched as in pope or emperor, for I hold humanity more dear in itself than the man I carry about with me.'[40]

But, as McGinn has argued,[41] Eckhart says practically nothing about the social or political situation of his time. He appears to have accepted the feudal system without qualm, even using it as an example of the divinely-willed hierarchical order of the cosmos. His harshest detractors never accused him of fomenting insurrection or even mouthing social criticism. No peasant rebellion or urban uprising ever dogged his steps. If Eckhart were in fact a social incendiary, he must have been dismally inept at it.

It seems far more evident that Eckhart remained unflinchingly loyal to the Church and submissive to legitimate state authority in every period of his life, not least in his submission to the inquisitions of Archbishop Henry of Virneburg and the papal commission, even despite his objections to their competence and motives, especially in Cologne. Eckhart was no toady, however. He is, rather, a supreme example of tragic fidelity to a judicial system unworthy of his loyalty – a brilliant scholar, able administrator and eloquent preacher who chose to work for spiritual reform from within an institution whose shortcomings and iniquities were plain for all to see. Eckhart simply saw past the human failings of the Church he loved to the Mystery within and beyond it. Nevertheless, in matters of right and truth, he remained staunchly unyielding in the face of ecclesiastical condemnation and political might.

Eckhart's preemption of the language and themes of the radical anarchists and spiritual rebels of the time, far from fueling opposition to the Church, forcefully and, I think, purposefully illustrated that such views were not only compatible with orthodox Christianity, but formed its abiding social message. Thus, Eckhart was a revolutionary figure in the most radical sense. He lived and worked within the complex, even disintegrating medieval edifice quite unmoved by its passion and power. He went his way, the way of the preacher, unaffected by partisan politics of whatever stripe. In so doing, he relativised all pretensions to absolute authority by both papal and imperial powers. He refused to side with peasant or potentate, concerned solely with the spiritual welfare of those who listened to his word, his students, his brethren and his beloved sisters.

In matters of truth, he stood ready to correct even his brother Thomas despite cautions against it by the Dominican order. Even so, his confreres with the exception of the renegades who witnessed falsely against him in Cologne never found cause to fault him, but rather entrusted him with even more responsible positions as teacher and administrator. Toward the end, he had been placed over the intellectual and spiritual formation of the young friars of his province as regent of the *studium generale* in Cologne. And to the end, he enjoyed the confidence and support of his provincial and brethren, several of whom accompanied him to Avignon. It is hardly surprising that after his death, when Eckhart's memory lay under the shadow of heresy, his former students Suso and Tauler endured censure and persecution out of loyalty to such a man and to the truth they had found in their Meister.

It is in this respect that Eckhart finds a place among the greatest revolutionaries of history, many of them true martyrs of conscience to the truth they served – Socrates, Jesus, Al Hallaj, Joan of Arc, Girolamo Savonarola, Thomas More, and in our own time, Pierre Teilhard de Chardin, Yves Congar, Mohandas Gandhi and Martin

Luther King, Jr, among them. Like the great eagle of German myth, Eckhart's spirit soars above all attempts to ensnare it for ideological purposes, whether those of Marxists today or those of Fascists, Hegelians, or Romantics of another time. His abiding and universal appeal lies in his transcendence of all such systems, his imperative pursuit of the properly human quest for freedom and ultimate integrity. For in the last account only three things mattered for Eckhart: the one God, the solidarity of humankind in Christ, and the world of creation that both distinguished and united them. All the rest was only commentary.

Conclusion
What does Eckhart say to us today?

Our times are as turbulent, perhaps more so, than his. Our sense of anguish as we face the potential horror of nuclear war, our feelings of outrage, compassion and helplessness as we watch the inexorable progression of famine and disease across the map of Africa or the brutalisation of small nations by the great powers of the earth are not different in kind from those remote ancestors of ours who lived in the midst of the Black Death, the incessant warfare between pope and emperor, France and England, serf and aristocrat, as well as famine, social disruption and religious persecution. The great hunger for ultimate meaning and eternal value in life in the fourteenth century is not incomprehensible to us in the twentieth. God is no less a mystery today than then, nor the presence of God less a desire of our prayer and common life as Christians or just human beings in search of truth and freedom, love, justice and peace.

We hear the Meister's voice today still preaching in accents comprehensible of homecoming, of the flow of love and creative energy from God, of the awakening deep within us of something uncreated dwelling in our souls – a seed, a spark, an unnameable Presence that wells up into the realisation of the wholeness of experience, the blessedness and warmth of personal solicitude and love. The call to healthy discipline in the inner world of the spirit, the invitation to let go of our petty concern with self, our clinging to others, our infantile grasping at images of God – these are not stale or hackneyed slogans of conventional piety or trendy whims of pop religiosity.

Eckhart calls us freshly to transformation, to a rebirth into God-centred contemplation of the world's weals and woes, to a greater, freer commitment to social justice, inclusive love and effective action. Eckhart does not call us back, but ahead, to a new humanity, renovated in the image and likeness of the living Word of God, the cosmic Christ, Lord of the Universe, child of woman.

In the end, Eckhart's way is the ordinary way – human, unspectacular, healthy because whole, divinely simple, an easy burden, a light yoke. His message is one of liberation, of the art of freeing ourselves and all creatures from the limitations of space, time and matter. More primordial than history, transcending death and sin, it is the gospel of Jesus interpreted and fulfilled by a man profoundly attuned to his own times and because of that in tune with our times, all times and all seasons.

NOTES

1. C.F. Kelley, *Meister Eckhart on Divine Knowledge*, New Haven, CT: Yale University Press, 1977, p. 107. Cf. also 108, n. 58: 'When God himself is acknowledged as the all-inclusive Principle there is nothing that can principially be affirmed as mystical.' Here, I believe, Kelley profoundly misunderstands not only Eckhart but mysticism as well. Kelley's important and influential work was republished in 2009 by Dharma Café Books, distributed by Random House (New York), with a foreword by William Stranger.

2. Cf. Lossky, op. cit., pp. 27 and especially 38, n. 76.

3. In 'Grundgedanken der deutschen Predigten', *Meister Eckhart der Prediger*, ed. U.M. Nix and R. Öchslin, Freiburg: Herder, 1960.

4. Stuttgart: Kohlhammer, 1969, p. 167.

5. Walshe, ed. cit., I, pp. xxxix. Cf. also H. Fischer, 'Zur Frage nach der Mystik in den Werken Meister Eckharts', *La Mystique Rhénane*, ed. cit., pp. 109–32.

6. Cf. 'Die Intention Meister Eckharts', *Sprache und Begriff. Festschrift für Bruno Liebrichs*, Meisenheim am Glan: Verlag Anton Hann, 1974.

7. 'Textverständnis und Textkritik in der Meister-Eckhart-Forschung', *Festschrift für Fritz Tschirch*, 1972, pp. 170–86. Cf. also Alois Haas, 'Das Verhältnis von Sprache und Erfahrung in der deutsche Mystik', *Deutsche Literatur des Späaten Mittelalters*, ed. W. Harms and L.P. Johnson, 1975, pp. 240–64.

8. Walshe, op. cit., I, pp. xxxix–xl.

9. Richard Kieckhefer, 'Meister Eckhart's Conception of Union with God', *Harvard Theological Review*, 71 (1978), p. 203.

10. Op. cit., p. 274.

11. W 19, pp. 157–8 (DW 71). It should not be overlooked that in this passage Eckhart is commenting on St Paul's vision in Acts 9:8.

12. Walshe, I, p. xxxii.

13. Richard Kieckhefer, art. cit. pp. 203–25.
14. Ibid., p. 224.
15. See ibid., pp. 205–7.
16. Ibid., p. 208.
17. Cited by Kieckhefer, ibid., p. 207.
18. Cf. ibid., pp. 214, 223.
19. See above, pp. 52, 105.
20. Cf. Théry, art. cit., pp. 186, 196–7 and Laurent, art. cit., p. 345.
21. See above, pp. 69, n. 36; 70, 156 and 161. Thirty-two of Eckhart's sermons were also posthumously included in a collection of sixty-four sermons intended for the training of Dominican preachers, the *Paradisus Animae Intelligentis* (Paradise of the Intelligent Soul), which was edited by Philip Strauch from the Oxford Laud manuscript Misc. 479 (Berlin, 1919).
22. Cf. John Loeschen, 'The God Who Becomes, Eckhart on Divine Relativity', *The Thomist*, 35 (No. 3, July, 1971), pp. 405–22. Also see above, pp. 42, 128, n. 37.
23. Op. cit., p. 6.
24. Ibid., p. 11.
25. Cf. Rahner, art. cit., passim, see above, p. 108, n. I.
26. Kertz, art. cit., pp. 330, 335–6, 359.
27. McGinn, 'Condemnation', pp. 398–414.
28. Cf. ibid., especially pp. 413–414.
29. McGinn's discussion of the condemned propositions can also be found in C-McG, pp. 32–3 n. 41; 33–4 n. 49; 36–8 n. 66; 41–3; 44 n. 140; 42 nn. 120–3; 44 n. 139; 48 n. 175; 51 n. 200–1; 52–3 n. 209; 54 n. 221; 58 n. 246–50; 59 n. 256. See also Appendix B, pp. 215f.
30. Cf. especially Ancelet-Hustache, pp. 133–8 and passim.
31. Knowles, art. cit., p. 4. Cf. also Hinnebusch, II, p. 310.
32. Schürmann, pp. 74–83. Cf. also Kieckhefer, art. cit., p. 216, n. 37.
33. Schürmann, pp. 221–5.
34. Colledge, art. cit., p. 257.
35. For an incisive discussion of the factors leading to the condemnation of Eckhart's teaching, see Oliver Davies, 'Why Were Eckhart's Propositions Condemned?' *New Blackfriars,* 71 (1990), pp. 433–44.
36. On Eckhart's emphatic language, cf. McGinn, 'Condemnation', pp. 403, 413. On the cross purposes of the commissioners and the defendant, cf. ibid., pp. 411–412. Schürmann similarly cites the opposition between the 'imperative' thought of Meister Eckhart and the 'indicative' thought of the theologians of the Curia: cf. pp. 29–31, 60–4, p. 235, n. 4. Cf. also Congar, 'Langage des spirituels et langage des théologiens', ed. cit., and above, pp. 121, 155, n. 4.
37. For a list of the condemned propositions and references refuting their alleged heretical content, see Appendix B, p. 215.
38. Cf. Schürmann, p. 164 n. 39 for discussion. See also Matthew Fox, OP, 'Meister Eckhart and Karl Marx: The Mystic as Political Theologian', in *Understanding Mysticism*, Richard Woods, ed., Garden City, NY: Doubleday, 1980, pp. 541–63.

39. Cf. H. Ley, *Geschichte der Aufklärung und des Atheismus*, Berlin, 1956, and *Studie zur Geschichte des Materialsmus im Mittelalter*, Berlin, reference by Schürmann, p. 264.

40. W 10, p. 95 (DW 25). Cf. W 56, p. 82 (DP 26): 'There are some poor people [here] who will go back home and say, "I shall settle down and eat my bread and serve God". By the eternal truth I declare that these people will remain in error, and will never be able to strive for and win what those others achieve who follow God in poverty and exile. Amen.'

41. Cf. McGinn. 'Introduction', p. 238.

ABBREVIATIONS

AFP   *Archivum Fratrum Praedicatorum*, Rome: Santa Sabina.

A-H   Ancelet-Hustache, Jeanne, *Master Eckhart and the Rhineland Mystics*, New York and London: Harper and Row (Longmans), 1957.

Bl   Blakney, R.B., *Meister Eckhart: A Modern Translation*, New York and London: Harper and Row, 1941.

Cl   Clark, James, *Meister Eckhart: An Introduction to the Study of His Works with an Anthology of His Sermons*, Edinburgh and London: Nelson, 1957.

Cl-Sk   Clark, James, and Skinner, John V., eds. and trans., *Treatises and Sermons of Meister Eckhart*, New York: Octagon Books, 1983. (Reprint of Harper and Row ed., 1958.)

C-McG   Colledge, Edmund and McGinn, Bernard, *Meister Eckhart: The Essential Sermons, Commentaries, Treatises and Defense*, New York: Paulist Press, 1981.

DP   *Meister Eckhart: Deutsche Predigten and Traktate*, ed. by Josef Quint, München: Karl Hansen, 1963 ed.

DW   *Deutsche Werke*, Josef Quint, ed., *Meister Eckhart: Die deutschen und lateinische Werke*, 5 vols., Stuttgart: Kohlhammer, 1936ff. (German works = Quint.)

Evans   Evans, C. de B., trans. and ed., *Meister Eckhart by Franz Pfeiffer*, 2 vols., London: Watkins, 1923, 1932.

Fox   Fox, Matthew, *Breakthrough: Meister Eckhart's Creation Spirituality in New Translation*, Garden City, New York: Doubleday and Co., 1981.

Jostes Jostes, Franz, *Meister Eckhart und seine Jünger*, Fribourg, 1895.

Jundt Jundt, A., *Histoire du pantheism populaire du moyen age*, Paris, 1875.

KS Koch, Josef, *Kleine Schriften*, 2 vols., Roma: Edizioni di Storia e Letteratura, 1973.

LW *Lateinischen Werke*, Ernst Benz, et al., eds., *Meister Eckhart: Die deutschen und lateinische Werke*, 5 vols., Stuttgart: Kohlhammer, 1936ff. (Benz = Latin Sermons, Koch = Latin Treatises).

M Maurer, Armand, ed., *Master Eckhart: Parisian Questions and Prologues*, Toronto, Canada: Pontifical Institute of Medieval Studies, 1974.

McG-T McGinn, Bernard with Tobin, Frank, *Meister Eckhart: Teacher and Preacher*, New York: Paulist Press/London: SPCK, 1987.

MOPH *Monumenta Ordinis Fratrum Praedicatorum Historica*, Rome: Santa Sabina.

Th Théry, G., 'Edition critique des pièces relatives au procès d'Eckhart continues dans le manuscrit 33b de la Bibliothèque de Soest', *Archives d'histoire doctrinale et litteraire du moyen âge*, Vol. 1 (1926–27), Paris: Vrin, 1926, pp. 129–268.

Pf Pfeiffer, F., *Deutsche Mystiker des 14. Jahrhunderts*, II: Meister Eckhart, Leipzig, 1857 (Aalen, 1962).

Sch Schürmann, Reiner, trans. and commentary, *Meister Eckhart: Mystic and Philosopher*, Bloomington and London: Indiana University Press, 1978.

Strauch Strauch, Ph., *Paradisus animae intelligentis* (DTM 30, from Oxford MS Laud Misc. 479), Berlin, 1919.

W Walshe, M. O'C., ed. and trans., *Meister Eckhart: Sermons and Treatises*, 3 vols., London and Dulverton: Watkins/Element, 1979, 1981 and 1985.

BIBLIOGRAPHY

I. SOURCE DOCUMENTS

Meister Eckhart: Die deutschen und lateinischen Werke. Herausgegeben im Auftrage der Deutschen Forschungsgemeinschaft. Stuttgart and Berlin: Verlag W. Kohlhammer, 11 Vols., 1936. Authentic treatises and sermons.

Augustine Daniels, OSB, ed., 'Eine lateinische Rechtfertigungsschrift des Meister Eckharts', *Beiträge zur Geschichte der Philosophie des Mittelalters*, 23, 5 (Münster, 1923): 1–4, 12–13, 34–35, 65–66. Eckhart's Defense at Cologne.

Franz Jostes, ed., *Meister Eckhart und seine Jünger: Ungedruckte zur Geschichte der deutschen Mystik*, De Gruyter, 1972 (Series: Deutsche Neudrucke Texte des Mittelalters). Sermons.

Thomas Kaepelli, 'Kurz Mitteilungen über mittelalterliche Dominikanerschriftsteller', *Archivum Fratrum Praedicatorum* 10 (1940), pp. 293–4. Letter fragment of Pope John XXII to Archbishop Henry II of Virneburg.

M.H. Laurent, 'Autour du procès de Maître Eckhart. Les documents des Archives Vaticanes', *Divus Thomas* (Piacenza) 39 (1936), pp. 331–48, 430–47. Records of Eckhart's trials at Cologne and Avignon with related documents.

Franz Pelster, SJ, ed., *Articuli contra Fratrem Aychardum Alamannum*, Vat. lat. 3899, f. 123r–130v, in 'Ein Gutachten aus dem Eckehart Prozess in Avignon', Aus der Geistewelt des Mittelalters, Festgabe Martin Grabmann, Beiträge Supplement 3, Munster, 1935, pp. 1099–1124. Opinion of Avignon Commission against Eckhart.

Josef Quint, ed. and trans., *Meister Eckehart: Deutsche Predigten und Traktate*, Munich: Carl Hanser, 1955. Authentic treatises and sermons.

Philip Strauch, ed., *Paradisus animae intelligentis* (Deutsche Texte des Mittelalters 30, from Oxford MS Laud Misc. 479), Berlin, 1919. Thirty-two authentic sermons from the period 1303–1311.

Gabriel Thèry, OP, 'Édition critique des pièces relatives au procès d'Eckhart continues dans le manuscrit 33b de la Bibliotheque de Soest', *Archives d'histoire littèraire et doctrinal du moyen âge*, 1 (1926), pp. 129–268. Eckhart's Defense at Cologne.

II. BOOKS ON ECKHART

A. ENGLISH TRANSLATIONS

James Midgely Clark, *Meister Eckhart:An Introduction to the Study of HisWorks with an Anthology of His Sermons*, Edinburgh and London: Nelson, 1957.

James M. Clark and John V. Skinner, eds. and trans., *Treatises and Sermons of Meister Eckhart*, NewYork: Octagon Books, 1983. (Reprint of Harper and Row ed., 1958.)

Edmund Colledge, OSA, and Bernard McGinn, trans. and eds., *Meister Eckhart:The Essential Sermons, Commentaries,Treatises and Defense*, NewYork: Paulist Press, 1981.

Oliver Davies, ed. and trans., *Meister Eckhart: SelectedWritings*, London and NewYork: Penguin, 1994.

C. de B. Evans, *Meister Eckhart by Franz Pfeiffer*, 2 vols., London:Watkins, 1924 and 1931.

Ursula Fleming, *Meister Eckhart:The Man from whom God Hid Nothing*, London: Fount, 1988.

Matthew Fox, OP, ed., *Breakthrough: Meister Eckhart's Creation Spirituality in New Translation*, Garden City, NY: Doubleday, 1980.

Armand Maurer, ed., *Master Eckhart: Parisian Questions and Prologues*, Toronto, Canada: Pontifical Institute of Medieval Studies, 1974.

Bernard McGinn with FrankTobin and Elvira Borgstädt, ed. and trans., preface by Kenneth Northcott, *Meister Eckhart:Teacher and Preacher*, New York: Paulist Press/London: SPCK, 1987.

Reiner Schürmann, *Wandering Joy: Meister Eckhart's Mystical Philosophy*, Barrington, MA: Lindisfarne Books, 2001 (a republication of *Meister Eckhart: Mystic and Philosopher*, Bloomington: Indiana University Press, 1978).

M. O'C. Walshe, *Meister Eckhart: Sermons and Treatises*, 3 vols., London/Shaftesbury, Dorset: Watkins/Element Books, 1979, 1981 and 1985.

B. Books in English on Eckhart

Jeanne Ancelet Hustache, *Master Eckhart,* New York and London: Harper and Row/Longmans, 1957.

James M. Clark, *The Great German Mystics*, New York: Russell and Russell, 1970 (reprint of Basil Blackwell edition, Oxford: 1949).

Oliver Davies, *Meister Eckhart: Mystical Theologian*, London: SPCK, 1991.

Michael Demkovich, *Introducing Meister Eckhart*, Ottawa/Notre Dame: Novalis/Fides, 2005.

Robert K. Forman, *Meister Eckhart: Mystic as Theologian*, Rockport, Mass./Shaftesbury, Dorset: Element Books, 1991.

Amy Hollywood, *The Soul as Virgin Wife: Mechthild of Magdeburg, Marguerite Porete, and Meister Eckhart*, Notre Dame and London: University of Notre Dame Press, 1996.

C.F. Kelley, *Meister Eckhart on Divine Knowledge*, New Haven, CT: Yale University Press, 1977. Reprinted with a foreword by William Stranger, Dharma Café Books (Random House), New York, 2009.

Bernard McGinn, *The Harvest of Mysticism: in Medieval Germany* (Volume 4 of *The Presence of God*), New York: Crossroad, 2005.

Bernard McGinn, ed., *Meister Eckhart and the Beguine Mystics Hadewijch of Brabant, Mechthild of Magdeburg, and Marguerite Porete*, New York: Continuum, 1994.

Bernard McGinn, *The Mystical Thought of Meister Eckhart: The Man from Whom God Hid Nothing*, New York: Crossroad, 2001.

Cyprian Smith, *TheWay of Paradox: Spiritual Life as Taught by Meister Eckhart*, London/NewYork: Darton, Longman and Todd/Paulist Press, 2004 ed. (1987).

Frank Tobin, *Meister Eckhart: Thought and Language*, Philadelphia: University of Pennsylvania Press, 1986.

C. GENERAL

S.M. Albert, OP, *Albert the Great*, Oxford: Blackwell Publications, 1948.

Angelus Silesius, *The Cherubic Wanderer*, trans. by Maria Shrady, New York: Paulist Press, 1986.

James M. Clark, trans., *Henry Suso: Little Book of EternalWisdom and Little Book of Truth*, London: Faber, 1953.

Norman Cohn, *The Pursuit of the Millennium: Revolutionary Millenarians and Mystical Anarchists of the Middle Ages*, NewYork: Oxford University Press, rev. ed., 1970.

Oliver Davies, *God Within: The Mystical Tradition of Northern Europe,* London: Darton, Longman and Todd, 1988.

Mary Jeremy Finnegan, OP, *The Women of Helfta*, Athens: University of Georgia Press, 1991.

St Gertrude the Great, *The Life and Revelations*, Westminster, MD: Christian Classics, 1986.

Gertrud the Great of Helfta, *Spiritual Exercises,* trans. and ed. by Gertrud Jaron Lewis and Jack Lewis (Kalamazoo: Cistercian Publications, 1989).

Canon John Gray, trans., *The True Prayers of St Gertrude and St Mechtilde*, NewYork: Sheed and Ward, 1936.

Leonard Hindsley, OP, and Margot Schmidt, eds. and intro., *Margareta Ebner: Revelations and Pater Noster*, preface by Richard Woods, OP, New York: Paulist Press, 1993.

Leonard Hindsley, *The Mystics of Engelthal: Writings from a Medieval Monastery*, NewYork: St Martin's Press, 1998.

William A. Hinnebusch, OP, *The History of the Dominican Order*, 2 vols., Staten Island, NY: Alba House, 1966 and 1973.

Johan Huizinga, *The Waning of the Middle Ages*, NY: Doubleday, 1954 (1924).

David Knowles, OSB, *The English Mystical Tradition*, New York: Harper and Brothers, 1961.

Emmanuel LeRoy Ladurie, Montaillou: *The Promised Land of Error*, trans. by Barbara Bray, New York: George Braziller, Inc., 1978.

Gordon Leff, *Heresy in the Later Middle Ages*, 2 vols., New York: Barnes and Noble, 1967.

Bernard J. Lonergan, SJ, *Verbum:Word and Idea in Aquinas*, ed. by David Burrell, CSC, Notre Dame: University of Notre Dame Press, 1967.

Robert Lopez, *The Commercial Revolution of the Middle Ages*, New York: Cambridge University Press, 1976.

Mechthild of Magdeburg, *The Flowing Light of the Godhead*, trans. by Frank Tobin, preface by Margot Schmidt, New York: Paulist Press, 1998.

Ernest W. McDonnell, *The Beguines and Beghards in Medieval Culture*, New Brunswick, NJ: Rutgers University Press, 1954.

Bernard McGinn, *The Harvest of Mysticism in Medieval Germany* (1300–1500), New York: Crossroad Publishing Co., 2005.

Steven Ozment, *Homo spiritualis: A Comparative Study of the Anthropology of J. Tauler, J. Gerson and M. Luther* (1509–16) *in the Context of their Theological Thought* (Studies in Medieval and Reformation Thought, Vol. 6) Leiden: Brill, 1969.

Steven Runciman, *The Medieval Manichee*, Cambridge: The University Press, 1960.

Jeffrey B. Russell, *Religious Dissent in the Middle Ages*, New York: John Wiley and Sons, 1971.

Maria Shrady, ed. and trans., *Johannes Tauler Sermons*, New York: Paulist Press, 1987.

Richard Southern, *Western Society and the Church in the Middle Ages*, New York: Penguin Books, 1970.

Frank Tobin, trans., ed. and commentary, *Henry Suso: The Exemplar with Two German Sermons*, preface by Bernard McGinn, New York: Paulist Press, 1989.

Simon Tugwell, OP, *Albert and Thomas: Selected Writings*, New York: Paulist Press, 1988.

Simon Tugwell, OP, ed. and trans., *Early Dominicans: Selected Writings*, New York: Paulist Press, 1982.

M.H. Vicaire, OP, *St Dominic and his Times*, trans. by Kathleen Pond, London: Darton, Longman and Todd, 1964.

Andrew Weeks, *German Mysticism from Hildegard of Bingen to Ludwig Wittgenstein: A Literary and Intellectual History*, Albany: State University of New York Press, 1993.

James A. Weisheipl, OP, *Friar Thomas d'Aquino: His Life, Thought and Works*, Garden City, NY: Doubleday and Co., 1974.

H. Wilms, OP, *Albert the Great*, London: Burns, Oates and Washbourne, 1933.

Frances A. Yates, *The Art of Memory*, Chicago: The University of Chicago Press, 1966.

D. FOREIGN WORKS: ECKHART

Bernard Barzel, *Mystique de l'ineffable dans l'hinduism et le christianisme: Sankara et Eckhart*, Paris: Editions du Cerf, 1982.

Jean Bédard, *Maître Eckhart* (roman), Canada: Stock, 1998.

Alain de Libera, *Introduction a la Mystique Rhènane d'Albert le Grand à Maitre Eckhart*, Paris: OEIL, 1984.

Reudi Imbach, *Deus Est Intelligere: Das Verhältnis von Sein und Denken in Seiner Bedeutung für das Gotterverständnis bei von Aquin und in der Pariser Questionen Meister Eckharts*, Freiburg: Universitätsverlag, 1976.

Nicholas Largier, *Meister Eckhart Werke*, 2 Vols. (Bibliothek des Mittelalters. Texte und Übersetzungen, Bd. 20), Frankfurt am Main, 1993.

Niklaus Largier, *Bibliographie zu Meister Eckhart*, Freiburg: Universitätsverlag, 1989.

Vladimir Lossky, *Théologie négative et connaissance de Dieu chez Maître Eckhart*, Paris: Vrin, 1960.

Kurt Ruh, *Meister Eckhart: Theologe, Prediger, Mystiker*, Munich: Beck, 1985.

Andres Speer and Lydia Wegener, eds., *Meister Eckhart in Erfurt*, Berlin and NewYork: Walter de Gruyter, 2005.

Heinrich Stirnimann and Ruedi Imbach (eds), *Eckardus Theutonicus, homo doctus et sanctus*, Fribourg: University of Fribourg, 1993. Report of the Commission set up by the Dominican Chapter of Walberburg.

Loris Sturlese, *Meister Eckhart: Ein Portrait,* Regensburg: Pustet, 1993.

Winfried Trusen, *Der Prozess gegen Meister Eckhart*, Fribourg: University of Fribourg, 1988.

Shizuteru Ueda, *Die Gottesgeburt in der Seele und der Durchbruch zur Gottheit. Die mystische Anthropologie Meister Eckharts und ihre Konfrontation mit der Mystik des Zen Buddhismus*, Gütersloh: Mohn, 1965.

Émilie Zum Brunn, Zénon Kalżua, Alain de Libera, Paul Vignaux, Eduoard Weber, *Maître Eckhart a Paris: Une critique médiévale de l'ontothéologie*, Paris: Presses Universitaires de France, 1984.

E. FOREIGN WORKS: OTHER

Carl Buecher, *Die Frauenfrage im Mittelalter,* Thbingen, 1882.

Chronicles of St Agnes, AOP (Analecta Sacris Ordinis Fratrum Praedicatorum) I, Rome, 1893–4.

H. Grundmann, *Religiöse Bewegungen im Mittelalter*, Hildesheim, 2nd ed., 1961.

A. Puccetti, OP, *Sant'Alberto Magno*, Rome: 1932.

Ferdinand Vetter, ed., *Das Leben des Schwestern zu Töss beschrieben von Elsbet Stagel samt der Vorrede von Johannes Meier und dem Leben der Prinzessin Elisabet von Ungarn*, Deutsche Texte des Mittelalters, Vol. VI, Berlin: Weidmann, 1906.

Hieronymus Wilms, OP, *Das Beten der Mystikerinnen dargestellt nach den Chroniken der Dominikanerinnenklöster zu Adelhausen, Diessenhoffen, Engeltal,*

Kirchberg, Oetenbach, Töss und Unterlinden, revised ed. (Quellen und Forschungen, Vol. 11), Freiburg im Breisgau, 1932.

_____ *Geschichte der deutschen Dominikanerinnen* (1206–1916), Dülmen i. W.: Laumann, 1920.

III. ARTICLES

A. ENGLISH: ECKHART

John Caputo, 'The Nothingness of the Intellect in Meister Eckhart's Parisian Questions', *The Thomist*, 39 (1975): 85–115.

Edmund Colledge, OSA, 'Meister Eckhart: His Times and His Writings', *The Thomist,* 42 (April, 1978) 2: 240–58.

Oliver Davies, 'Why Were Eckhart's Propositions Condemned?' *New Blackfriars*, 71 (1990): 433–44.

Donald F. Duclow, '"My Suffering is God": Meister Eckhart's Book of Divine Consolation', *Theological Studies*, 44 (Dec. 1983): 570–86.

Henry L. Finch, 'A Note on Two Traditions in Western Mysticism: Meister Eckhart and Jacob Boehme', *Centerpoint*, 3 (1978) 1: 41–50.

Gundolf Gieraths, OP, 'Spiritual Riches', *Cross and Crown*, 14 (1962): 160–72, 311–32, 338–48, 456–67; and 15 (1963): 78–89, 186–97, 444 – 62. Translation of *Reichtum des Lebens. Die deutsche Dominikanermystik des 14. Jahrhunderts*, Düsseldorf, 1956, by Edward Schuster and Sister Mary of the Immaculate Heart, OP.

Alois M. Haas, 'The Nothingness of God and its Explosive Metaphors', *Eckhart Review,* 8 (1999): 6–17.

Rufus Jones, 'Meister Eckhart: The Peak of the Range', *The Flowering of Mysticism in the Fourteenth Century*, New York: Hafner Publishing Co., 1971 (facsimile of 1939 ed.), pp. 61–85.

Karl Kertz, 'Meister Eckhart's Teaching on the Birth of the Divine Word in the Soul', *Traditio*, 15 (1959): 327–363.

Richard Kieckhefer, 'Meister Eckhart's Conception of Union with God', *Harvard Theological Review,* 71 (1978): 203–25.

M.D. Knowles, 'Denifle and Ehrle', *History,* 54 (1969), 1–12.

Niklaus Largier, 'Recent Work on Meister Eckhart. Positions, Problems, New Perspectives, 1990–1997', *Recherches de théologie et philosophie médiévales,* 65 (1998) 1: 147–167.

Bernard McGinn, 'Meister Eckhart: An Introduction', *An Introduction to the Medieval Mystics of Europe,* ed. by Paul E. Szarmach, Albany: State University of New York Press, 1984, pp. 237–57.

_____ 'Meister Eckhart on God as Absolute Unity', *Neoplatonism and Christian Thought,* ed. by Dominic J. O'Meara, Albany: State University of New York Press, 1982, pp. 128–39.

_____ 'The God beyond God', *Journal of Religion,* 61 (1981): 1–19.

_____ 'Meister Eckhart's Condemnation Reconsidered', *The Thomist,* 44 (1980): 390–414.

_____ 'St Bernard and Meister Eckhart,' *Citeaux,* 31 (1980): 373–86.

Sr Margaret R. Miles, 'The Mystical Method of Meister Eckhart', *Studia Mystica,* 4 (Winter 1981) 4: 57–71.

Steven Ozment, 'Eckhart and Luther: German Mysticism and Protestantism', *The Thomist,* 42 (April 1978) 2: 259–80.

Josiah Royce, 'Meister Eckhart', *Studies of Good and Evil,* Hamden, CT: Archon Books, 1964, pp. 261–97 (reprint of 1906 ed.).

Reiner Schürmann, 'Meister Eckhart's "Verbal" Understanding of Being as a Ground for Destruction of Practical Teleology', *Sprache und Erkenntnis im Mittelalter,* Jan P. Beckmann et al., eds., Berlin and New York: Walter de Gruyter, 1981, pp. 803–9.

Ernst H. Soudek, 'Eckhart, Meister', in *Dictionary of the Middle Ages,* Vol. 4, New York: Charles Scribner's, 1984.

Loris Sturlese, 'Mysticism and Theology in Meister Eckhart's Theory of the Image', *Eckhart Review,* 2 (Spring 1993): 18–31.

Loris Sturlese, 'A Portrait of Meister Eckhart', *Eckhart Review,* 5 (Spring 1996): 7–12.

Frank Tobin, 'The Mystic as Poet: Meister Eckhart's German Sermon 69', *Studia Mystica*, 2 (1979) 4: 61–75.

Shizuteru Ueda, '"Nothingness" in Meister Eckhart and Zen Buddhism', *The Buddha Eye: An Anthology of the Kyoto School*, ed. by Frederick Franck, New York: Crossroad, 1982 (repr. from *Tranzendenz und Immanenz: Philosophie und Theologie in der veränderten Welt*, ed. D. Papenfuss und J. Söring, Berlin: 1977). Trans. by James W. Heisig.

Felix Vernet, 'The Dominicans', *Mediaeval Spirituality*, trans. by the Benedictines of Talacre, St Louis, MO: B. Herder Book Co., 1930, pp. 53–65.

Wolfgang Wackernagel, 'Establishing the Being of Images: Master Eckhart and the Concept of Disimagination', Thomas Epstein, trans., *Diogenes*, 162 (1993): 77–98.

Wolfgang Wackernagel, 'Some Legendary Aspects of Meister Eckhart: The Aphorisms of the Twelve Masters', *Eckhart Review*, 7 (Spring 1998): 30–41.

Richard Woods, OP, '"I Am the Son of God": Eckhart and Aquinas on the Incarnation', *Eckhart Review*, 1 (June 1992): 27–46.

_____ 'Meister Eckhart and the Neoplatonic Heritage: The Thinker's Way to God', *The Thomist* (October 1990): 609–39.

_____ 'Meister Eckhart's Wayless Way and the Nothingness of God', *Mysticism and Prophecy: The Dominican Tradition*, London and New York: Darton, Longman and Todd/ Orbis Books, 1998, pp. 77–91.

B. FOREIGN: ECKHART

Fernand Brunner, 'Le Mysticisme de Maître Eckhart: Etude Comparative', *Das 'Einig Ein': Studien zur Theorie und Sprache des deutschen Mystik*, Alois M. Haas and Heinrich Stirimann (eds), Freiburg: University Press, 1980, pp. 63–86.

W. Goris, 'Dietrich von Freiberg und Meister Eckhart über das Gute', in Karl-Hermann Kandler, Burkhard Mojsisch und Franz-Bernhard Stammkötter (eds), *Dietrich von Freiberg. Neue Perspektiven seiner Philosophie,*

Theologie und Naturwissenschaft (Bochumer Studien zur Philosophie, Bd. 28), Amsterdam/Philadelphia: B.R. Grüner, 1999, pp. 169–88.

B. Geyer, 'Albertus Magnus und Meister Eckhart', *Festschrift Josef Quint anlässliche seines 65. Geburtstages hberreicht*, Bonn: 1964. (On Albert and Eckhart, pp. 253–4.)

Josef Koch, OP, 'Meister Eckhart: Versuch eines Gesamtbildes', *Kleine Schriften*, 2 vols., Roma: Edizioni di Storia e Letteratura, 1973, I, pp. 201–38 (from *Die Kirche in der Zitenwende*, ed. by O. Kuss und E. Kleineidam, 3 Aug. 1939, pp. 277–309).

_____ 'Kritische Studien zum Leben Meister Eckharts', *Kleine Schriften*, ed. cit., I, pp. 247–347.

Niklaus Largier, 'Negativität, Möglichkeit, Freiheit: Zur Differenz zwischen der Philosophie Dietrichs von Freiberg und Meister Eckharts', in *Dietrich von Freiberg: Neue Perspektiven seiner Philosophie, Theologie und Naturwissenschaft*, ed by. Karl-Hermann Kandler, Burkhard Mojsisch und Franz-Bernhard Stammkötter (Bochumer Studien zur Philosophie 28), Amsterdam-Philadelphia: Grüner, 1999, pp. 149–68.

Hugo Rahner, SJ, 'Die Gottesgeburt. Die Lehre der Kirchenväter von der Geburt Christi im Herzen der Glahbigen', *Zeitschrift für katholische Theologie*, 59 (1935), pp. 333–418.

Reiner Schürmann, 'Trois penseurs du relaissement, Maître Eckhart, Heidegger, Suzuki', *J. Hist. Phil.*, 12, 4 (October, 1974), pp. 455–78 and 13, 1 (January, 1975), pp. 43–60.

Édouard-Henri Wéber, OP, 'À propos de Maître Eckhart et de son procès', *Mémoire Dominicaine*, 2 (Printemps 1993): 135–37.

C. OTHER

Francis A. Catania, 'Albert the Great', *Encyclopedia of Philosophy*, New York: Macmillan and The Free Press, 1967, I, pp. 64–6.

Louise Gnädinger, ed. and commentary, *Johannes Tauler: Gotteserfahrung und Weg in die Welt*, Olten und Frieburg-im-Breisgau: Walter Verlag, 1983. Fifteen sermons of Tauler in modern German.

Johann Huizinga, *The Autumn of the Middle Ages*, trans. by Rodney Payton and Ulrich Mammitzsch, Chicago: University of Chicago Press, 1996.

Josef Koch, OP, 'Der Kardinal Jacques Fournier (Benedikt XII.) als Gutachter in theologischen Prozessen', *Kleine Schriften*, Roma: Edizioni di Storia e Letteratura, 1973, Vol. II, pp. 367–86. (From *Die Kirche und ihre Ämter und Stände. Festgrabe für Joseph Kardinal Frings*, ed. by W. Corsten, A. Frotz, P. Linden, 1960, pp. 441–52.)

Valerie Lagorio, 'The Medieval Continental Women Mystics', *An Introduction to the Medieval Mystics of Europe*, ed. by Paul Szarmach, Albany: State University of New York Press, 1984, pp. 161–93.

Walter Nigg, 'Johannes Tauler', in *Das mystische Dreigestirn*, Diogenes: Zurich, 1990, pp. 130–31.

Kurt Ruh, 'Deutsche Predigtbücher des Mittelalters', *Beiträge zur Geschichte der Predigt*, Heimo Reinitzer, ed., Hamburg: F. Wittig, 1981, pp. 11–30.

I.P. Sheldon Williams, 'The Greek Christian Platonist Tradition from the Cappadocians to Maximus and Eriugena', *The Cambridge History of Later Greek and Early Medieval Philosophy*, ed. by A.H. Armstrong, Cambridge University Press, 1970, pp. 425–533.

Richard Weber, 'The Search for Identity and Community in the Fourteenth Century', *The Thomist*, 42 (No. 2, April, 1978), pp. 182–96.

APPENDIX A

ECKHART'S WORKS: A COMPARISON OF WALSHE AND OTHER TRANSLATIONS

1. German Sermons:

W (*Vol. 1*)	DW	DP	Pf	Bl	Cl	Cl-Sk	Sch	C-McG	McG-T	Fox	Davies
1	-	57	1	1						21	
2	-	58	2	2						18	24
3	-		3	3							
4	-	59	4	4						17	25
5	65		5								
6	1	1	6	13	i				p. 239	32	12
7	76	35	7				p. 131		p. 327	23	
8	2	2	8	24	ii		p. 3	p. 177		20	13
9	86	28	9						p. 338	34	21
10	25	38	10	17	iii					16	
11	26	49	11				p. 55				
12	27	50	12							22	
13a	5a				xxii						19
13b	5b	6	13	5					p. 181	14	
14a	16a										20
14b	16b		14		iv				p. 275		
15		44	15								
16	29	29	74	21					p. 287	25	
17	28	31	81	20							3
18	30	43	66			p. 39	p. 181		p. 292	2	4
19	71	37	19				p. 122		p. 320		
20	44		20								

German Sermons Vol 1 continued:

W (Vol. 1)	DW	DP	Pf	Bl	Cl	Cl-Sk	Sch	C-McG	McG-T	Fox	Davies
21	17		21		v					1	5
22	53		22					p. 203			
23	47		23							7	
24a	13				xxiii						
24b	13a		24								
25	3		25	9	vi				p. 244		
26	57										
27	34		27								
28	78		28								
29	38		29								2
30	45		30								
31	37		31								
32a	20a		32		vii						
32b	20b										
33		35	33								
34	55		34								
35	19		35		viii						
36	18		36		ix						
37			37								
38	36a		38								
39	36b										
40	4	4	40	19	x				p. 247	29	
41	70	53	41						p. 316		
42	69	40	42	15	xi				p. 311		23

German Sermons Vol 2:

W (Vol. 2)	DW	DP	Pf	Bl	Cl	Cl-Sk	Sch	C-McG	McG-T	Fox	Davies
43	41	46	43								9
44	58										
45	60	45	45							27	6
46	54b		46								
47	46		47						p. 304		
48	31	47									
49	77		49								
50	14				xxv				p. 271		
51	15				xxiv				p. 189	11	
52	32	30		14							
53	22	23	88		xviii				p. 192		
54	23										
55	62	48	55								
56			56		xii						27
57	12	13	96		xx				p. 267		16
58	26	27	58								
59	39	25	59			p. 43			p. 296	33	10
60	48	34	60						p. 197		7
61			61								
62	82	54	62								
63	40		63						p. 300		11
64	81		64							26	
65	6	7	65	18	xiii				p. 185		
66	10	11	83		xvi				p. 261		15
67	9	10	84		xvii				p. 255		
68	11	12	90	12	xix						
69	68	36	69	6						9	

German Sermons Vol 2 continued:

W (Vol. 2)	DW	DP	Pf	Bl	Cl	Cl-Sk	Sch	C-McG	McG-T	Fox	Davies
70	67									28	
71	59								p. 307		
72	7	8	72		xiv				p. 252	31	
73	73	33	73								
74	74		86								
75			75								
76	61										
77	63										
78	64										
79	43	52	79								
80	42	39	80	7						8	18
81	33										1
82	8	9	82	16	xv					4	14
83	51	24	102	11							
84	84								p. 335		
85	85									19	26
86	56										
87	52	32	87	28				p. 214	p. 199	15	22
88	75		85							5	
89	49		89							24	
90			103								
91	79	41	91	10						10	
92	24		94						p. 284	6	
93	50		95								8
94	80	55	97						p. 332		
95	72	56	98								
96	83	42	99						p. 206	12	28
97	21	22	100		xxi				p. 280	13	17

2. Additional German Sermons:

Jostes 46								21	29
Jostes 82								18	30

3. German Treatises:

	Walshe III	DW	Pf	Bl	Cl-Sk	C-McG	Davies
I: Talks of Instruction	p. 11–60	V: 135–376	p. 53	pp. 3–42	pp. 47–89	p. 247	p. 1
II: Book Divine Comfort	p. 61–104	V: 3–61	p. 101	pp. 43–73	pp. 90–126	p. 209	p. 53
III: On the Noble Man	p. 105–16	V: 101–19	p. 140	pp. 74–81	pp. 127–35	p. 240	p. 97
IV: On Detachment	p. 117–29	V: 400–34	II, 9	pp. 82–91	pp. 136–46	p. 285	
V: (German Sermon 98)	p. 131–5						

4. Additional German works:

	Walshe III	Pfeiffer	Blakney	DP	McG-T
1. 'Good Morning'	p. 137–38	III, 67	p. 251		
2. The Naked Boy	p. 138	III, 68	p. 251		
3. M. Eckhart's Daughter	p. 138–39	III, 69	p. 252		
4. M. Eckhart's Feast	p. 139–43	III, 70		pp. 529–31	
5. 'Final Words'	p. 147–49	pp. 685–6	p. 249		
6. Sister Katherine					pp. 347f.

5. *Latin Sermons:*

LW	Cl-Sk	McG-T	Fox	Davies
2. IV, i	pp. 161–4			
4. IV, 22–32		p. 207		
6. IV, 50–74		p. 212		
11. IV, ii	pp. 165–8			
12. IV,			pp. 417–28	
21. IV,	pp. 169–70			
22. IV,	pp. 171–8			
24. IV, 2-				p. 255
25. IV, 230–44		p. 216		
29. IV, 263–70	pp. 179–83	p. 223		p. 258
30. IV,	pp. 184–91		pp. 531–37	
40. IV, 3-				p. 263
45. IV, 374–87		p. 227		
47. IV, 2-				p. 264
49. IV, 421–28		p. 234		
52. IV,	pp. 192–3			

6. Latin Treatises:

Prologue to Opus Expos.	LW I, 183			p. 82		
Comm. On Genesis	LW I, 185–206			pp. 82–91		
Book of Parables of Genesis	LW I, 447–636 (passim)			pp. 92–121		
Comm. on John	LW III, c. 1–130 (pp. 3-114)		c.1-52 (pp. 202–25)	pp. 122–73		
Comm. on Exodus	LW II, 1–227		pp. 197–201		pp. 41–129	
Comm. on Wisdom 1:14–18:15	LW II, 339–62				pp. 147–74	
Comm. on Ecclus. 24–29	LW II, 270–90				pp. 174–81	
Comm. on John 14:8	LW III., 477–506				pp. 182–93	
'Creavit enim'	II, 359–69	I, 343–50				
'Ego Sum Qui Sum'*	II, 20ff.		pp. 197–201			
'In Principio erat verbum'**	LW III, c. 1		pp. 202–25			
On the Lord's Prayer	V, 109–30					pp. 495 –503***

* From the Commentary on the Book of Exodus

** From the Commentary on St John's Gospel: 1–52

*** Klibansky, ed., pp. 1–17, from Migne, *Patrologia Latina* 35, 1377. (LW V = E. Seeberg ed.)

APPENDIX B

Sources of Condemned Propositions: Koch and Laurent.[1] Q = Quint.

Bull No.	Koch	Laurent

A. *15 articles condemned as heretical:*

1.	1 Comm. Gen., n. 7, LW I, 190, 5–9[2]	
2.	Comm. John, n. 216, LW III, 181, 7	
3.	1 Comm. Gen., n. 7, LW I, 190, 11	
4.	Comm. John, n. 494	
5.	Comm. John, n. 494	
6.	Comm. John, n. 494	
7.	Comm. John, n. 611 LW III, 534	
8.	Serm. 6 (Q) DW I, 100, 4–6[3]	
9.	Serm. 6 (Q) DW I, 112, 6–9[4]	
10.	Serm. 6 (Q) DW I, 110, 8–11, 2ff.[5]	
11.	? Serm. 5a (Q) DW I, 77, 11–17[6]	Serm. 3 (Q)
12.	Serm. 24 (Q) DW I, 421f., I–4[7]	? (*Book Div. Con.*)
13.	? (Serm. ?) *Book Div. Con.* I[8]	? (Serm. (Q) 11)
14.	Book Div. Con. DW V, 22, 5–8. 10[9]	
15.	Ibid.? (*Couns. Disc.*)[10]	*Couns. Disc.*[11]

B. *11 articles condemned as rash and evil-sounding, but capable of a Catholic interpretation:*

16.	2 Comm. Gen., n. 165, LW II, 635, 11[12]	2 Comm. Gen.
17.	2 Comm. Gen., n. 165, LW II, 635, 3–4[13]	2 Comm. Gen.
18.	Comm. John, n. 646	Comm. John 15, 16
19.	Comm. Wisdom, n. 226	Comm. Wisdom, 11, 27
20.	? Ibid. (*Book Div. Con.* DW V, 44, 19 + 26?)[14]	Serm. 14 (Q)
21.	Serm. 14 (Q) DW I, 239, 4[15]	Serm. 14 (Q)
22.	Serm. 6 (Q) DW I, 109, 7ff. + 110, 1ff.[16]	Serm. 6 (Q)

23.	Comm. Exodus n. 58–60, LW II, 65–66	Comm. Exodus, 15, 3
24.	'On the Noble Man' DW V, 114, 21–115, 3[17]	Book Benedictus
25.	Comm. John, n. 728	Comm. John 21, 15
26.	Serm. 4 (Q) DW I, 69, 8ff.[18]	Comm. John 21, 15

C. *Articles condemned as heretical but not ascribed to Eckhart:*

| 27. | Serm. 13 (Q) DW I, 220, 4ff.[19] | Serm. 12 (Q) |
| 28. | Serm. 9 (Q) DW I, 148, 5 – 7[20] | Serm. 9 (Q) |

NOTES

1. Based on Koch, KS I, 325–27, Laurent, op. cit., pp. 436–43, nn. 74–102. Cf. also C-McG, pp. 316f., nn. 2–28, and Walshe, passim.
2. C-McG, p. 85.
3. C-McG, p. 185, W 65, p. 131.
4. C-McG, p. 188, W 65, p. 136.
5. C-McG, p. 188, W 65, p. 135.
6. C-McG, p. 182, W 84, p. 259 = DW 84.
7. W 92, p. 314. Cf. W 65 (Q 6), p. 135–36.
8. C-McG, p. 228.
9. C-McG, pp. 216., 261, 306.
10. Diederichs ed., p. 20, II. 32–34, C-McG, pp. 261f.
11. Pfeiffer ed. II, p. 557.
12. C-McG, p. 121.
13. Ibid.
14. C-McG, p. 229.
15. W 50, p. 46. (= Art. 22: Walshe)
16. C-McG, p. 187, W 65, p. 135.
17. C-McG, p. 244.
18. W 40. p. 284.
19. C-McG, p. 80 and C-McG, p. 198, W 24a, p. 190.
20. W 67, p. 151; cf. Serm 83, C-McG, p. 207, W 96, p. 332.

SUBJECT INDEX

NAME INDEX